[Available]

A *VERY* HONEST
ACCOUNT OF LIFE
AFTER DIVORCE

LAURA FRIEDMAN WILLIAMS

THE BOROUGH PRESS

The Borough Press
An imprint of HarperCollins*Publishers* Ltd
1 London Bridge Street
London SE1 9GF

www.harpercollins.co.uk

HarperCollins*Publishers*
1st Floor, Watermarque Building, Ringsend Road,
Dublin 4, Ireland

This paperback edition 2022
2

First published by HarperCollins*Publishers* 2021

This book is a work of non-fiction based on
the author's experiences. In order to protect privacy, names,
identifying characteristics and details have been changed.

A catalogue record for this book is available from the British Library

ISBN: 978-0-00-839593-3

Set in Minion by
Palimpsest Book Production Limited, Falkirk, Stirlingshire

Printed and Bound in the UK using 100% Renewable Electricity
at CPI Group (UK) Ltd

MIX
Paper from
responsible sources
FSC™ C007454

This book is produced from independently certified FSC™ paper
to ensure responsible forest management.

For more information visit: www.harpercollins.co.uk/green

[Available]

LAURA FRIEDMAN WILLIAMS credits her degree in English and the 10 formative years she spent in book publishing for giving her a deep love and respect for the written word, and she credits the break-up of her marriage for giving her the subject matter about which she both needed and wanted to write. She lives in Manhattan with her three children. This is her first book.

Praise for *Available*:

'This memoir is a real page-turner. What happens when you start dating after 22 years of marriage? Unexpected, original, funny and sometimes deeply infuriating, Laura Friedman Williams has so much to say about what we expect of women's sexuality. Confronting without being sleazy and intelligent without being preachy. I loved it'   **Viv Groskop**, author of *How to Own the Room*

'*Available* offers far more than just a wild romp through the Wild West of the post-marital dating world [. . .] Curling up with this memoir is like settling in for a night with a hilarious girlfriend, listening to her best sexual anecdotes. *Available* is also a serious exploration of womanhood. Laura reminds us of the importance of regaining all the parts of who we are as women, despite how easy it is to become consumed by the mammoth roles of Mother and Wife. [. . .] We deserve to reawaken the parts of ourselves that often become dormant once we enter maternal roles. We deserve to live life to the fullest, embracing each facet of our identities, even (especially!) the parts society teaches us to shove aside when we become mothers'

Caroline Mackenzie, author of *One Year of Ugly*

For my mother, whose steadfast
love and faith in me keeps me aloft,
and for my three remarkable children, who rally
and rise and continue to awe me every day.

Introduction

In February 2018, I discovered that my husband was having an affair. We had been together for 27 years, and I believed we would be together into our golden years. I envisioned us jockeying to be the first to hold our grandbabies when they were brought to visit us and reading the *Sunday Times* together with a pair of reading glasses we would pass back and forth. That we would not be married forever had not so much as crossed my mind, nor had I ever had a fleeting concern that he would have an affair. We loved each other deeply and truly and his tendency to think like an absent-minded professor seemed likely to preclude him from being able to organize and sustain such a thing as an affair anyway.

We were young when we started dating – I had just turned 20 and a few weeks after we started dating he turned 21. Up to that point my dating and sexual experience had been limited. My best friend and I had been desperate to lose our virginity the summer before our senior year of high school and I succeeded a few weeks after she did, on the plaid pull-out sofa in the basement of my family's house in the suburbs of New York. I had wanted to understand the allure of sex and why certain girls I knew had a sophisticated swagger. I was dating a boy named Rob who was home from art school for the summer and drove a yellow school bus for the camp at which I was a counselor. He took me out to a hibachi restaurant to celebrate my 17th birthday and by the time the chef had finished flipping grilled shrimp in the air for me to catch on my plate, I knew that Rob was the one I would cede my virginity to.

The first few times we had sex, I found it painful and, frankly, embarrassing. It seemed bizarre that we would be caught up in unspeakable lust one moment and then the next he would come and our bodies would simply deflate. Were we supposed to resume our conversation at that point and pretend something both magical and calamitous had not just taken place? Mostly, relieved not to have been caught by my parents, we would hurriedly pull our clothes back on, smooth our voluminous '80s hair and part ways.

When Rob returned to the city for the fall semester of school, he moved into an apartment, which was where I learned to enjoy sex, not having to worry about the potential appearance of disap-proving parents. We saw each other on weekends, tumbling in and out of his narrow, unkempt bed, emerging bleary-eyed to pick up Chinese take-out. Our romps were hasty but fun, and I learned to be quick to come so that I wouldn't be left wanting when he was done – an ability that I took in stride until decades later when I learned from friends and books this was not a God-given skill.

I went away to college in the Midwest the following year and a few months into the first semester, I broke up with Rob. It didn't take me long to settle into a relationship with Julian, who lived in a fraternity house. Minus the scent of stale beer that permeated his bedding, and the sounds of his frat brothers throwing up in the bathroom across the hall after a night of partying, I took refuge in his full-sized bed, relishing the space and privacy his room afforded us.

Julian and I broke up two years later and I wasted no time, within days going out with Michael, who had been my next-door neighbor the year before. Although I had never before thought of him romantically, sitting in his white Volvo after he took me out to a Jamaican restaurant for dinner, a James Taylor cassette tape tucked into the stereo, I looked at him anew. He kissed me, but then told me that between the tennis team and architecture school, he didn't have much time for a girlfriend. I told him I liked my independence and wouldn't require much of his time anyway. We spent our days separately, but when bedtime came I would practically skip across the lawn separating our on-campus apartments and sleep over in his room. His roommate had left for London for the semester and by the time he returned we had broken his wooden futon frame with the copious and vigorous sex we were having every night.

Marriage, three kids, and twenty-seven years after that first kiss in his Volvo, he fell in love with another woman. For several months after finding out, I did little aside from scrape myself off the floor and care for our kids, through my misery and theirs. But then that dismal winter turned into a blustery spring which evolved into a lush, fragrant summer. I had a vague memory of what it felt like when I had been wildly confident, when I had laughed with ease, when I had cared if I looked good, when

I had felt content, even joyful. I wanted it back and I decided to actively figure out how to accomplish that.

My ensuing dating and sexual experiences were empowering, sexy and exhilarating, but they were also full of humanity. By the time we arrive at middle age, most of us have a long, twisting story of failed relationships, shifting life goals, heartbreak, abandonment, love, hope and loneliness. I found all these things in myself and in the men I slept with over the next few months. I had sex that made me feel euphoric and sex that made me feel dirty, sex that helped me find the sensuality well hidden in me most of my life and sex that left me craving intimacy and love, sex that was fumbling and cringeworthy, and sex that made me curl my toes when I recounted it to friends later.

I openly shared my dating and sexual experiences with friends – all of it, the good, the bad and the ugly – and was told over and over again that these stories were unusual and I should write them down. I didn't want to write about dating and sex though, I just wanted to live it and I didn't believe there was anything special to share anyway. Marriages end all the time and people move on. Mine was a story as old as time and embarrassingly clichéd. Still, friends kept insisting. They said my stories were hilarious and educational, inspiring even. They all had sisters or friends whose marriages had likewise imploded but who had turned inward, not wanting to go out, feeling reduced and undesirable. These women had not embraced their newly single status with my vigor and ferocity. Friends asked me to meet these sisters or talk to their friends and give them pep talks, explain how I was moving on, let them know that the seemingly impossible was actually completely within their ability and control. Matthew, my staunchly supportive brother, was adamant that writing about my experiences would be cathartic and made me promise that just five minutes a day I would sit at the computer, even if it meant staring at a blank screen.

I would like to say that I boldly took the bull by the horns and confidently started spinning tales out of my trysts, but in truth it was more like I plopped down sulkily at my computer because Matthew wore me down. I eked out a few clumsy sentences, not knowing how to speak a language of loss and love and lust, and carefully watched the clock until I had met my five-minute daily requirement. The next day I repeated the process, deleting most of what I had written the day before and replacing it with language that gradually, over the course of days and then weeks and months, became more confident and fluent. I was in fact learning an entirely new language, translating my complex web of emotions and experiences into the written word. My goal was to be raw and real when I had to be, but mostly to be funny. I had plenty of amusing anecdotes about my dating trials and travails and I envisioned a breezy page-turner of the kind I was too much of a literary snob to read myself.

Though the pages I was writing were slowly accumulating, I had no intention of sharing them outside my small circle of friends. I had kids and parents and a soon-to-be ex-husband with whom I was working hard to peacefully co-parent and the idea of publicly sharing my sexual escapades and most intimate thoughts terrified me. What I looked like on the outside was different from who I was turning into under the façade, I knew, and I neither understood why anyone else would care, nor why I should feel so bold as to reveal myself this way. I told one of my friends I was going to stop, but she persuaded me to keep going as the writing process would be cathartic, if nothing else.

I reluctantly agreed. By now I had grown to both love and hate the process of writing, and could procrastinate like I was aiming for a world record, but was fascinated by how my often confused and unspoken feelings found words and meaning on the written page.

So, I kept writing, friends read my pages and cheered me on and eventually a book took shape. It did not come out as I had intended. The zippy story of the single, middle-aged mother-of-three striking out and finding her sexual mojo was not, in fact, the only story I had to tell. The deeper story was how I came to the revelation that I had become complacent in my married life, beatifically coasting through it while roiling underneath was a woman yearning to live life on her own terms. My story, ultimately, is not simply an amusing collection of anecdotes about my sexual escapades, though these are certainly plentiful, but a narrative of how I gradually shifted roles from wife and mother to woman with a rich and complex private life.

Still, like so many other women, I seek approval from those close to me and also from strangers. I'm a rule follower and a pleaser. This so-called book would reveal my entire ecosystem, exposing desires that extended beyond those allowed for a woman my age with kids to raise and a reputation to keep intact. I would be denuding the flaws in my marriage and in myself and doing the entirely unspeakable act of acknowledging and acting on my own needs, not just those of my children. Even more unseemly, I would be telling anyone who listened that I had strong, seemingly insatiable sexual curiosity and longing. I decided that presenting myself this holistically would be too much, too outside the boundaries of the image I had carefully cultivated for myself. I called the same friend who had urged me along when I had wanted to stop and who had since become my literary agent and asked her not to do anything with the material I had been working on for well over a year – I was putting this project to sleep.

Over the next few days I was surprised to find myself feeling – more than the relief I had anticipated – profound disappointment. I had seen the spark of a vital woman in the pages I had written and I was effectively burying her. Late one night after dinner with friends I arrived home and found my mother sitting on the couch reading, having babysat for me that night. I confessed everything to her – the dating, the sex, the mishaps, the writing. My mother and I are close. She is a strong, accomplished, fiercely loving woman, but sexuality has always been an uncomfortable subject for us. By the time she had asked me when I was nineteen if I had a diaphragm "or something," I had already been sexually active for years; I reddened and nodded and that was the extent of our dialogue about birth control and sex. Now, I needed her to see that my recent discovery of myself as a sexual being could still fit within the parameters of being an "acceptable" daughter and mother. I wanted her approval, not of the book but of my decision not to write it. I knew that her squeamishness on the topic of sex would confirm I was making the right decision.

My mother, though, is nothing if not full of surprises. In her own steady, determined way, she refuses to conform. I explained to her that I was worried I would scandalize her with this book, but she stared straight at me with her crystal blue eyes and said, "I will never be embarrassed by anything you do, only proud." When I told her I wouldn't want her to read the book for its many graphic scenes, she said, "So I won't read it, or I will and I'll be sorry I didn't do all the things you did." When I told her I was worried the book would embarrass my kids, she said, "Your kids are resilient, they might feel embarrassed but they'll also see that you're living life on your own terms and they'll grow from that." She refused to let me off the hook; she would not approve of me closing myself back inside the box from which I had just recently emerged.

Many women ascribe to long-standing notions of femininity and maternalism to the extent that they become all that matter. The desires of our youth become trapped beneath the carefully crafted veneer we paint on as we age until the exterior layers are so thick that those desires become distant memories of an inner life we vaguely recall from our days pre-marriage, pre-kids, pre-middle age. But it doesn't have to be that way and I am living proof. If someone had asked me during the many years of my married life what I would do if I found out my husband was in love with another woman, I'm fairly certain the last answer I would come up with would be what actually happened: that I started dating and having sex with wild abandon and in doing so awakened a part of myself that I had neither known I needed nor wanted. I wouldn't take my old life back even if it was offered to me, which would come as a shock to the woman who a mere two years ago believed that she had been destroyed by losing the love of her life.

Introduction

I hope that anyone who reads this recognizes the part of herself she's locked away and considers giving her a chance to emerge. It's scary to open that door, terrifying even, but once we so much as unlock it, we may be surprised not by who comes in but who walks out. That's what happened to me one humid, rainy night in July 2018.

CHAPTER 1

An Opening

I stand paralyzed next to the hotel bed, staring at the closed bathroom door, behind which is the stranger who is about to end my post-marriage virginity. I am completely unsure of what to do with myself. It occurs to me that I have a beast of a strapless bra on – it holds me in place perfectly but with a wide back and four hooks. There's no way he will be able to get it off gracefully and I don't even want to imagine how matronly it will look to him. Then there's my belt! It has a clasp in the middle that you have to twist just so to undo and if he has to tackle that he will surely feel defeated before he even gets to the bra. Game time decision: I quickly remove all of my clothes – all of them, even the thong – and fold them neatly in a pile on the desk next to his motorcycle helmet because even in this moment, incredibly, I am concerned about the thin, delicate fabric of my dress becoming wrinkled. By the time he emerges from the bathroom, I am standing back in the spot where I started a few minutes ago, completely naked. I cannot think of a time in my 47 years when I have ever felt so wholly out of my body, so certain that I do not belong where I am. It's not too late to retreat, to reach for the clothes a mere arm's length away, to get in my car and backtrack to the life I have known for decades, the only life I ever wanted for myself. I hold my breath; he looks at me, unflinchingly. The air between us is charged as we each wait for the other to make the first move now that I have surprised him and bared myself.

Jump, Laura, I hear the voice in my head instruct me.

Ever so slightly, I nod my head in assent. This is the only way forward.

*

Five months have passed since our separation, which began 48 hours after I discovered that Michael was having an affair with a woman twenty years my junior. He moved into a two-bedroom rental in a brownstone while I stayed in the spacious "forever" apartment we finished a painstaking year-long renovation of just a few months before he moved out, also forever. Six nights a week, I have all three of our kids at home with me; Saturday nights, I'm down to just the two teenagers while our seven-year-old daughter goes to Michael's apartment for a sleepover. The older kids refuse to talk to him, so I'm suddenly a single mother to them.

Although Michael and I had agreed when we separated that we could – and should – date other people while we try to figure out if reconciliation is possible, dating has been just about the furthest thing from my mind. With a broken heart, a young child underfoot and two teenagers carefully assessing my comings and goings (whoever thinks teenagers don't care what their parents are doing clearly hasn't lived with two teens watching for signs their parents might reunite), the mere idea of dating has been laughable.

But now it's early July 2018 and I am conscious that my senses, long dulled by a dark and oppressive winter, are beginning to stir. Even noting the sweet scents and gentle sounds of summer feels like a reawakening as I have been numb for months. Though reluctant to disrupt our newly established summer routine, I pull Georgia out of day camp so that we can spend a few days with my friend Tina and her family at their house in Nantucket. Tina has been insistent that a few days away will do me good and I don't have the stamina to come up with more excuses. I want to burrow in my grief and hibernate, but my friends keep digging me out. I love them for their tenacity, but wish they would let me be. Countless mornings I walked through my apartment from bedroom to bedroom, attempting to rouse my kids for school with a chipper "Good morning, sunshine!" and watching them instead pull blankets over their heads without so much as opening an eye. I would disentangle and then pull off twisted blankets from their slumbering bodies as they reached out to hold on for a few more minutes, seconds even. That's how I feel now – friends keep throwing my blankets off to wake me up, but I want to be left alone to sleep through the pain.

Of course, Tina had been right. A change of scenery, her bracingly strong cocktails and the sight of Georgia frolicking on the wide expanse of beach are a welcome respite from my misery. If I can't feel joy right now, I can at least find occasional moments of peace. It has been months since I have been able to get through more than a few hours of the day without weeping and these small bits of calm give me a glimmer of hope, reminding me of the person I was before. My current life is framed in the before and the after: before, I was happily married, comfortable, my path laid out in a neat, unbroken line. After is the dystopian alternative of that narrative, the pitiful remains left after the version I wanted was taken away from me. I need to get back to the before version of myself – the one who smiled easily and often, who embraced her life with purposefulness, a can-do attitude and joie de vivre – but without marriage, stability and a clear footpath I cannot figure out how to begin the journey to find her, if she in fact still exists.

We arrive sandy and sunburnt back at our house in rural Upstate New York after a choppy ferry ride and a long drive home. Michael is there, ready to take over for a couple of days. I turn Georgia over to him and close myself in my – formerly *our* – bedroom. We are sharing our country home so that the kids don't have to come and go; it's awkward on a good day, a slap in the face on a bad one. Now it's 6 p.m. on Saturday and I'm facing a long evening shut in my room so that I can avoid interacting with him. I can't even bring myself to look straight at him yet, unable to have anything more than a halting conversation while my eyes frantically dart and roam so they'll land anywhere but on him.

It was here in this house, where we come to escape our hectic city lives two hours away and spend quality family time, that I discovered that Michael was not only sleeping with a woman I knew, but also that he had been contemplating divorcing me to be with her. Over the course of our many years together he and I had

14

discussed the concept of infidelity and I had always maintained that I thought I had it in me to understand and forgive a one-night stand; anything more, no way. The exposition of his affair had brought me to my knees – he wasn't just with her physically, he had fallen in love with her and in the process had fallen out of love with me and our life together.

However, my "no way" is not so easy to sustain now that it's a reality and I'm actually facing down the violation, not just the vague idea of what it might feel like. Our lives are inextricably linked; we share kids and friends and two homes and a dentist and a Netflix account. We were together from such a young age that he still remembers when I had the blemished skin of an acne-prone teenager and I vividly recall the layout of his childhood room before his stepmother threw out his tennis trophies and Andre Agassi posters to transform the room into a den. I was with him when first his father and then his mother died of cancer. Just a couple of years ago, I nursed his mother during the last month of her life, breaking it to her that she was too ill for further medical treatments when Michael could not find the courage to tell her himself. He is my partner, my co-parent, my best friend, my family – family being a concept that apparently only I had believed to be unalterable and essential. I hate him for how he's hurt me and our kids, but I'm not ready to throw in the towel on our marriage and I don't know if I have it in me to be alone. For over thirty years, I have continuously had a boyfriend or husband, moving from one to the next as if an interruption in the sequence would be fatal. I have no evidence to the contrary and cling to the notion I was raised on: any man is better than no man at all.

Michael, in turn, believes our marriage can be revived, albeit with sweeping changes. Instead of crawling back to me as I had expected, he's infuriated with me, as if I caused him to have an affair and am now being uncooperative in our recovery. To him, a bomb detonated after a years-long countdown and my not having heard the ticking is evidence of how little I understand him. The weight of having to decide our fate feels firmly planted on my shoulders. He wants me, pieced back together differently than I was before, but still, he says he wants me. It's me now who can't find my way back to him. There have been moments that flood me with shame in which I have wished he had died instead of having an affair so that the kids and I would have beautiful memories of him, not this painful and confusing knowledge that our life together wasn't what I thought it had been. Now the kids have a father two of them refuse to see and I can't find solid ground to stand on. If he had died, our life together would have ended, but at least it wouldn't have proven itself to be a total fraud. I'm in a holding pattern, unwilling to move forward with him, unable to walk away.

Barricaded in my room in the country house, I am at loose ends. Because this is not our primary residence, I have few friends here and a limited social life. I see myself with Tina on her deck yesterday, the two of us sipping watermelon margaritas amidst deep purple hydrangeas as the sun set, her advising me to put on a cute strapless sundress, show off my tan and go out and flirt – a good old-fashioned, non-committal flirt to shake off some of the sadness and attempt to locate the part of myself that is ready to move forward. I had adamantly protested: I'm not ready, I want to stay

16

home with the kids and I don't know how it's done anymore and anyway, any man who looks at me will know I'm just a shell of a formerly decent flirt. Now her words echo through my mind – I could indeed go out, there's really nothing to stop me but myself and the barrier of my bedroom door. It would be uncomfortable, but staying here is uncomfortable too, with the added downside of giving me way too much solitude in which to ruminate.

I think strategically: if I can find a band playing, it'll be less awkward to sit at a bar by myself as I will have something on which to focus my attention. I start googling places on my phone and it doesn't take long to find a possibility – a music venue in town has a soul singer on the schedule. Tickets are still available, standing room only. If I get there early, maybe I can snag a seat at the bar. This is a pivotal moment for me and I hover indecisively over the "purchase ticket" option on the bar's website as for months I've done little aside from force myself out of bed every morning, paste on a tentative smile for my kids and carry on with copious tears and a rage I hadn't previously known I could even muster up. My daily theme song has been from 'Santa Claus Is Coming To Town' in which Frosty is learning to walk: "Put one foot in front of the other, and soon you'll be walking across the floor. Put one foot in front of the other, and soon you'll be walking out the door." I've done nothing but walk across the floor for the past five months, but something inside of me has subtly shifted and I am suddenly aware that there is indeed a door, one that I have the power to open, even if just a crack to peek at what's on the other side. I click the button and quickly enter my credit card details before I can change my mind.

I shower, grooming long-neglected parts of my body, and in a burst of optimism douse my sun-kissed skin with fragrant rose body oil that Tina brought me back from Paris (by the way, there's apparently not a guide available to suggest cheer-up gifts for your girlfriend whose marriage has just imploded, and I both adored and felt for my friends as they plied me with things they thought might help: fancy herbal teas with names like Calm and Serenity and healing bath salts and body scrubs, aromatherapy candles, a delicate gold bracelet that said "You can do this," a small blue porcelain elephant that had been passed from friend to friend going through hard times, jars of freshly canned tomatoes, a case of my favorite yellow marshmallow Easter Peeps and, of course, the (requisite) vibrator. I unearth a black lace thong dormant at the back of my underwear drawer, pull on a strapless navy blue dress with a summery beaded belt and barely have time to strap on my wooden-heeled clog sandals before I'm flying out the door, hair still dripping, racing to exit before Michael and Georgia arrive home from their bike ride and ask me where I'm going.

As I drive down the road, fat raindrops start splattering on the car windows. My heart sinks; I should circle the neighborhood to find Michael and Georgia on their bikes and give them a ride home, but then my escape won't be clean. In a first for me in my 18 years as a mother, I put myself before my kids, telling myself Georgia will be soaked but fine, and I drive on down the long country road before I lose my nerve.

CHAPTER 2

Is This Too Much?

As I pull onto the side street where the bar is, I see couples streaming down the block. This is not exactly what I had in mind: they're all walking in pairs and they mostly have white hair. I grimace at what an amateur I am, at the quaint notion that I would drive myself into town and find a single man to sweep me off my feet. Unless that man is 70-something and looking for a threesome, I've clearly come to the wrong place.

But I've already put myself together and I'm really looking forward to that cocktail with which I lured myself here, plus I can't exactly go home now that I'm dolled up and smell like I'm hoping to be devoured, so I park my car and reluctantly walk in on my own. I feel equal parts brave and foolish: less "I am woman, hear me roar," and more "I am lonely, newly single, timid woman, hear me whisper." With empty stools on either side of me, I sit down and order a Margarita in a voice the bartender has to lean in close to hear and nurse that drink for all its worth. *I can do this*, I think, *just one drink, some people watching and I'm out.* I listen to the young, pig-tailed bartender tell her older, white-bearded counterpart about her visit home to introduce her boyfriend to her parents. I eavesdrop on two women at the end of the bar who are discussing strategies for organic gardening, stopping only when I realize I am nodding along with their suggestions. I watch the tables in front of the bar fill up and wonder if my parents might turn up; they don't live far and this looks like their crowd. I remember how ill at ease I felt in bars even when I was in college and was supposed to thrive in them, finding them loud and pointless, preferring to snuggle up with my friends in our own apartment where we could talk without yelling and sip our peach wine coolers in a room that didn't smell like rank beer.

A boisterous group files into the bar and fills the seats to my left. My radar goes up. A man whose back is turned to me is tall, muscular and has a full head of dark hair. I casually lean forward to check his ring finger and raise my eyebrows when I see that it is bare. The group seems to be his family, so I assume a girlfriend will soon appear and I can then relax my lifted eyebrows and go back to feeling sorry for myself. I impatiently wait a few more minutes, closely monitoring the group dynamics. When a girlfriend does not appear, I slide my stool back noisily, hop off it and make a big show of moving it away from him to try and grab his attention. It works.

"Oh, hey, sorry," he says, turning his warm brown eyes to me. "I didn't mean to crowd you.'"

"No, no," I say, smiling. "I just realized that I have a football field open to the right of me and you're crammed in here with a big group, so I was giving you more room."

And that's it.

Clearly, I don't know how this is done, but I do now know that dragging your stool away from the man you're trying to get to pay attention to you is not effective in the long run. His back is turned again and now I'm not only alone but adrift at sea, gaping spaces to my right and left. I did not know it was possible to feel both conspicuous and invisible at the same time and I squeeze my eyes shut as if that could make me disappear altogether.

Sip, breathe, sip, breathe, I instruct myself.

"That's an interesting bag," a deep voice says, interrupting my one-woman pity party.

"Sorry, what?" I ask, startled and looking around to see if this handsome stranger is speaking to me or someone near me.

"Your bag. What's it made of?" he asks, nodding his head towards my clutch purse resting on the bar.

"Cork," I say, testing out my voice, and I hand it to him to touch.

"Very fancy."

"Not exactly," I say. "It's from one of the outlet stores over in Lee. But thanks," I foolishly say and cringe, thinking about how I am always quick to deflect a compliment – *learn how to just say thank you,* I think to myself.

"I passed those stores earlier today on my bike," he says.

"That's a hilly bike ride."

"No, not a bicycle, I mean my motorcycle. I'm on a quick getaway trip, just checking out this area. I'm Jack," he says, sticking out his hand toward me. "And this is Don," he says of the short, balding man next to him.

They continue talking, but include me in their conversation. I'm the only one from around here, so I give them tips for local restaurants and scenic highways. Jack gestures to my nearly empty glass and asks what I'm drinking. I tell him a Margarita and he asks if I've ever had a Cadillac. When I say no, he calls over the bartender and orders one for himself and one for me, asking the bartender to put it on his tab. The bartender's eyes flicker over to me and he gives me a small smile and nod, as if relieved that I seem to have made a friend. I suppress a laugh. A man is buying me a drink? The last time I went on a date I was still using a fake ID, not even of legal drinking age yet.

Don tells us that he traveled here from hours away to hear the singer tonight, then he drifts off to his wife and friends, leaving Jack and me alone. Jack emphasizes that he is on his own on this weekend trip; his daughter spends most of her time with her boyfriend, leaving him lonely, as his wife died many years earlier and he just ended a relationship with a girlfriend. I tell him I am separated from my husband and have three kids. This whole interaction feels so surreal that I decide to adopt the old adage "Fake it till you make it" and play the role of a poised, confident single woman as best I can. As if I am auditioning for the role of divorcée out on the town on a Saturday night, I become increasingly coquettish, shrugging my bare tan shoulders toward him, delicately setting my bright pink nails on the dark mahogany bar. Finally, the lights dim and musicians start to fill the small stage.

"You won't be able to see the stage from your seat," he says, so I pop up from my perch on the barstool. When I do, my hair, finally dry and in tight, messy curls from having been left to its own devices, brushes against his face and he says, "Your hair smells amazing." I'm a literary snob yet here I am trapped in my own Danielle Steel romance novel.

The singer is dreadful. I look at Jack, shrugging and grimacing. He leans over my shoulder and whispers into my ear, "I can't believe Don traveled hours for this." A man with a girth like a linebacker in front of us turns around and with a withering look, asks Jack if he plays any instruments.

Jack responds that he plays a little guitar and the man says he hopes he will play in public one day so that people will come and heckle him as we are doing to this singer. Abashedly silenced, we make it through one more song before Jack presses close to me again to ask, "Will you eat something if I order food?" I see now that we are in this together, but I don't have time to answer before we get shushed again. The proper girl in me needs to escape before getting in trouble yet again. I whisper back, "If you're hungry, I can show you somewhere good to eat and we can talk without getting in trouble."

"OK," he whispers. "You leave first. Say goodbye to Don. I'll meet you outside in a few minutes so it won't be obvious that we're leaving together."

Though I am not certain why it would matter, it seems like fun to play along. Later, I will wonder if he thought this was a common scene for me and I will feel touched that he wanted to protect my reputation in this small town. Don is surprised that I'm leaving already, but I tell him it's been a long day and slip out. The street outside is deserted and wet from the rain. I lean against a lamp post and wonder if Jack is really coming out or if he might find a backdoor to sidestep me. Maybe this is his way of getting rid of me, an obvious imposter, so that he can flirt with the *real* sexy divorcée he spotted in the crowd. After a few minutes in which I fear that I will actually die of embarrassment, Jack noiselessly appears next to me. We smile shyly at each other now that we are alone with only the crickets as background noise and I lead the way through muddy puddles to the more populated part of town.

At the entrance to a noisy barbecue place, he asks if I will eat with him.

"No, probably not," I say. I love to eat, but how can I possibly do so right now with my stomach doing its own unique form of nervous acrobatics? "I'm not hungry, but I'll sit with you."

"I don't want to eat alone," he says. "Will you have a drink?"

"No, I can't," I say, shaking my head, my curls bouncing in the humidity. "I've reached my two-drink maximum and have to drive home." I'm pretty sure this goes against the bold, carefree persona I'm trying to put forth, but the practical mom in me keeps breaking through.

We face each other, contemplating.

"I'm happy to sit with you while you eat," I say, and then add in a rush of words that I can't believe are coming from my mouth, "but are you really that hungry?" The words themselves are less meaningful than the impassioned look I am giving him that basically says, ravish me instead.

"I guess not," he says carefully, taking a moment to register my meaning, and then suddenly he is pressed against me, kissing me so hard that I back up to the brick wall behind me and brace myself against it. His lips, soft and full, are pushing against mine with a sense of urgency that I recognize and reciprocate. Like water being poured over a wilting plant, I immediately perk up. I haven't been kissed like this, with passion and curiosity, since I was barely more than a teenager. I am astonished. How have I survived until now without this source of nourishment?

When he pulls back, he breathlessly tells me, "My hotel is up the street."

I know it and it's kind of seedy, not exactly what I imagined for my first (or really any other) tryst. But I know better than to pass up a seemingly perfect opportunity like this, so I smile demurely, nod my head and we start walking up the hill of the main street in town. On every corner, as we wait to cross the street, he kisses me – not just kisses me, but sucks the very breath out of me as if sustaining himself one more block until he can do it again. I pray none of the few passing cars contain people who know me here because I feel powerless to stop the rapture that has been set in motion, whether or not I'm seen.

The hotel lobby is brightly and fluorescently lit and I can guess what I look like to the knowing eyes of the schoolmarm receptionist at the front desk as I click against the tiled floor. I want to explain myself, but right now I'm a character in a romance novel and explaining myself is not part of my role. I have always cared so much about how I appear to other people, even if I doubt they'll ever see me again, but it occurs to me at this moment that I should start caring less and simply live my life; I should care about what I look like to myself, but maybe I don't need to care so much about what I look like to people who don't even know my name.

Jack and I are silent and palpably tense with anticipation as we ride the elevator and approach his room. A few fumbles with the key card and then we are in this man's room with a king-size bed and motorcycle helmet on the desk. I excuse myself to use the bathroom, where I lock the door and stare hard at myself in the mirror while giving myself a silent, rushed pep talk: *It doesn't matter what happens here, if you cry or laugh or embarrass yourself, just make sure all your parts are in working order.* It's like the first attempt at a jog after years of being sedentary, a breaking in of new sneakers, knowing you won't last very long and you'll still end up with blisters, and anyway, he isn't a local guy and will never see you again. I nod along with the words in my head – *Yes, yes, I can do this, just knock it out and it'll be over and done with, a post-marriage virgin no more.* With all the courage I can muster, I fling open the door of the bathroom and pass him as he takes his turn inside.

This is how I come to find myself standing naked in a stranger's hotel room, shedding my clothes as he does his own preparations for me in the privacy of the bathroom. I am not versed in the rules of this game, and since I have, in the past hour, successfully impersonated a confident single woman, I am determined that my act must go on. I am showing him that I'm ready and willing. I'm not pretending that we aren't here for the sole purpose of having sex; this seems like the only logical next play – but why is he just staring at me now that he's out of the bathroom and just a few feet away? Shouldn't he be voraciously feasting on me already? Should I not have acted so boldly? Is there any chance the ground will open and swallow me whole right now, teleporting me from the faux pas I seem to have committed?

"Is this too much?" I finally break the silence and ask more timidly than I intend to, eyes wide, eyebrows raised – and, I realize, somewhat ridiculously for a woman who has just brazenly undressed for a man she met an hour ago.

He matches my look with eyes just as wide and eyebrows equally raised and says, to my great relief, "Definitely not too much," while picking me up like a newlywed and half placing, half tossing me on the bed. To say this moment feels dreamlike is an understatement of epic proportion. For 27 years, since I was little more than a teenager, I have had sex with only one man and expected that I would continue to have sex with this one man for the rest of my life. Since that first night with Michael, I have given birth three times, nursed three babies, fought gravity with only middling success and just – frankly – aged. I am terrified of what Jack – who has clearly been living a full life with his Cadillac Margaritas and his motorcycle and condoms in his wallet – will find when he gets closer to my body, but I'm expecting nothing less than horror, perhaps even some pity.

Within seconds he has worked his way down my body and it is no *small* surprise when he whispers up to me, "You have a really nice pussy." A sound bursts out of me that I pray is more laugh than cackle, prompting him to ask what's funny. For starters, I hadn't known this was a word men actually used outside of lewd conversations with their friends. Second, I can't believe he thinks this line will work on me – am I supposed to believe that one so-called middle-aged "pussy" looks qualitatively different from another? But the well-mannered girl in me rushes to apologize, "No, it's not funny, I'm sorry, it's so nice, thank you, it just surprised me as no one has ever told me that before."

"Really?" he asks. "Come on. No one? I don't believe that."

"I swear," I insist. "Don't they all kind of look the same? I mean, more or less?"

"No, not at all. They all look different, smell different, taste different. Don't you ever take a close look at your own to know how good it looks?"

"Um no, I never have," I say, thinking the last time I got a good look was probably when I caught an accidental, horrified glimpse in a mirror when I gave birth to Georgia seven years ago. "But now I'm intrigued." And I truly am, making a mental note to take a look later and try to see what he's seeing – I have so much to learn.

"Please be gentle," I say, hesitating to admit the truth of this situation. "I have a confession to make: this is my first time having sex with a man since I've separated from my husband. I'm very nervous." My unabashed act falls away at that moment despite my best efforts to keep up the façade. I am here and I am determined to stay here, but I can no longer pretend not to feel afraid. The idea of another man being inside me, a man who is not my husband, flat out terrifies me.

"I understand, it's OK. This is my first time too since breaking up with my girlfriend. I had promised myself that I wouldn't make this getaway weekend about a woman," he says. I am relieved by his sharing his own ambivalent feelings, impressed and grateful that he isn't shying away from my vulnerability, but staying with me in this moment.

Within seconds I am a bundle of contradictions as I tell him that what I really want is to be fucked. I've never used these words before and I'm fairly certain that according to how I would define what it means to be fucked – the vulgarity of the word, the lack of love and warmth and intimacy that comes with the transactional nature of it, the idea that something is literally being banged out of you – I never have been. If the opposite of being fucked is being made love to – a phrase that always makes me recoil with its cheesy evocation of '70s love songs, giving me an image of a couple pouring enduring love and tenderness into each against the backdrop of a setting sun – I'm not certain I've ever been made love to either. I've simply had sex, the safest, most banal term I can think of; slightly clinical, devoid of all emotion, whether loving or intense, middle of the road.

He hesitates and says, "First, you asked me to be gentle and now you're telling me you want to be fucked. I'm confused by what you want."

"You and me both," I say, attempting a light-hearted tone, trying to get back the bravado I felt a few minutes earlier when I undressed. "How about you proceed without me giving further directions and I'll let you know if it's too much?"

It occurs to me for a fleeting moment that I don't know this man and no one knows I'm here. I don't even know if Jack is his real name. I've spent more time worrying about how this will all play out and the state of what I now know is called my pussy and maybe not enough time worrying about who this stranger is and if he reels women in by claiming to be a lonely widower. But, against my nature, I've boldly jumped into the deep end and I'm damned if I'm not going to swim. I may have lost my virginity thirty years earlier, but this experience feels remarkably similar. All that's missing is the worry that I will be found out by my parents in their bedroom two flights up from the basement and the nubby wool of the plaid sofa.

Being intimate with Jack is surprising in all the best ways: fun, sensual, even transporting. It is liberating to give up control and stop dictating what end of the spectrum between making love and fucking our intercourse will be. The fact that he doesn't know me and thus has no expectation of how my body will respond allows me to be whoever I want to be sexually at this moment in time. I had worried that I would miss Michael like a stabbing pain during whatever my first encounter would be, but having shed self-consciousness and assumptions of who I am once my clothes come off is profoundly freeing, giving me a reprieve from the sexual identity I steadfastly adhered to over the course of almost three decades with Michael.

As Jack works his way back up my body, he places one hand on my stomach and reaches the other hand up to gently place his palm on one of my nipples. His touch on my stomach is the one that feels decidedly intimate; I've always equated arousing touches with private parts of the body that are reserved for sex, but his interest in the more mundane parts of my body – my calves, thighs, stomach – enthralls me.

"You're in great shape," he says. "It's hard to believe you have three kids."

"Thank you," I say. "But yes, they're all mine. I've got some stretching and sagging to prove it." Immediately I regret saying this: *learn just to say thank you*, I think for the second time tonight. If he's not noticing where I've lost my elasticity, it's not my job to draw a map for him.

He playfully squeezes my arm muscles, admiring them. I feel aglow from these compliments. He's not saying that I'm lithe or I'm voluptuous, words I associate with sexiness – he's saying I'm strong. I know that no one can create strength in another person and that you can't fake strength, which means I can take full credit for this aspect of myself. I realize that's exactly what I want – to be a little badass, a little unexpected, willing and able to take care of myself.

He reaches over for the condom that he had earlier placed on the nightstand, but I catch his forearm and say, "Wait."

I roll over so that I am straddling him and I put my hands on his bare, buff chest. His skin is soft and smooth, not a hair in sight. I take my index finger and trace the tattoo on his left bicep. It's the size of my fist, a large bird with Latin words underneath.

"What does this mean?" I ask.

"It's a long story. I got it during a stint in the military a long time ago," he says.

Shimmying my hips back until I am kneeling on the bed, his legs on either side of me, I pause to fully take in what's in front of me: his penis is erect and his entire pubic area hairless. I ponder what I had just asked him minutes earlier about what makes one pussy different from another and I am struck by how different his penis is from what I'm used to. It's been 27 years since I've seen a penis that did not belong to my husband and to my surprise, this one really does look very different, but I can't say exactly how. Suddenly I'm aware that I couldn't adequately describe Michael's penis if I tried to. When was the last time I really looked at it? And when was the last time I lustfully (or even with complete boredom) wrapped my lips around it?

I stroke his balls; I like the way they feel without hair, like baby skin. Tentatively, I flick my tongue against them and he grabs my hair and groans. I slide back up, pressing my body against his, and now reach for the condom myself, opening it and helping him unroll it down the length of his penis. I had been certain that condoms must have changed drastically in the thirty years since I last used one, but no – the sensation of a synthetic, sticky object rather than warm, soft skin is the first thing I notice when he slides into me. The second thing I notice is that a man who is not my husband is now deep inside me and I'm still very much intact.

We remain in his bed for hours, touching and kissing and talking in between. Whatever I think 'it' is, I'm proving to myself that I might actually still have it. I had expected tears, nostalgia for the way it had been with Michael who knew so well what I did and didn't like in bed. It turns out I'm an expert at achieving an orgasm and many women aren't, according to Jack in what is admittedly a limited research study. For all the ways in which I've assumed I'm out of touch with myself sexually, I've just discovered that I understand what my body responds to, and that I enjoy the physical sensations that come with having sex. Sure, I've been having it for decades, but with the same man mostly the same way and with sleeping children a thin wall away. This is the sex I remember from my youth – ravenous, raw, and thrilling – the kind of sex that takes my breath away and makes me greedy for more. It occurs to me that I'm free to reinvent myself now in whatever way I choose, to shed the sexual persona that I rigidly assigned myself.

If I'm being honest, it wasn't Michael's fault that our sex life had become humdrum and monotonous – he was a passionate lover; had I even slightly reciprocated his desire, he would have been thrilled. Whether I was no longer attracted to him or whether I was no longer attracted to myself when I was with him, I can't determine. The only thing I'm certain of now is that there is something inside of me stirring – not just sexual arousal but sexual curiosity too. I have always gagged giving blow jobs. Maybe I like them now? I was always fairly quiet in bed. Maybe I'm ready to make some noise? The possibilities seem vast and wondrous, presenting me with something I haven't felt for years: desire.

Jack asks me to lie to him and tell him I will stay all night.

"I can't stay," I say. "I have to go home."

"I know," he says. "That's why I said lie to me."

So I do, I say I won't leave his side all night, and the loneliness behind his request fills me with deep sadness but also tenderness for the way he has been unguarded with me. He makes me laugh by relaying that when I left the bar earlier to wait outside for him, Don expressed surprise that I had left because he was sure Jack was going to 'get lucky' with me, so our ruse was successful and my reputation intact. He tells me he thinks I am beautiful, sexy and fierce and even though he sees my raw and open wound, he feels sure I will be more than OK someday. This is the only moment in which my breath catches. That this man, who is a stranger to me, and yet has now seen me intimately in a way no one but my husband has, should show me compassion and express confidence in me injects me with a dose of optimism I hadn't realized I desperately needed. I thought I had been doing an excellent job of playacting the happy-go-lucky, freewheeling, soon-to-be divorcée, but he saw through those superficial layers to my core where grief resides, yet wasn't scared away.

It's well after midnight and we are both starting to nod off as we lie entwined. I whisper that I have to go home and ask if he will walk me to my car, which is several blocks away in this now-deserted town. We dress in silence and it feels like our protective armor goes back on, thicker with each article of clothing we don. I wonder if sex with men who aren't Michael will always feel this profoundly intimate, or if Jack and I have simply been fortunate to have found kindred spirits in one another: to have really seen each other even knowing this would be a one-night stand.

As we leave the hotel, a heavy rain starts to fall and he asks if he should run back upstairs for an umbrella. I say no, because now that our clothes are on and we are back to the business of practicalities, I'm anxious to be on my way. We walk quietly and quickly.

"Wow, you walk fast! I've never walked with a woman who can match my pace and definitely not in heels in the rain," he says.

"I'm a city girl," I tell him, remembering how little he knows about me aside from my body and the basic facts of my life.

When we reach my car, I offer to drive him back up the hill to the hotel. Stepping into the driver's seat, I do a quick swipe of the passenger seat, which is still filled with the remnants of my trip with Georgia: Ziplocs of goldfish crackers, granola bar wrappers, a bag of cherry pits. I feel totally and suddenly exposed for who I really am: a harried housewife and busy mom. How does this fit with the woman who a few hours ago stripped off her clothes and practically begged to be debauched?

Back in the driveway under the stark, too-bright lights of the hotel, I turn to him and shyly say, "Well, thank you. It was really nice meeting you."

"Yeah, it was great to meet you too. Maybe I'll run into you one of these weekends when I'm back up here," he says, but he doesn't ask for my phone number and I don't ask for his. Within seconds I'm pulling out of the parking lot and driving back to my house. I've been gone only seven hours, but I am returning home a changed woman.

*

The next morning, I wake up bewildered. It seems impossible that last night happened the way I replay it in my imagination. I feel like I've been hit by lightning. I look down at my naked body, put my hand over my heart. Everything looks as it did just a day ago, my skin deeply tanned from the Nantucket beaches, my stomach slightly rounded, breasts spilling over toward the sides of my body. I'm not as taut or as buoyant as I was the last time I had sex with someone for the first time. My edges seem to be both harder, having lost the supple baby fat of my youth, and softer, having experienced gravity and childbirth and age. I survey myself, every freckle and vein and scar and hair, and think, *it's all mine, for better or for worse, and I can do whatever I want with it.* This knowledge is liberating and riveting. For months I have felt numb when I'm having a good day and despondent when it's a rough day, but I feel a flicker of myself coming back to life. It's both a physical sensation and a sudden awareness of myself as a person. Not just a mother, not just a wife, not just a jilted lover. I am all these things but not just that. It's like seeing an old friend again. Flooded with gratitude, I am intrigued by the possibilities that lie ahead.

I am certain Jack must have hit the road on his motorcycle hours ago but I hop into my car anyway and drive back into town. It seems impossible that the man who woke me up from this long and deep slumber could be a mere ten minutes away from me right now. When I pull into the hotel parking lot, it is almost empty, the weekend crowd having cleared out; the corner spot that contained his motorcycle nothing but a blazing slab of cement now. I am both disappointed and relieved as I don't know what I would have done if I had found him there, but I wanted proof that he really existed. Sighing, I drive back home to the summer day ahead of me, to my daughter and the man who is still my husband.

CHAPTER 3

Looking for Men, Everywhere

By Monday morning, it feels like my Saturday night sexcapade may as well have taken place in another lifetime. Knowing my girlfriends will be thrilled for me, having witnessed up close my deep sorrow of the past months, I call them one by one and tell them of my great victory, never tiring of recounting the story from the moment I decided to dress up and go out, to when I pulled out of the parking lot to go home. It's been entertaining to tell them and have a tale of success to share instead of my usual sob story, and they are an appreciative audience, demanding details, shrieking at all the right moments and exclaiming surprise at my boldness. I had felt especially triumphant on a FaceTime call with Tina when I told her that I had done so much more than simply follow her advice to put on a dress and go out – that I had slept with a stranger. She and her husband, sitting by a bonfire on the beach, had yelled "Mazel tov!" and toasted me with their Martinis, beaming with pride as they said, "We knew you could do it, Momma" as if I had just achieved a lifelong dream.

My friends' happiness on my behalf moves me, as my path has suddenly veered wildly from theirs, but they don't judge me or try to burden me with their own agendas. I had announced early on that there was a good chance that Michael and I would get back together and to please refrain from saying anything bad about him in my presence. Katherine had asked me for guidance, "Tell me what you want, to leave him or to reunite, and I will come up with every good reason for it." Mara had sat with me at Starbucks when I told her my news, straight through an appointment I knew she was missing in order to stay with me, and reassured me that if I took Michael back, she and my other friends would too. Jacqueline heeded my request not to speak badly of Michael, but besieged him with angry texts for hurting me. Jen, Lauren and Jessica sat with me in Jessica's living room for hours at a time, listening and asking questions and holding my hand. If I expressed anger at Michael, they nodded along but otherwise used self-restraint I could see caused their lips to press together in a tight line. Johanna and Stephen took me and the kids to our favorite dim sum restaurant. When Stephen asked if I was feeling better on the no-sugar diet I had started just a couple of weeks earlier, before my marriage came to a screeching halt, I gave him a quizzical look and repeated in a dazed tone, "Do I feel better?" and we both laughed at the absurdity of the question until we cried. Julie texted emojis from her home in Chicago, apologizing that she could not be at my side but letting me know every single day that she was thinking of me.

I could feel the vibrations of the love these friends had for me and admired them for facing my grief head-on without trying to manage it. They had offered solace and hugs and tissues, but not advice, understanding that I had to figure this out on my own. Now, as I tell them my brazen story, they gracefully change course, cheering for me, expressing delight that I have momentarily emerged from my paralyzed stupor, showering me with praise for my boldness. They joke that somehow I've ended up ahead, that the tragedy of my fall and then excitement of my rise is a surprise and wonder, something to envy if they didn't love me so much. Even so, I'm keenly aware that my life – my real, mundane life – goes on much as it did before, and that at the moment it's pretty bleak. I'm still furious at Michael, tender with Georgia and equal parts terrified of the once-clear future now hazy in front of me and miserably alone. For all the chutzpah that had me soaring on Saturday night, I've landed back on my little square of the earth and am certain that the entire episode was a fluke, something I will likely not experience again.

*

By Wednesday afternoon, the momentary high of Saturday night has only served to remind me of how low I actually am now that I'm back in my routine with Georgia and feeling more than a little sorry for myself. It seems silly to me now that I had felt hopeful, lying in bed with the man I was hoping would be #1 on a long list of men. It seemed effortless to feel a spark of confidence in my potential to find happiness as I came down from the high of my first orgasm in who knows how long – but now, in the quiet of my day-to-day life, I feel abandoned by both Michael and my own burgeoning self.

Georgia and I walk through the market that's part of the farm where she attends day camp. We come in here every afternoon after camp to inhale the scent of freshly baked bread and choose an ice pop for a treat. I notice a familiar-looking man standing by the salad bar and my gaze lingers a moment too long so that he catches and returns it as we try to figure out if we know each other. He is maybe ten years older than me, with a salt and pepper goatee, deep lines around his eyes and tattoos creeping beyond the short sleeves of his T-shirt. I squint trying to place him and then, having no choice but to follow Georgia who is making a beeline for the salad bar, walk toward him.

"Oh, Johnny!" I loudly exclaim, relieved to have finally made the connection.

"Hey Laura, I thought that might be you. It's been so long."

We smile warmly at each other and embrace in a quick hug. Johnny had been my contractor years earlier when we were in the midst of a house renovation. He had been in and out of my house for weeks, and one night showed up at about 9pm in his pickup truck with his German Shepherd hanging out the passenger window. He said he wanted to see how the outdoor lights looked after dark, so we turned them all on and stood outside while my son threw sticks for his dog to fetch. I had suspected that he had a crush on me as the night-time visit seemed odd, and often he had idled in the house for what seemed a little longer than necessary to chat with me after he was done for the day. Now he expresses surprise at how big Georgia has gotten and tells me he's been working at a job close by. When I ask how he's doing, he shakes his head, saying this has been a terrible year, that he'd been in a near-fatal motorcycle accident and recovered to find out that he had lung cancer, so surgery and treatments and a difficult recovery ensued.

"Yikes, what a year, I'm sorry. You look healthy but thinner, which is why I guess I didn't recognize you right away. You're so tough, I have no doubt you'll be back to your robust self soon."

"Well, Laura, I'm getting better and stronger every day. God is good, and I'm grateful. How are you? How's Michael?"

"I had a rough year too, trying to get back on my feet. Michael and I split up," I say quietly, glancing at Georgia, who is peering into the salad bar a few feet away. My throat instantly constricts. I know that his sympathetic look will reduce me to tears so I reach out to hug him again and say I have to get going.

"Oh, wow, I'm shocked. I'm sorry, I don't know what to say. If you ever want to talk or need a friend, I'm a good listener."

I thank him and give him my cell number, suggesting that he reach out at some point. Then Georgia is tugging me over to the freezer aisle and Johnny is gone.

Fifteen minutes later, Georgia and I are en route to her gymnastics class when I get a text from Johnny: "I'm sorry about you and Michael. You guys seemed so solid to me. You're the last couple I would have expected this from. I know you'll get through it, but it's got to be hard right now."

I respond that it is indeed very difficult and within a few texts we have made a plan to have a drink the coming Sunday after I drop Georgia at sleepaway camp.

*

As we drive home from my parents' house on Saturday afternoon after Georgia has said her goodbyes and instructed them on exactly what they should include in their upcoming care packages to her, she requests a send-off dinner with me and Michael that evening. I want to fulfill this simple request and I'm furious at myself that I can't bring myself to do it, and at Michael for putting us in this position.

"I'm so sorry, sweet girl. Daddy and I aren't able to do that yet. We're very upset with each other and need time to calm down and move on. We're trying hard to forgive each other, we just need more time."

"Whose fault is it that you're mad at each other?" she asks.

"Both of ours," I say. I don't like having to accept responsibility for our current situation, but I want her to have healthy relationships with both of us and I will bend the truth to help make that happen. "I always tell you that it takes two to tango, right? It's not one person's fault, it's about how two people are together."

"OK," she murmurs so quietly that it breaks my heart.

"I can't promise that Daddy and I will stay married, but I can promise that someday we'll do better than we're doing now. I will always be your mom and Dad will always be your dad and we will always love you and Daisy and Hudson the most in the world. That won't ever change, whether we're together or apart."

She remains quiet and I'm grateful this conversation is happening while I'm driving and she's in the backseat, so she doesn't have to see my tears and I don't have to see hers.

"Are you OK?" I ask and even as I do so, I know I'm looking to her to reassure me that she will make it through our split intact.

"I mean . . ." she starts and pauses. "This isn't the best thing that's ever happened to me but yeah, I'm OK."

I burst out laughing. I am so in awe of this brave, resilient and funny little girl and I know that I will do whatever I can to keep her this way. She's not quite done with me yet though, wanting to know if I will someday marry another man and if so, if that means she will have an entirely new father. I am grateful that we have moved past some of the heaviness and grief of our conversation to imagine what the future could look like and I laugh again, teasing her that she's getting ahead of herself and moving way too fast for me.

"Oh yeah, I forgot," she says, giggling. "Daddy stays my daddy no matter what."

"Exactly," I say. "And our feelings for each other might change but our feelings for you never will." This much, at least, I know is true, and it feels good to be able to declare the words authoritatively.

*

Sunday, drop-off day, arrives. Michael and I both want to bring Georgia for her first time at overnight camp, but even if I can manage to sit in the car for the ride there with him and Georgia, there's no way I'm getting back in that car with him alone afterwards. After a flurry of text negotiations, we agree to take two cars.

The drop-off itself is as uncomfortable as it is quick. In the cabin, I smooth new sheets on Georgia's bed and direct Michael with short and sharp words. We take pictures of her in her pastel tie-dyed sundress in front of her small rustic cabin and are effusive with our goodbyes, but the second she runs off, we are silent.

"Bye, Laura," he says quietly as I open my car door.

I hold up my hand in what is both a wave and a stop sign and pull out. There's no reason I can think of that I will need to see or speak to him for the next two weeks and I feel nothing but relief. I've had no choice but to frequently interact with him about money and schedules and kids, and every time it has felt akin to pouring salt in a wound. That I'm about to get a break from him and maybe from my own anger makes me feel lighter and freer than I have in months.

CHAPTER 4

Never Come Between a Man and His Dog

Back home a few hours later, Johnny texts to see where I want to meet. He says he doesn't know my part of town well and do I want to suggest a place. I can't picture him in the hipster boutique cocktail bars that our town is filled with, so I pick a local dive bar between his house and mine on a sleepy main street.

I arrive a few minutes early and choose a stool in the center of the bar, away from the few other people there. I'm in a black tank top with spaghetti straps that show off my tanned shoulders, a cut-off jean mini-skirt and flip-flops. The bartender is an older woman who says "Sure, hon" when I order a Margarita and I immediately feel like a child playing grown-up.

When Johnny arrives I'm already halfway through my drink, not because he's late but because I'm so nervous. He's wearing jeans and a striped shirt with buttons at the top and a thick gold chain; compared to his usual work uniform, he looks dressed up. When he leans over to kiss my cheek, I catch a whiff of cologne; if I hadn't quite been sure if this was a date, the cologne has confirmed that it indeed is.

We sit for a couple of hours while he nurses a beer and I do not let myself have the second drink I want because I know that I will soon have to drive the twenty minutes back home. He tells me about his long-ago divorce, the wife who cheated on him and the strained relationships he has with his grown sons. He also talks about his newfound religion and I realize his gold chain has a cross dangling from it. He quotes his pastor and I try to figure out if the church is evangelical or if he's born-again, but I'm Jewish so this Jesus talk is pretty foreign to me. His religious beliefs are deep and sustaining, so even though I don't share his convictions I appreciate that he is a genuine and decent person who, like me, is trying to find his way again after a battering. An empathetic listener, he acknowledges my broken heart without shying away from it. Since he knows Michael from the time he worked on our house, I find it comforting that he personally knows the players involved.

When we get up to leave, I tell him I've already paid for my drink and we head outside. He tells me that he drove to meet me in his new pickup truck, walking over to it and opening the driver's side door to show me the inside.

"Oh, I love pickups," I say rapturously, inhaling the new car scent as I lean into the driver's seat. The novelty of riding in a big truck on country roads is incredibly alluring to me. I've been listening to country music all summer, and I imagine myself in the front seat with my feet up on the dashboard, driving past corn fields and peach orchards. He leaves me to revel in my country fantasies as he runs back inside to use the restroom.

I lean against the driver's seat as I wait for him and then I hear a woman's voice yelling at me to get out of the street. It's dark out and I can't find the body attached to the voice until she tells me to look up. She is standing on a second-storey balcony and tells me the cars come up this road too fast and she doesn't want me to get hurt. I feel a passing worry for myself, wondering if I'm losing common sense in my attempt to be coquettish: first, entering a man's hotel room without telling anyone I'm there and now standing blithely in the middle of a dark street. I thank her and wait on the sidewalk, wondering how many awkward goodbyes she's witnessed from her perch. When Johnny emerges, I ask him if he wants to walk me to my car even though it's right across the street.

I am ambivalent about how to say goodbye. Does he want nothing more than to send me on my way, or is he attracted to me but keeping his distance because he knows my husband, or is he trying to follow my lead, which is unfollowable since I don't know where I'm going? I open my car door and am once again standing in the street.

"OK, well then," I say slowly as I gaze intently at him with my eyebrows raised, daring him to make a move or lose his chance. We regard each other without speaking.

Finally, he takes my not-so-subtle hint, leans in and kisses me softly on the lips. The coarse hairs of his goatee rub against my face; I've never kissed a man with a beard except for the short period when Michael experimented with growing one before I made him shave it off. Johnny's beard is scratchy but not unpleasant. He pulls away and we look at each other again, and then when he leans back in, I put my hand behind his neck and pull him toward me. This time when he pulls away, I say "So would you like to go back to my house or to your house or . . .?"

That's about as cliché a line as I have ever uttered and I wince as the words tumble out, but I understand innately there's momentum needed to move from a kiss goodnight to having sex, and tonight a mere kiss is not going to do the trick for me. There are a million things I need right now – numbing, fun, validation, physical attention, distraction, proof that paramour #1 is not really #1-and-done, and I will clumsily barrel ahead to close a deal.

Johnny lets out a quick breath of air, a cross between a sigh and a chuckle. He's thinking about it. I bite my lip and wait for a response. I know I'm probably bright red so I'm thankful we are standing in the dark. Is a kiss sometimes just a kiss? Am I scandalizing him with my forwardness?

"OK, let's go back to my house. I can't leave the dog alone much longer. Do you want to follow me?" he asks.

Much as what I really want is a ride in that shiny red pickup with its fresh upholstery, I agree to follow him. His house is at least twenty minutes north of here and I don't want to do a walk of shame back to my car later with the busybody on the balcony watching. I'm already judging myself more harshly than she possibly can and when Johnny gets into his car, I'm tempted to yell up to her, "Don't judge me! My husband of 27 years shattered my heart and I'm trying to put it back together! I'm just starting to figure it out on the most infinitesimal level, so be kind!" But honestly, do I really care? I want to be desired and I'm about to have sex with another man. I pull out, spin around in a quick U-turn and Johnny and I are on our way to his house.

Ten minutes on dark rural roads, and then ten more minutes on the Interstate. A few miles off the highway, we pull into a suburban enclave, ranch houses with long driveways and mailboxes in front. I'm surprised by the mundanity. I had imagined him and his big dog out in a starry field somewhere, in a cabin he'd built himself over time. I laugh at my romanticism as Johnny pulls into a driveway next to a split-level and points me off to the side. He drives his pickup into the detached garage and then minutes tick by as he moves other cars around, pulling his work van out of the garage and then a second work van back into the garage. I can't help but feel this is a delay tactic and he regrets having invited me here.

After an uncomfortably long wait in which I try to lean sultrily against my car but finally give up and do a crossword puzzle on my phone instead, he's ready to go inside. As we enter, I see a set of weights to one side and a washer/dryer with dirty laundry piled on top on the other side. I'm suddenly aware that going to an anonymous hotel room with a man in which the most personal item on display was a motorcycle helmet is very different from being inside a man's home and seeing how he lives, what he lifts and what his laundry habits are. And now here comes Floyd, his 80-pound German Shepherd, running in absolute ecstasy – the one I recall running for sticks in my backyard years ago. He jumps on me, panting and drooling, and I know this dog is the love of Johnny's life, but to put it mildly and regretfully, I'm not a dog person.

Johnny comes to my rescue, pushing the dog's paws from where they landed on my stomach, and we head up a short flight of stairs to the kitchen. His house is tidy and comfortable with a few attempts at decor thrown in – a vase with a sprig of fake flowers, a scented candle, a 'Bless This House' print framed on the wall – though I am surprised to see a dozen bath mats scattered all over the kitchen. I am tempted to mention that inexpensive rag rugs can easily be purchased online, but I remind myself that I'm here for a few hours, I'm not moving in, and instead gladly accept the glass of wine he offers me. He takes me on a quick tour of the living area and I feel confused; I don't want to be rude so I express enthusiasm over the small details he proudly points out, but I'm not quite sure what we're doing here. I was expecting the "You run to the bathroom and I'll take all my clothes off and you'll throw me on the bed" routine, but instead I'm admiring the wood floor he just laid in his enclosed porch.

I nestle into the couch with my glass of wine and curl my feet underneath me, trying to exude availability. He perches next to me for a second before he pops back up again saying something about needing to check on the state of affairs upstairs. It finally dawns on me: he's nervous! I've been so focused on how new I am to this that it hasn't occurred to me how strange it must be for this man, who knew me as a client and has seen me in my element with my husband and kids, to have me invite myself over and present myself on his sofa, scantily clad and there for the taking.

He has been upstairs a few minutes when I accept that nothing is going to happen unless I make it happen. I climb the stairs and find him down a carpeted hallway in his bedroom, taking clothes off the bed and smoothing down the blankets.

"Hey," I say, poking my head in. "Just seeing what's going on up here."

"Sorry," he says. "I wanted to straighten up a bit."

"No need to do it for my sake," I say and take a quick inventory: queen-sized bed, shiny mahogany dresser set, Floyd standing at the end of the bed. I place my glass of wine on a coaster on the dresser and sit on the edge of the bed. When he continues to putter around the small room, I pat the space on the bed next to me and beckon him to sit.

It is amusing and surprising to me that I seem to have moved from being the downtrodden to the aggressor but I feel compelled to coax this tryst along as best I can. I am so nervous that I can't believe I have the power to make someone else nervous, but in spite of my anxiety, I am determined. I don't quite understand why I feel like I absolutely must have sex and with no particular concern for who it is that joins me in this pursuit, I just know that ever since my night with #1, I feel like I'm blindly stumbling into the sunlight after a long period of hibernation. I want to feel wanted and I need to prove to myself that my first try was not just a one-time windfall. That I'm here with someone who is at least ten years older than me, who has just had half a lung removed, who has worked for me in my home, who wears a cross and talks a lot about his passion for his church and has an inexplicable constellation of bath mats on his kitchen floor – none of that matters to me as much as the fact that he's a muscular, fit man who is not repelled by me and there are no children on my radar at the moment.

I almost whisper "hallelujah" when he finally leans toward me to kiss me. I pull my tank top off and help him with that damn strapless bra that I was worried would stymie #1 the last time (a note about the bra: when you have substantial boobs and you've nursed three children and you find a strapless bra that holds your boobs in place and miraculously makes them look firm and buoyant, not just like one solid row of breasts, you continue to wear that strapless bra no matter how hard it is to unhook). His shirt is off too and I see tattoos sprinkled across his chest, contributing to my excitement over doing slightly illicit, dangerous things – which is silly as Johnny could not be less threatening, but I try to go with the vibe I've conjured up. We are lying down now and the only noise in the room is the incredibly loud panting of the dog standing guard. I eye Floyd furtively and I swear the dog is shooting me looks of pure loathing – it's more than a little distracting.

"Johnny," I pull back and whisper, "is there any chance you can put Floyd out of the room for a little while?"

"No, I can't, I'm sorry. He's used to being here alone with me and he'll get upset if I put him out. Trust me, the barking and crying will be even worse than having him in here."

"Um, OK," I say and try not to be preoccupied with our audience. As I reach for his belt buckle and start to undo it, I ask if he has a condom. He shakes his head.

"Seriously?" I ask skeptically. "A single man with not one condom in his house?"

"Sorry," he says. "I really don't. I wasn't expecting this."

Now we have paused mid-air like a still from a public service announcement in which a voiceover comes on and reminds us that to prevent diseases, we must use a condom. I have an IUD, so I'm not worried about getting pregnant (plus I am, ahem, a bit old for that), but I can't tell my kids to use condoms every single time they even think about having sex and then not use one myself. I mean, I can't, right? Because there's a part of me that's desperate enough for this to happen that I would be willing to.

Luckily he saves me from myself, pulling away to check for a condom in the other room. When he steps into the hallway, I hear him cursing and muttering to himself, and then he's yelling at the dog, who apparently in a jealous rage has defecated all over the hallway.

"I cannot believe this. Floyd, did you do this? I just cannot believe this," I hear him complaining over and over to himself.

This seems like a good time to pull a blanket over myself and pretend I don't know what is happening. A minute later he reappears and gives me the update as if I didn't hear everything already. I turn my back to the door as I see him, shirtless, jeans unbuttoned and belt buckle flapping, bend down to the carpet with a roll of paper towels and cleaning spray, all the while muttering to himself and talking sternly to Floyd. This is not exactly the seduction I had in mind, but I'm not sure what to do other than wait it out.

Back in the room a few minutes later, still condom-less but with Floyd hot on his heels, he announces that out of respect for me, he will run to the 24-hour Walmart. He puts his shirt back on and hands me a remote control so I can watch TV while he's gone. I tell him I'm going to listen to music on my phone instead and then hallelujah again, he's telling me that he will take the dog with him. He takes my car key so he can move it out of the way of the car he wants to drive and heads out.

Five minutes later, he's back with a sheepish look on his face, apologizing that he can't get my car to start. I sigh, roll my eyes and hold out my hand for the car key. Surely this is a sign that I should stop things, but who knows when my next opportunity for sex will be, so I wait as he rummages through his dresser for a T-shirt for me to pull on. The one he hands me is black and from a Harley-Davidson event. It hangs down to my thighs and I like it, feeling so delicate in this man's oversized motorcycle T-shirt. It has started to drizzle outside so we run to my car, which I instantly turn on. I shoot him a quizzical look.

"How did you do that?" he asks.

"I turned the ignition," I say and shrug, trying to keep the annoyance out of my voice. I smile encouragingly at him, then run through the rain to get back inside. Keeping the T-shirt on, I crawl back under the covers and try to find a playlist on Spotify that seems appropriate. Country Kind of Love? Happy Chill? Walk Like A Badass? Confidence Boost? I settle for Indie Chill and manage to lie still and nod off.

An hour later, I wake up to car doors opening and closing and then it seems to take an inordinately long time once again for Johnny to reappear. I try to pretend that I'm still sleeping so he can sneak in next to me and we can get right back to where we left off without any further small talk, but by the time he finally arrives, I'm too antsy to even feign sleep.

"I'm so sorry, Laura, that took forever," he says.

"Yes, I know," I say dryly.

"I almost gave up. There was only one register open in the store and a long line and there I am standing with my box of condoms.

Then when it's finally my turn, the cashiers change shifts and I stand there still holding my box of condoms while one cashier counts out her register and the other sets up. It's as if they were messing with me. I almost walked out."

I laugh and thank him for his determination and ultimate triumph, and here he goes again, nervously shuffling around the room and in again comes Floyd, revved up and ready for round two.

He undresses and joins me under the blankets. I have to give myself a silent pep talk to get back in the spirit of things as the time lapse, series of unfortunate events and watchful eyes of the dog have gotten in my head. As he burrows under the blankets to go down on me I close my eyes and hold my breath, as anxious as I had been with #1 that he might find something down there that alarms him.

It's a great relief when he compliments me instead, tells me that I smell good and my skin is so soft. More importantly, two men have now independently surveyed the state of my vagina and given it the all-clear. If I'm lucky enough to have sex with another man, I can probably stop worrying about this part of my anatomy. I don't want to rely on male approval, and frown when I think of my distinctly non-feminist dependence on it, but I have lost faith in the power and beauty of my body that I took for granted the last time I was single. I'm realistic about the inevitable changes that result from childbirth and age. Even though I'm grateful to have had a chance to experience both, and believe on a fundamental level that they only add to a woman's power and beauty, I worry that for me they don't sweeten the pot but mark me instead as if

I am decaying. Over the years, I've worked to maintain my physique, but I did so to stay attractive and appealing to Michael, not for myself. Now I see that I need to do a search-and-rescue mission for the confidence I once had in my physical prowess, that I need to embrace the imperfections I see as battle scars and not apologize for them.

Johnny is suddenly inside of me and thrusting, fast and hard. Within a couple of minutes, I worry that he is disconcertingly breathless – not lustful panting, but more the way I sound like I'm wheezing after an intense workout.

"Are you OK, Johnny?'"

"Yes, sorry, I'm fine."

But he does not sound fine to me; unbidden, my caretaking instincts kick in.

"I think we should stop. Just lie with me while you catch your breath."

He lies next to me and I put my hand on his chest over his heart.

"I'm so embarrassed," he says, shaking his head. "I'm still recovering. I can't do all the things I did before. It's frustrating but also just so embarrassing."

"Shhhh," I say, like I'm soothing a child. "It's OK. Recovery is a process. Don't feel bad if this is too much for you."

"I cannot believe I have a sexy woman lying naked in my bed and I can't keep up."

"Please, don't apologize or feel bad. You'll get back to yourself eventually. I'm sure most men would fare much worse after having half a lung removed!"

We lie quietly for a few minutes, my hand remaining firmly over his heart as it slows to its normal rhythm, and it occurs to me that just being here, being held by a man, may be enough for now.

"I don't know how you like your coffee in the morning," he says, breaking the silence.

I hesitate. I'm enjoying being held but I was not planning to spend the night and his assumption that I will makes me panic. My mind starts racing – what if I'm thinking this is a fun one-night stand but to him it's the start of something? What if he thinks we're embarking on a relationship of some sort? He's such a kind man at a vulnerable moment in his life, and in my own vulnerability I have overlooked where he's coming from. I'm terrified that I will hurt him.

Instead of answering that I like my coffee with a splash of soy vanilla creamer, I decide that just lying here will in fact not be enough for me and I turn to kiss him. His breath is calm again and I roll on top of him and whisper that he should lie still and I will do all the work this time. Having been trained to be quick to avoid interrupting children, I wrap my hand around his penis and push it deep inside of me and then move my hips until I orgasm and he says he can't because of the limited sensation he's getting through the condom and we are done. I lie next to him again and he's quiet and breathing deeply, his cheeks flushed and his mouth falling open.

"Johnny," I whisper. "I'm going home."

"What?" he says, opening his eyes. "No, don't go. It's too late for you to drive all the way home."

"I won't be able to sleep if I stay."

"OK,' he says with resignation. "Give me a minute to get up to walk you out."

"No, stay here, I insist. You look so comfortable. I can see myself out," I say.

"You'll text when you get home so I know you made it safely?" he asks.

"Yes, I promise," I say. I give him a quick kiss on his cheek and then I'm back out in the warm drizzle of a summer night at 2am. I text him when I arrive home half-asleep close to 3am, but by then he's sleeping off our tragicomic night and my text goes unanswered.

CHAPTER 5

The Grief Game

I lived at home with my family until I left for college, where I lived with the same four roommates for the duration of my time there. Within weeks of graduating, Michael and I moved into our first apartment together on the Upper West Side, close to Columbia University, where he earned a Master's degree in architecture while I started my career in book publishing. There had been two brief periods in which I had been on my own, each time for two months during the summer when he worked as an intern in faraway cities, and I busied myself with weekends at friends' beach shares or with my parents in the suburbs, as if staying home alone was not a viable option. The most vivid memory I have of those months alone is buying an Entenmann's low-fat raspberry Danish and thinking how thrilling it was that a) Entenmann's now had a line of low-fat baked goods and b) that I would be the only one eating it. That was the extent to which I had recognized my independence and took advantage of my freedom. I had known that Michael would be back soon and for good, so it felt a bit like when my parents used to leave us in the house as teens when they went on tropical vacations. It had felt like I was playing an adult living on her own more than I really was one, but I understand now that my current state of aloneness is permanent. It doesn't feel exciting to me, just scary and lonely.

Early Tuesday morning, I drive to Pennsylvania to meet my childhood friend Jessica, who is treating me to a few nights at a spa. For years, she has tried to convince me to go away for a few days, but she knew that much as I craved a break from my kids, I would never take one. Partly out of anxiety from being away from them, partly from the difficulty of getting childcare since Michael worked such long and erratic hours, and partly because I would not give up control of their care for even a day if it wasn't imperative. First and foremost, I was at all times a mother, and stepping away from that role to do something just for myself was inconceivable; even thinking about it used to flood me with guilt.

Our first afternoon at the spa, we throw ourselves into the Zen spirit of the place and take a mala bead meditation class. The instructor says we will go around in a circle and express what we are hoping to achieve with this meditation. She starts the circle by sharing that she is grappling with a huge loss that's been very difficult for her to talk about, the recent passing of her tabby cat. As soon as the words leave her mouth, I panic that I will burst into uncontrollable nervous laughter if I look at Jess. *This is your pain?* I want to snort. *I know we're not having a contest, but come on, I'm obviously the winner.* There are fifteen women before it's my turn and each says what she wants – serenity, love, patience, emotional connectedness. When it's my turn I surprise myself and try to set the record straight of who is ahead in this grief game by blurting out that I am reeling from the sudden rupture of a decades-long marriage and I am looking for clarity as to what to do next and how to begin my recovery. The instructor looks at me with such genuine warmth and compassion that my eyes fill with tears and I scold myself for not having taken the loss of her cat seriously. I have recently become aware of how often I make hasty, biting judgments about people I don't know; I am determined to change that. Being in the throes of grief does not make me the owner of it or give me the right to make light of others' sorrow that I have blithely determined is less than mine. I make a note to myself: we don't know what people have gone through or are going through or will go through, so always be kind.

The next day, Jessica and I are hanging out in the second-floor lounge overlooking the lobby when we notice a large group file in. There are about fifty people and they're all 20/30something, mostly male and casually but intentionally dressed: narrow jeans rolled up just so, cool retro T-shirts, carefully groomed hipster beards. We assess which men are the cutest and which of those are wearing wedding bands. We lean further and further over the ledge to see more clearly until a couple of them spot us and look up quizzically. In our embarrassment, we quickly duck behind the plants and laugh about how we must appear to them: two middle-aged women in yoga pants ogling the fresh blood. In truth, I would willingly throw myself at any of them, so badly do I want to be wanted. A new and essential understanding of my current status is starting to become clear to me: I'm looking for men all the time now. I want to be noticed, I want to be flirted with and touched, and there's no limit – aside from when I'm with my kids – as to when or where that can happen. For better or for worse, I am free and very, very available.

*

On Friday, I say goodbye to Jessica and drive to Upstate New York, where Hudson is performing in a play at a theatre camp. I'm eager to see him and hear about his time at camp, but my heart is heavy: it's been five months since he has spoken to Michael, with whom he had always been close – in fact, much closer than he had been with me – and there's no way around the fact that Michael's absence this weekend is going to be keenly felt. I feel like sloppy seconds, knowing I am not the parent Hudson would have chosen loyalty to if he had had an option. I pull into the motel parking lot, where my mother is sitting on a bench near the entrance waiting for me to arrive, watching Hasidic Jewish families bustle in and out of the kosher grocery store in the adjacent parking lot before Shabbat beckons them home. Alarmed by the squalid state of the motel, she decides she will spend the whole weekend with me as she cannot bear the idea of my spending any time in this decrepit place alone. I insist that I will be fine but she's stalwart, her eyes fixing leerily on the man who has come to deliver a broken-down cot so that I have a place to sleep now that she will be in the bed. I feel a flutter of anxiety, knowing I will not get so much as five minutes alone this weekend and that she will be watching me like a hawk. It takes everything I've got to pull myself together for a full day of being upbeat, and now I won't have privacy at night to retreat. Plus, she's chattier than usual, which means she has something important to say and is unloading herself of all minutiae until she has no choice but to spit it out.

Over an early dinner of Greek salads at a diner, she finally divulges that a week ago Michael had visited her and my father; it was strained and distressing, as he had for decades been a son to her but now felt like an unwelcome stranger. Over the years I had often felt that she actually preferred him to me – he was open and inclusive, always inviting her to stay for dinner or join us on family vacations while I subtly shook my head no at him, wanting time with just him and the kids. She is loyal and vehemently dedicated to her children, so I know that she's not upset that she got stuck with me instead of with him, but still, his fall from grace has been difficult for her to wrap her head around.

Ever the optimist, after a long rant about how she barely recognized him as the man she's come to know and adore, she throws in, "I'm still hopeful you'll be able to work it out, so we'll see, maybe he'll come back to himself."

"We won't be able to fix this, Mom," I say sadly and with a degree of certainty I haven't felt until now. "I can't find a way."

"Well, you don't know how you'll feel in a few months. Take your time, that's what a separation is for. There's no need to decide anything right now," she says.

"I do need to decide though and I don't feel I have endless time to do it. Living with the uncertainty of what will become of us is killing me and causing the kids horrible anxiety. I can't stay in this state of purgatory. I would rather face what I know deep down, that I'm done. Then I can start to figure out what's next rather than reside in this ambivalent state in which I'm consumed with the question of should I stay or should I go and pondering if it's just fear that's stopping me from doing what I see as inevitable. I hate him so much right now, I don't see how I will ever not hold this against him. If you were in my position, would you be able to move forward with him? I mean, even if I'm able to forgive him, even if I can someday move past the anger and hurt I feel, to actually be with him physically again?"

Her face falls and she answers swiftly, "No, I don't think I could do that either."

We are quiet for a moment – a rarity for both of us – and then she says, "You're going to find someone special who is going to love and respect you, I have no doubt of it. You still have so much time ahead of you. You're my daughter so I'm biased, but people always seem drawn to you. You'll find love again."

I eye her skeptically, so she continues, "When your father died, I felt like I had a mark on me. You and your sister had been through so much and I had to get you through the trauma of his death and also make a living, so there was no time to think about dating."

"And yet somehow one year later you remarried!" I say.

"You know faster the second time around. Plus, Dad was willing to adopt you and Jennifer and raise you as his own kids. Not many men would do that. I had to look out for all of us," she says.

"My kids don't need another father, they need back the one they had. And I don't want to move from one long marriage to another. I understand why it was important to you, but I need to learn how to stand on my own two feet. I'm sure someday I'll move on, but it's not going to be anytime soon. It could be years before Hudson and Daisy speak to Michael again. How can I move on when they have to continue to carry the pain of his betrayal with them? I can't be OK if they're not, so I'm stuck in this miserable holding pattern."

"You know what, Laura? You're 47 and I'm still trying to figure out how to be happy when you're not. Mothers always want their children to be happy, but we have little control over it. I so badly wanted you to have what I didn't have – a lifelong marriage, a stable family – but I don't have the power to give you that. You can't control what your kids feel and what they'll have to face as they move through their lives, so maybe focus less on happiness and more on resilience. Having determination and a positive attitude are things you can teach them. Happiness they will find or not find on their own, it can't be up to you," my mother says.

I look closely at her: 76 years old, abandoned by her father as a child, widowed with two young kids at 35 but going on to earn a doctorate in computer science, becoming an award-winning pioneer in her field, raising three children and becoming a proud Jewish grandmother. She marks her life by what she has, not by what she's lost. I realize that I've got resilience in my DNA – hopefully my kids do, too.

*

A few days later, I drop Hudson at the airport for his trip to a camp in Israel and I am child-free again for the next four days. I head straight from the airport to the Jersey Shore, where my friend

Lauren and I have planned a few days together at her condo on the beach. She is my most ardent cheerleader; I am relieved that I won't have to pull myself together to be with her as she is not skittish around my pain.

Our first morning, we bike to a yoga studio to take a class and then to a nearby restaurant for a late breakfast. I had told Lauren I didn't want to ride a bike – I'm an extremely nervous bike rider – but she had insisted I try her beach cruiser and now as I coast along the wooden slats of the boardwalk, weaving around families toting red wagons filled with sand toys, I don't know if I've ever been more content. Construction workers whistle as we fly by and I wave back cheerfully. I tell Lauren that I'll take any attention I can get and she laughs and eggs me on, saying, "OK, keep waving to all your new friends, you're making them very happy." I feel young and free with a sense of liberty I haven't known since my 20s. My kids are at camp, they're settled and busy, and I have no one to take care of aside from myself for the next few days. The utter lack of restraint and responsibility make me giddy.

We are lounging with green smoothies and English muffins at an outdoor café when two men park themselves at a table near ours. They're at least twenty years older than us, excessively tanned and lizard-like. Lauren and I are easily distracted by people around us even when the conversations we're eavesdropping in on aren't all that interesting, but this one is a doozy.

"I don't know what's with Gina. She spent all her money on fake tits and now all she does is complain that she has no money. She was in no position to get them in the first place," says one.

"Well, the cancer," says the other mournfully.

"Sure, it's not her fault she had to get a double mastectomy but still, if you can't afford fake tits, you shouldn't get them."

"You wouldn't be saying this if it was Marla."

"That's true, that's true. I had a lot more patience for Marla."

"You wouldn't even take Gina out to P.F. Chang's and a comedy club! You never took her out."

Lauren and I have been rolling our eyes during this conversation, but now I'm looking at her in terror. The revelry of the bike ride and calming breathing during hot yoga has been replaced by cold sweat and panic.

Back on our bikes, I announce to Lauren, "I'm staying with Michael. I have to find a way. Gina has no health insurance for reconstructive surgery because her husband probably left her, and now this cheap tan bastard won't even treat her to dinner and a comedy club? And by the way, I hate comedy clubs. I can't do this. An uncertain future is not for me. I'm going back to Michael, there's no choice. I don't know why I thought I had this in me."

"Laura, those men were disgusting. You're going to find someone top notch, I promise," she says soothingly.

"No, I see the writing on the wall for middle-aged women like me. I'm scarred by that conversation – it was an eye-opener and a reality check," I say, shaking my head. "It's like the old adage, why buy the cow when you can get the milk for free? I'm disposable now. I'm not young, I can't give a man a family – and oh, by the way, my sagging boobs and crepe-y stomach aren't all you'll get with me – I come attached to three kids! My demographic is a dime a dozen. We're all fighting gravity and trying to look like we're still relevant, but men can see the truth about us."

We bike back down the boardwalk, stiffly and silently.

Plunked down in chairs on the beach a few hours later, Lauren convinces me it will cheer me up to send a picture of myself in a bikini to #2. We've exchanged a few texts since our ill-fated night together a week ago and I've been hinting to him that I'll be free when I'm back upstate Friday night, my last night before I have to pick Georgia up from camp. I don't know what I'm hoping for by spending another evening with him, given the challenges of the last time, but I'm grasping at straws here. I spend the next hour trying to take a sexy selfie, but after a series of failed attempts at seductive poses leaves me and Lauren laughing and gasping for air, I settle for a photo of my toes in the sand, bright pink nail polish peeking through.

I demand that Lauren also send a picture of her toes in the sand to her husband, who is at work in the city, and he writes back that the sand looks white and clean. We laugh even harder and agree that being jilted as I've been has its perks because now my toes are sexy and hers are just a backdrop to the sand. #2 responds to me that he would love to be on a beach with me, that it's been ages since he's had a proper vacation, and this is all the encouragement I need to start tormenting him with texts. Lauren's goading and the bottle of wine we are now drinking on her terrace lend me bravado and I send some of the failed selfies from the beach as well as insist that he see me when I return on Friday night. He's evasive, cagily says maybe. When I scan the texts the next morning, I wish I could erase them all: they start out playful and flirty, but as they go on become bolder and obnoxiously persistent. The photos of my toes in the sand move fairly quickly to photos of my legs and then my bikini bottom and then my cleavage. I'm pretty sure I'll never hear from him again.

I reek of desperation.

*

As I drive the four hours from the Jersey Shore back to my home in Upstate New York, I can feel the ease and freedom of the past two weeks recede with each passing mile. After a refreshing hiatus from being a round-the-clock caregiver, now I must return to my real life as a responsible mother, which first and foremost means dealing with the fallout of my crumbling marriage. I want so badly to believe that I have it in me to be happy and whole, even without Michael and without being 100 percent focused on my kids all the time. I'm doubtful that I can get there even though I am starting to see a glimpse of who I am when I don't define myself first as a mother and second as a wife and I actually like it.

This is a somewhat shocking revelation to me. Ever since I became a mother over 18 years ago, I've thrown myself into the role with single-minded gusto. There's not a PTA I haven't joined, a school auction I haven't run, a bake sale I haven't contributed to, a craft project I haven't attempted. No holiday has passed without my marking the occasion with special celebratory meals and decorations for our front door. My kids have never been late to school, I've never missed a slot at a camp or afterschool registration, and they get their check-ups and shots right on time. In other words, I take parenting as seriously as the United Nations takes world peace. If I haven't made my mark in the world outside my home, I've at least made sure my home itself has been a veritable bastion of maternal warmth and order. Most of my close friends are women I've met at the kids' schools, who are now also stay-home moms: former lawyers, teachers, social workers, literary agents, marketing executives, stylists and artists. We've formed tight circles of friendship, but our conversations and plans are usually centered around our families. In my case, just as my kids were getting older and becoming more self-sufficient, I had another baby – so I'm awestruck by a peek at life outside this realm. My own needs and desires? I have not acknowledged them in decades. Now that I'm aware of them, they're not going to so easily be swept back under the rug, but this begs a very difficult question: which is stronger, my hunger to establish myself as an independent woman or my fear of establishing myself as an independent woman?

I arrive home to a thunderstorm and a text from #2 saying that the week has wiped him out and he's going to stay in for the night, though he's sorry to disappoint me. Even though my night with him was a debacle, I am disappointed and also more than a bit embarrassed. What seems like daring fun when having a Girls Gone Wild weekend on the beaches of the Jersey Shore doesn't translate to the quiet of your home in the countryside with the scent of cow manure wafting down the dirt road. But I've got this one last night to myself and I'm determined not to let it slip by as I have a void in me that needs filling, and this may well be my last shot for quite some time. The bar in town where I hit pay dirt last time doesn't have anything on the schedule tonight, but I remember another place a bit further away in a converted barn. It seems like fate that they have a young, folksy band playing tonight. Though weather looms large for me when making decisions about whether or not to go out and I'm fretfully watching the thunderstorm create mud puddles in my driveway, I drag myself to the shower and begin the grooming process: shaving, trimming, scenting, oiling and finally donning a long, silky navy blue slip dress, along with high-heeled strappy sandals. I suspect I'm overdressed for a barn but hey, I've only got this one night.

CHAPTER 6

A Question of Availability

The rain is tapering off by the time I pull into the gravel parking lot next to the barn. There are only a handful of cars here and I rue my sandal choice as I dodge puddles and mosquitoes on my way to the entrance. The small tables inside are occupied by couples – again, mostly older – but there are plenty of empty seats at the bar, and I sit in the center of them and order a glass of rosé, which quickly arrives in a can. I survey the room as it starts filling up. The only people younger than their fifties are to my right – the college-aged band members. As I listen to them talk about their summer travels through Europe and what they will do until school starts again, I feel old and used up, neither tethered to another person as everyone else is here nor young and fresh enough to be noticed. My last bar tryst was likely a once-in-a-lifetime event and these rural areas are probably not fertile grounds for meeting single men. I am definitely overdressed for the casual crowd and feel ridiculously and conspicuously alone, but I'm following the new rule I made for myself: one drink, a few songs and then it's fair to call it a night. As my kids used to chant when they were in nursery school: if you don't try, you don't know – so I'm trying, and when I return home alone later still feeling empty, perhaps it will provide some consolation that I did, at least, try.

What are the chances that at this very moment as I admit defeat, a tall, handsome man will walk in alone? He is heading toward me as if we are in a movie in which the music fades to the background while our hearts draw magnetically toward one another, but at the last minute he veers to the side and takes a stool two seats away that the band member, who is now warming up, has vacated. He is dressed in an untucked white button-down shirt over jeans, with black-framed glasses and no wedding ring. I know that I need to hear him order as evidence of whether or not someone is joining him, so I lean less subtly than I would like to the side while bracing myself against the bar so I don't fall off my seat, and listen to him order food and one – only one – beer. Encouraged, I feel a bit like a cat who has just spotted her mouse.

"Do you know this band?" he leans over to ask after a couple of minutes during which I not all that casually eye him.

My eyes flare open – *is this really happening?*

"Yes, a bit," I say.

"What kind of music do they play?"

"Well, when I say I know them, I mean I looked them up on Spotify on the way here and listened to one song," I admit, and then add, "but I like what I heard so I guess you could say I'm an expert."

"So you're actually the band's manager?" he asks and we laugh.

I deflate as a woman appears between us. No-nonsense, outfitted in rain gear and with cropped grey hair, she asks if the seat between us is free. We both say yes and then I turn back to my can of wine, he to his beer, and we quietly watch the band warm up. Should I have said no and then moved over a seat? Would that have seemed too eager? I am once again wishing there was a manual for how this is done.

A few minutes later, he passes by on his way back from the food window and offers me French fries from his basket. I smile and take one and note that he's eating my ideal dinner – fries and a salad – but then he sits down on his stool, and I am alone again.

Is he passing fries to any other women here?

"Since you're the manager, do you know when the band is going to start?" he leans over the woman between us a few minutes later to ask.

"It's going to be a while," I say.

"What?" he shouts. It's loud in here and we are gracelessly leaning over this poor woman as we attempt to keep our conversation going.

"Would you like to trade seats with me?" she asks, looking at me and then at him and then back at me when he doesn't answer.

I hesitate for a second, remembering that moment weeks ago of indecisively lingering over the "purchase tickets" button that set my newly active single life in motion and then say "Sure" and hop off my stool to switch with her. This makes me feel almost like I've accepted an invitation to a date, but it wasn't his invitation so I hope I'm not misreading his cues. And now here comes another woman, much younger than me, with a sweet smile and straight, compliant hair pulled back in a ponytail. She leans in with a kiss on the cheek for my new friend and I want to die for getting this whole thing wrong. He attempts to introduce me but we don't know each other's names, so we clumsily exchange them and now we are stuck here together, an awkward threesome. When the band welcomes the small crowd and starts playing, I am beyond relieved that I can stop trying to participate in their conversation. Bonus: soon the woman says she's going to find her sister and wanders away, and she doesn't say she is coming back so I am hopeful she won't: we are fighting for limited supplies here and I am a scrappy but determined contender.

The band is fun, upbeat and quirky. We are both smiling watching them and it feels like music that it would be impossible not to feel happy listening to. The hour that they play passes quickly and soon enough, they call it a night.

"Do you want another drink?" he asks as the room quiets down.

"I do, but then I'll have to stay here a while until I can drive home," I say.

"I will take responsibility for keeping you company until you're ready to go," he says solemnly.

I am incredulous. It does not seem possible that for the second time I have found and ensnared the one single man in the room, but I gratefully accept this gift from the universe. It will occur to me later that on both these nights, there were few other single women present, so it will seem less remarkable, possibly even comic that I gave myself and the universe so much credit.

It's quiet now, so we can talk without shouting. He lives nearby and this is his regular weekend haunt. He is a freelance writer whose passion for books, podcasts and music matches my own. I tell him I am struggling through an old Michael Chabon novel; he tells me he tried that one but couldn't get through it. We talk about how we ended up in this area and marvel when we realize that not only did we grow up in the same suburban town, we even attended the same elementary school. He is three years older than me, so we don't know many of the same people but we land on one or two in common. He seems familiar to me, not that I know him, but I feel like I could. Our conversation meanders and is thoroughly enjoyable; he is witty, charming, and attentive. My conversations with #1 and 2 were fun and flirty, but this is something different – he feels like a friend.

We've passed a couple of hours without running out of steam, but it's just us and the bartender now and I suggest that we should probably let him close up, so we reluctantly get up to leave. The rain has stopped, but the air outside is heavy and damp.

"I would love to see you again if you want to share your number with me?" he asks.

"Yes, that would be lovely," I respond, and he puts my number into his phone. We are standing at my car already so it's do-or-die time.

"When are you available?" he asks. "I'm sure it's hard for you to get away with your kids at home."

I raise my eyebrows. I don't have an easy answer to this question: tomorrow, Georgia will return from sleepaway camp and then I've got kids home for the rest of the summer.

"Well," I say very slowly, "I'm available right now."

The meaning of my words sinks in and he chuckles softly.

"That's a more literal answer than I was expecting," he says.

"Just grabbing the bull by the horns," I say with a soft laugh. "And the question of my future availability is anyone's guess."

"What are you thinking about doing with your current availability?" he asks.

"Going back to my house or yours," I say, letting my forwardness float between us.

"I'm not sure," he says hesitantly. "I wasn't expecting this tonight. My girlfriend and I broke up a few months ago and I haven't been with anyone since."

"It's OK," I say. "I don't have any expectations, it's just that I'm not sure when I'll be free again, so . . ."

He leans down toward me and kisses me. He's tall, and I lean forward onto my toes to reach him. His kiss is soft and gentle.

"OK," he says, pulling back. "Let's go to my house. It's closer than yours plus I have to walk my dog."

Another dog, I think, my heart sinking.

I follow him along dark winding roads. He knows the area well and drives fast; I have to concentrate to keep up. After a few minutes he turns up a dirt road and parks in front of a small weathered farmhouse. I get out of my car and hear a cacophony of honking noises – ducks! He assures me they'll settle down but I don't care, I'm thoroughly charmed by the whole scene. When he opens the screen door after crossing a ramshackle porch filled with rubber boots and gardening tools, two cats and a chocolate Labrador come running to greet us. He looks down at my feet and asks if I have a more practical pair of shoes in my car to take the dog for a walk. I do not, so he reaches for my hand to guide me as we walk up a damp grassy path behind the dog. It is serene under the inky black sky, but impossible to see more than a foot ahead and we are walking with purpose to keep up with the dog, wet grass tickling my feet while my delicate sandals rebel against the pastoral conditions. Terrified that even with him protectively clutching my hand I am merely steps away from wiping out, I'm doing everything I can to simultaneously secure my footing, casually swat away mosquitoes and reassure him this is a lovely walk and of course I am loving every second of my time outdoors! My relief when we are back inside and I can kick off my ridiculous heels is so great that one might have thought I was returning from a ten-mile hike in the depths of the jungle. Settling into a cane-backed rocking chair to wait while he feeds his cats, I take in the living room, which, like the house, is unpretentious and charming, simply furnished with a stack of astronomy magazines and copies of *The New York Review of Books* on the coffee table.

Soon he is back, wasting no words while he sinks down to his knees next to the rocking chair, kissing me gently and then with increasing urgency. He asks if I want to go upstairs and then we are on the rickety staircase with him holding out a hand behind him for me to hold as we head to his bedroom. The windows are open and it sounds like pouring rain outside, but he says it is the river rushing by, one on his property that I could not see in the dark. It's hard for me to imagine a more romantic spot than the one I am standing in. I have a flash of the hugely best-selling book *The Bridges of Madison County*: at the time I read it I thought it was absurd, the idea of a lonely housewife on a farm having a brief affair with a stranger she stays in love with forever and never sees again, but now it comes back to me and makes sense.

I don't expect this night to be my great reprisal and for #3 to become the keeper of my soul, but I can see how these just-right conditions could create a backdrop for an affair that encapsulates the essence of a love that was meant to be. Slipping off the thin straps of my dress, I let it fall down into a dark heap, step out of it onto the creaky wooden floorboards and stand in my strapless bra (yes, *that* one) and thong. I see the dog standing politely in the hallway as if waiting for an invitation and think *oh boy, here we go again*, but #3 gently kicks the door closed and tells me to ignore the dog when she starts whining. *Progress*, I think.

We lie naked on his bed and I take note of his body. This is the third man I've been with in the past few weeks and, naïve as it may sound, it genuinely surprises me to find each one so different from the one before, and so different from the one I knew as my own for the past few decades. I haven't thought about men's bodies for so many years, as if the mere notion of what lay under their clothes had been completely erased from my brain with marriage. This man is tall, sturdy and fit, with hair on his chest and a well-endowed penis embedded in a mess of hair. The men I've been with so far have manscaped and I've liked it – how it makes them clean and smooth. It strikes me as ironic that women's pubic hair is slangily called a bush as if offensively uncultivated and in need of landscaping, while men seem to have avoided any kind of moniker associated with nature and flora even though theirs are probably more like overgrown hedges unwinding over a larger region. He reaches over me for a condom in the night table drawer, but once he has it opened, he hesitates.

"I'm sorry, I'm nervous," he says. "It's really strange to be here with you. I thought my girlfriend and I were going to get married and our breakup has been rough. I haven't even thought about being with someone else for the past few months. The last thing I expected tonight when I walked into my usual watering hole was to find a beautiful woman in a slinky dress sitting alone."

I'm surprised to hear that he noticed me as I have felt invisible both times I have gone out to bars on my own. I assumed both when #1 and #3 started talking to me, they did so because they stumbled upon me, not because they actively noticed me. In my mind, when I'm alone in public, I am not much more than an apparition. It's not that I don't think I'm attractive – I think I'm pretty but not conventionally beautiful, that I have a nice figure but not one that commands attention. I'm petite with a voluminous head of curly hair, neither sleek nor statuesque. When I look at photos of myself, I see a genuine smile, complete with dimples, but one that makes my eyes disappear. So not until now has it occurred to me that I might be attractive according to the literal definition of the word – not necessarily beautiful, but appealing to people – and that that appeal is not because of my hair color or figure or blue eyes but from something as subtle as the way I sit or smile. Or maybe it comes from something I have only just learned about myself: I hold my head high. I'm proud to be myself, to be recovering from this broken mess of a year, to be present and alive when the alternative of closing into myself would have been so much easier and more comfortable. I'm bruised but not shattered as I've been regarding myself, my head is most certainly not hanging low, and if I'm not actually a shadow of my former self, can it be that I'm stronger and more capable than I ever knew?

#3 is sweet, gentle and, as he has pointed out, nervous. He puts on a brave face and the condom he's opened and when I orgasm and he doesn't, he is embarrassed and apologetic.

"Please don't worry," I say. "I basically forced myself on you, so it's only fair you weren't ready for me." I can't help noting that this is the second time this has happened, so my track record is starting to take on a troubling pattern: I come, but the men can't. Is it the condoms? Am I doing something wrong? Is it possible I've had it all wrong, thinking men could come on a dime but women had to really work for it? Should I feel the guilt that rises up in me that I am leaving these experiences sexually satisfied but the men are not?

"Can I see you again?" he asks. "I need to get my head in the right place. It'll be better next time, I assure you. I really liked spending time with you."

I nod my head and smile.

It's late, after two in the morning, and I have to be en route to retrieve Georgia in six hours. He walks me outside in the muggy night air, crickets serenading us, and opens my car door for me. Pausing before I get in, I tell him that I think I will be available on Sunday afternoon. We both softly chuckle at my usage of the word "available", knowing I mean it in more than one way, and I fold myself into my car. He bends down to the open window to kiss me goodbye; from my rearview mirror as I pull out, I see him standing in the driveway, barefoot, rumpled, hands tucked in the pockets of his jeans.

By the time I arrive home in the dead of the night half an hour later, there's a text from him saying how great it was to meet me and jokingly wishing me well in my future as a band manager. This is a new situation for me: a man I have enough of a connection with that we have already made plans to see each other again. I like how he isn't playing games with me – he likes me and isn't afraid to let me know it. I like him too, which means this could be more than just the one-night stands I've recently come to know.

CHAPTER 7

Homemade

A few hours later, I pull into the camp parking lot and see Georgia and her bunk-mates assembled by the main building. She looks tanned and robust, wearing an oversize T-shirt and messy braids. I am eager to get my hands on her, but she pulls away quickly – she wants to soak up all the affection she can from her counselors before she has to leave. A mom I know starts chatting with me and then Michael approaches, his arms open wide for a hug. My eyes dart to my left and then to my right to figure out who this hug is intended for and I feel dismay as he gets closer and I realize it's for me. I reflexively take a step backward and hold up my hands to stop him. He stops short and his arms fall and dangle at his sides as he says, "Oh, OK, sorry, hi Laura." I know that I have embarrassed him but I don't know if I will ever be able to receive even the most basic affection from him again, and I'm most certainly not ready now. When he walks away to find Georgia, I look up at the mom I had been talking to and shrug my shoulders.

"I'm sorry you had to witness that," I say, wincing. "The very definition of awkward."

"Been there, done that," she kindly replies. "If you ever want to talk about it, I'm here."

I am aware once again that I am part of a new club, one that I wish I could refuse admittance into even though I do appreciate the camaraderie in it. I want to set the record straight, demand that people understand Michael and I were different – we're not together now, sure, but we meant to stay together forever, we were a family, I am not supposed to be here. I don't know how to pretend I'm one of the divorced moms' crew while also maintaining the steadfast belief that I am not, that if one of them would just give me a map back to the road I had been on, I would gladly stay on the recommended route forever.

A memory comes back to me in a painful flash. Months earlier, in the spring, when I was at Georgia's school selling tickets to the talent show I was organizing, a mother approached with her daughter. When I realized that she was the mother of the one child from whom I did not yet have music, I asked her to please get it to me right away. She dramatically rolled her eyes and shook her head at me, saying, "That's her father's job."

"OK," I said, "well then can you tell him I need it today?"

"We're divorced," she said.

"I feel your pain, I'm going through it myself right now. I just need the music though," I said.

She became animated then, leaning across the table toward me conspiratorially as she asked, "Who's your judge?"

"What do you mean?" I asked, confused.

"There are only two judges at the court who handle divorce. I'm curious if you have the good one," she said.

"Oh, no, we're not up to that yet," I said.

"Who's your lawyer?" she asked as I continued to shake my head.

"We're not up to that yet either," I said. "Anyway, I just really need the music."

"I'll tell him, but I can't promise that he'll send it," she said brusquely, while her daughter stood next to her, silently listening to our interaction. I wanted to reach over the table and hug her, reassure her that we would make this work for her no matter what, but she turned, shoulders drooping, and went into the school building while her mother strode purposefully down the sidewalk. I watched her until she turned the corner, absorbing the critical information I had just unwittingly received: this is what bitterness and anger look like after years of unchecked growth. If I buy into the negative behavior I've read about in newspaper accounts of ugly divorces or in dramatic retellings on TV or in books – or in live exchanges like the one that just took place – I will soon be a hostile, spiteful shadow of myself.

Standing now at Georgia's camp, having rejected Michael's hug, I know I have to do better. If I am resolute that I want to move forward in my life without him, I have to find a way to soften my anger so that my kids are not in the line of fire – or better yet, so there is no line of fire, just a soft dissolution. I won't be hugging him any time soon – after all, I'm still working on making eye contact – but the venom inside me has to be treated before it poisons me.

*

I arrive home before Michael and Georgia. He was indulgent with the kids even before we separated but now that he's got only one child who will talk to him, all the spoiling goes into her. I've warned him that buying her treats all the time and taking her from one activity to the next is having a negative effect on her. When she's with me she constantly asks, what are we doing today? Can we go to the arcade? Can we go skating? Bowling? Daddy lets me have bubble tea and ice cream. Daddy doesn't care about bedtime. Daddy is more fun. By the time she returns home to me, I have to run her through a detox program. Now that he's got his hands on her, I can only imagine how he's pampering her. I'm seething, not only because I fear he's ruining her, but also because I feel I have a right to be with her after an absence and sharing her like this feels patently unfair. *She's mine*, I think possessively, as if I'm doing him a favor by granting him access to her, and anxiously peer out the window waiting for them to return. *Didn't all those years glued to my kids' sides entitle me to VIP privileges now when I want them?*

Then comes my silver lining: a text from #3 suggesting that if I'm still available tomorrow, he will pack a picnic and we can head over to Tanglewood to listen to classical music and read the Sunday *NYTimes*. I am astonished. I've never been with a man who cooked or prepared food for me. The idea that someone would take care of this aspect of an outing is a wonderful novelty. To add to that the suggestion of having this kind of adult time, to be with someone in a companionable way coexisting as we listen to music and read the newspaper without children around: mind-blowing.

I check the weather report and am dismayed to see that the

heatwave we are in the midst of has a couple more days in its clutches. Now instead of picturing us leisurely reading side by side on a grassy lawn, I am worrying about the lack of shade at Tanglewood, how we'll be smudged from the newsprint that will rub off on our sweaty fingers and smacking at mosquitoes that will be feasting on us. I confess my practical concerns to him despite the fact that his plan represents my idea of a perfect day, and he proposes a compromise: we will picnic by the river on his property, where we will be guaranteed a shady spot, while listening to the Tanglewood concert on the radio, and he will provide me with a hazmat suit for the bugs.

I am practically swooning. We set a date for the next afternoon.

In the meantime, I have been invited to a dinner party tonight by a mom I recently met at Georgia's camp. Since Michael is going to be with Georgia until he leaves for the city Sunday evening, on goes a bright orange floor-length strapless sundress I recently scored at a thrift shop, a flat pair of silver sandals, and some of my lucky rose oil just in case.

When I arrive, the party is in full swing in a beautiful enclosed porch at the side of a rambling farmhouse. I hesitate at the entryway, noting the six couples who are already there. Being the odd man out and conspicuously single is still new to me. So far, on the few occasions I've shown up to parties alone, it's been in the presence of close friends who have instinctively encircled me. This is my first time flying completely solo, and I wonder if there is some behavior that is expected of me: party roamer, double-fisted cocktail taker, spirited floozy? Or is the expectation the opposite: stay quiet and demure, don't come too close, signal in some way that I'm not a threat to anyone? *Head high*, I remind myself, *you're alone and that's the beginning and end of it.*

A glass of rosé in her hand, I am approached by the hostess, a lovely Australian woman named Kate. Next to her stands a man who she says is here from Sweden for the summer. She introduces us and quietly slips away. Aha, so this explains the last-minute invitation. The Swedish man is friendly, but when he shows me pictures of his babies and girlfriend back home, I am quietly stung. I realize that Kate is not trying to set me up with this man, just round out her dinner table. I don't want to be a seat filler. These are new friends who don't understand what an alien feeling it is for me to be on my own, and how horrifying it is to find myself the only single woman in a room filled almost entirely with couples. Just six months earlier I was one of them – safely ensconced in a pair, eyeing my husband to signal no more drinks since he would inevitably be the one driving home. Kate and her husband are gracious and I know their invitation was purely kind, but I feel out of place nonetheless and hyper aware of my new status. I've always had such a solid sense of my role in my family and in social settings, but I'm not sure where I belong anymore.

*

The next day is as hot and humid as the weather reports had predicted, so I don the skimpiest outfit I can find: very short chambray shorts and a flimsy black tank top. I realize I have my elementary school yearbooks in the house and scan the books on the shelves until I find them, then I pull out all seven and dump them in a tote bag as a surprise to show #3. If all else fails at least we can spend some time going down memory lane together.

When I pull up to his house half an hour later, I feel like I've just entered Dr. Dolittle's yard. Ducks are waddling down the driveway, cats are purring on the back porch and the chocolate Lab is barking from inside the door. Now that I can fully see the house in daylight, its many charms are fully exposed, and what's more charming about an old farmhouse than a little decay? Paint is peeling, weeds are flourishing, creaky uneven wooden floor-boards lead to the back door and I am thoroughly captivated by every detail. I shout hello and he yells for me to come in, the rickety screen door banging shut behind me. I find him busily puttering around his rustic kitchen, surrounded by piles of greens and fruit, bread and olives, a tall vase of wildflowers holding command at the center. The kitchen has a fresh, yeasty smell and I notice a bread machine on the floor, an appliance I haven't seen in at least 25 years since the one my mother bought me when I was newly married and my entire kitchen was the size of the bread machine. I'm enchanted. If there is an antidote to the ferocity of my emotions of late, I'm certain it may well be found right here in this kitchen with its freshly baked bread and just-picked flowers.

I am not sure how to greet him. We are too new for perfunctory kisses hello, but it seems cold and slightly absurd at this point to keep my physical distance. I approach him and he bends down to give me a quick kiss on the lips. It gives me a stabbing pang of sadness, this kiss – the informality and ease of it a reminder of my marriage that I hadn't realized I missed. The acknowledgement of familiarity embedded in this greeting jars me from my revelry: do I even want this level of ease with a man? It feels too much like it should be happening with Michael instead. My recent forays have been all about sex, but this one is embarking on new territory: intimacy.

To mask my confused feelings, I pull out my treasure trove of yearbooks and fan them out for him to see. His face lights up and he grins, pulling me into the living room where we sit on the loveseat and start with the first yearbook, when I was in second grade and he was in fifth. We find my photo first, pint-sized and smiling broadly with a mouth of crooked teeth and a head of unruly curly hair; then we find him, tall, grinning mischievously. We are delighted to find ourselves in the same yearbook from 1979, 39 years earlier. What are the odds? I have always loved thinking about the surprising ways people we have circled in the past resurface again later in life and the fact that #2 and #3 are both men I have known in some way in the past makes me wonder who else might be coming down my path.

It is not long before he neatly stacks the yearbooks on the coffee table, takes my hand and leads me up the slanted wooden staircase to his room. He is less nervous and more assured this time, and I can see that he's made preparations for me: he is clean-shaven, his body missing much of the hair that was in abundance on Friday night, and I catch a whiff of a clean, fresh scent.

Sex with him is fun and comfortable, not mind-blowing like it was with #1, but I feel relaxed with him. I am relieved when he comes, breaking the curse I was convinced I was burdened with. The best part is after, when we lie naked on the bed with the fan gently blowing on us and bright golden sunlight streaming into the room. Neither of us try to cover our bodies, and the comfort we feel with each other is lovely. He tells me about his ex-girlfriend, who he dated for six years and who he had thought he would marry. Never having been married or had kids, he says he does not want to let years pass again with a woman with whom he can't see a definite future.

I tell him I understand that, even though I feel the opposite, that I can't imagine ever being married again. I confess that I don't know if I believe there is anything sacred about marriage anyway, though I hate to sound jaded about it. My experience turned out so differently than I had expected – just because I thought it was inviolable ultimately amounted to nothing. I know I sound bitter – I *am* bitter. I was raised on the notion of happily ever after and it turned out to be a farce. I explain that I don't even know how to break it to my kids that I'm dating, that I'm intrigued by meeting men and seeing all the different types who are out there, and that settling down seems light years away. He floats his fingers delicately over my bare skin as he listens and nods. I appreciate that he seems to understand that we are each emerging from such different situations, that my lack of interest in a relationship is not a personal affront but simply a statement about where I am. It seems crass to bluntly tell him the bottom line, that right now I want to sleep with as many men as I can to the degree that I don't even refer to them by name but by number.

And yet, I really, really like him. He wears his heart on his sleeve as I often do and is kind, honest, empathetic and well-read. He is a left-leaning vegan Democrat (we depart here – I could never give up cheese, butter or ice cream) who won't even kill a mosquito (we depart here too – I kill mosquitoes with fervor) and lives comfortably, but not luxuriously. For years I have questioned Michael's insatiable need to always have more, bigger, better while I often buy clothing second-hand and love nothing more than a cabinet full of mismatched chipped china picked up at yard sales. #3 has strong beliefs and adheres to them, which impresses me.

We spend the entire afternoon in bed until the intensity of the light from outside begins to fade. We have sex multiple times, reaching for each other in between conversations that ramble from our families to gardening to our favorite books. We make each other laugh and I like how when he laughs it is with a heartiness that makes me feel I said something truly witty.

"I better feed you," he finally says with a sigh. "I promised lunch and now it's almost dinner and I think we've missed the concert."

"Yes, good idea. I'm famished," I say.

In the kitchen he directs me to sit on a wooden stool at the counter while he busies himself preparing salads and slicing freshly baked nine-grain bread. I watch intently, more than a little over-whelmed at being cared for this way. I ask for a job, but he shakes his head. Swinging my feet from my perch on the high stool and tapping my fingers on the butcher block in front of me, I ask again, telling him sitting still is not in my wheelhouse and is making me anxious. Laughing, he hands me a bowl of lemons and instructs me to juice them so that he can make us lemonade.

My mind is officially blown. I can think of nothing sweeter and more sincere than a man making me fresh lemonade. My voice catches in my throat.

"I think this may be the nicest thing anyone has ever done for me," I say quietly. "Thank you."

"This?" he sweeps his arm across the counter. "This is very simple and it's being served hours late, after I've practically starved you."

"No, really. Don't underestimate yourself. No man has ever prepared a meal for me before. This is so lovely. I mean it. Thank you."

"Come on. I'm sure your husband or another man made you a few decent meals over the years," he says.

"No, none. The kitchen has always been solely my domain. Trust me. I'm touched and grateful."

Truthfully, the kitchen has been more than just my domain. For years I have attempted to express my love to Michael through food, cooking his favorite meal of paella on his birthday and elaborate Indian curries, homemade chicken soup, Korean stir-fried noodles, and spanakopita for weeknight meals, leaving a plate of food on the counter for him to eat when he came home late and the rest of us had already eaten and cleaned up. He had exuberantly praised my cooking, always insisting the kids take notice of the healthy and creative meals I attempted. I was not physically demonstrative like he was and sometimes even pulled back when he kissed me hello, but food was a love language I had mastered, so it was a shocking blow when he told me recently that he would have traded all of my meals for some tenderness and affection from me. I had wept in response, insisting those meals *were* my tangible displays of the tenderness and affection he craved. He had shaken his head sadly, reiterating that it wasn't what he had wanted, leaving me bereft and mystified. If that was the love I had to give and I had thought it had been enough but it wasn't even close, what did I understand about loving people the way they needed to be loved?

Would what I have to give be adequate for anyone?

Now, watching #3 spread a faded gingham tablecloth on the picnic table outside, setting the vase of wildflowers in the center, bringing out his pitcher of lemonade and plates of salads and bread, I feel a stolen piece of myself being gifted back to me. Making someone a meal, it does count for something. What I gave Michael before he wholeheartedly rejected it, that counted for something too.

We face each other at the picnic table and are shy again. We've spent hours naked in his bed, but facing each other now, eating, is yet another form of intimacy. I am barefoot and, as the ducks waddle under the table looking for scraps, they nibble on my toes. I'm squeamish about it so I swing my feet up onto the bench, realizing in horror that what I thought was mud squished between my toes is actually duck poop. Too embarrassed to call attention to it, I pull a handful of grass and try to wipe it off surreptitiously, but the blades of grass are narrow and flimsy, no match for runny duck poop, so now it's streaking across my fingers and I can't eat for fear that I will get E. coli by accidentally consuming it. I finally give up on both eating and cleaning my toes and walk around the table to sit on the bench next to #3 for a moment.

"This day with you was absolutely delightful. And I know the planning and preparation of this meal doesn't mean much to you, but it means everything to me. Also, I urgently need to wash my feet. Perhaps you have a hose?"

"Ugh, sorry, I should have warned you not to walk around here barefoot," he says, grimacing.

"It's OK. I just pretend to be a country girl, but in real life I'm as city as they come," I say laughing.

When I hear the late evening chirps of the crickets start to swell, I tell him that as much as I want to stay, it's way past time for me to head home. Michael has to return to the city, so I need to get back to Georgia. He leans against my car door as we draw out our goodbye, asking when he can see me again. We tentatively set a date for the following weekend, when Michael will take Georgia to the beach and Hudson will still be in Israel. I make him promise that he will let me cook for him on our next date, and with one last kiss through the car window, I am once again on my way back home.

CHAPTER 8

A Hug Won't Fix This

I've added #3's contact information in my phone under the name Jen. Since I have a handful of friends and a sister named Jen, I hope that when his texts pop up on my phone the kids won't think twice about who it is. I'm not ready to tell them that I have started dating, but sneaking around makes me feel like I'm doing something illicit. I'm confused about my status with Michael, moving further and further away from him as the summer progresses but unwilling to commit to staying apart. If the kids know I'm dating they'll feel it is a definitive statement about our future; given my own ambivalence, the last thing I need is for them to throw their own addled feelings into the mix.

Like a woman on the run who has to be in motion all the time now, I take Georgia to Pennsylvania for a few days to visit our friends at their lake house. I have always been a busy person, working on messy baking or craft projects or cleaning out closets. I claim that I want to be left alone with a good book but given the opportunity to do so, I rarely let myself relax. Now it's like I'm on speed. When I read, my eyes aimlessly scan pages without taking words in and I start books only to give up on them a few pages in. If I'm sitting still, chances are that I'm keeping myself busy with disconcerting thoughts about my past and unanswerable questions about my future. My mind is in a constant, unpleasant state of overdrive.

One night as we lounge in my friend Alexandra's living room with a bottle of Prosecco after putting the kids to sleep, I ask her 80-year-old mom how she first met her husband fifty years earlier. He has recently passed away after a long illness, and I think it might be cathartic for her to talk about him in his younger and healthier years.

"I lived in a decrepit walk-up on St. Mark's Place and one day I bumped into this guy who had just spilled groceries all over the hallway. He had brought them for a friend but it was pouring out and the bag had gotten wet and ripped and his friend wasn't home, but he couldn't just leave the food in the hallway, so he gave it to me. We started talking and he invited me to a party that was being thrown by his friend, an artist named Stephen who lived uptown with his girlfriend. I went and there was this interesting group of artists and writers who threw parties all the time. I became close with them over the next few months. One day, I heard loud banging on my door and when I opened it, Stephen was there, looking wretched. He rushed in and said he couldn't wait another minute to tell me that he was in love with me. Well, I was in love with him too but he lived with his girlfriend, who had become my friend. He said he had to be with me and was going home to get his things and would come back to stay with me."

I think sadly of the unnamed girlfriend, knowing well what it feels like when the love you rely on is redirected to another woman.

"To spend the night or to move in with you?" I asked.

"To move in, because he couldn't stay with the girlfriend once he told her about me. So he left to go back uptown," she continues.

"Wait, so he comes, declares his love for you, you say yes same and then he just leaves?" I ask.

"Yes, I guess so," she says.

"You didn't sleep with him first? This man appears at your door, you admit your feelings for each other and then nothing else?" I ask dubiously.

"I guess I slept with him," she says contemplatively. Alexandra and I howl with laughter. I ask if she's being coy or if she really can't recall.

"OK fine, I slept with him. But then he left and was supposed to come right back and he didn't. He was gone for hours. I was crushed but of course I had no way to reach him because I couldn't call his apartment. I assumed he had decided to stay with his girlfriend. Well, he finally appeared and do you know where he had been?" she asks.

"Outside on the street collecting his things after his girlfriend threw them out the window?" I ask.

"No, he had stopped at a bar to watch the Super Bowl. It was the first year of the Super Bowl and a very big deal. He came over after it ended," she says triumphantly.

Setting aside my feelings of compassion for the jilted girlfriend, I am thoroughly charmed by this story – the passion and ardor involved, the parts she clearly remembered and those that were fuzzier to her. It wasn't the sex that had been so astounding to her, it was his sudden declaration of love, the moment they acknowledged their feelings for each other even though it came at the cost of heartache to a third party. There is something else I realize, which is that sex is part of every love story, but not one that we openly talk about. We ask each other, how did you meet or when did you know it was forever? But we don't ask how was the sex, was it explosive or beside the point, was it exciting or a bit of a letdown? Sex is an integral part of all intimate relationships, so why don't we talk about it as freely as we talk about feelings? I not only want to be having sex, but I want to talk about it too; I want to understand it, what makes it powerful and what doesn't, what makes it sustainable, what it means to other people.

*

Back from Pennsylvania, I set off with Georgia to drop her with Michael at a rest stop along the highway for their weekend trip to the beach. Halfway there, my phone rings, a foreign exchange flashing across on the screen. I answer with a sense of dread and a man from Hudson's camp in Israel announces himself and tersely tells me that I must arrange for my son to leave immediately, that he has been caught smoking marijuana and has admitted to smoking it every day since he arrived. If I want to avoid the police being called in, I must make arrangements for Hudson and the two friends he went to camp with to leave the premises at once – in fact, right now before it gets any later as it's already 10pm there.

With a promise to call back within the hour, I hang up the

phone. Immediately, Georgia pipes up from the backseat with questions. What happened to Hudson? What's he smoking? Where is he going to go? Will he be left alone? Is he in trouble? I snap at her to stop talking until I reach the rest stop. I know that I have to tell Michael what has happened but I'm reticent. For the five months that he hasn't spoken to Hudson, he has been irate with me as if I'm fueling Hudson's anger by not allowing him in our apartment and not agreeing to spend family time together. I feel I have been more than fair; I don't speak badly of Michael to the kids and I encourage them to see him, telling them that I want them to have a relationship with him – they don't need to prove their loyalty to me by severing ties with him. Daisy and Hudson have complained to me that my efforts at reuniting them feel heavy-handed, that when they're ready to see him they will, but I shouldn't expect it for a long time. I didn't cause this disturbance in our family and I can't fix it. I'm doing my best on my own to keep it all together, but this latest news is going to be my downfall – proof that I have neither authority nor control and that I am failing woefully short of the parenting my kids need.

I send Georgia into Michael's car so that we can speak privately. Shaking and crying, I relay the phone call.

"I'm sorry," he says sympathetically. "Can I give you a hug?"

"A hug?" I hurl back at him, the word becoming a grenade. "A fucking hug? What I need is a co-parent and a partner. I need a husband, a father for my kids. I need you back but the you that was you before. I've never felt so alone. What I don't need is a fucking hug." With that, I storm back into my car.

The camp director calls again from Israel. I am usually respectful and polite, but, truly, hell hath no fury like a woman scorned. What little self-control I've been able to cling onto until now slips away. I have constructed a delicate and precarious house of cards and I am watching it spectacularly topple down, so I don't have an update for this man, just a broken heart, a troubled son and a husband whom I no longer recognize. I scoff that he is overreacting, that Hudson was caught with marijuana not a gun, and demand that he put my son on the phone right away.

In a moment, I hear Hudson's voice, faraway, subdued and angry. If he wants to be angry, I will meet him there, I will show him a new level of anger he's never seen from me. It erupts out of me, grief and rage spewing across the international phone line.

"Mom, you have to calm down, I can't talk to you like this," he pleads.

"Calm down? *Calm down?* I just got a call from a man telling me they'll call the police if I don't immediately get my son off premises in a foreign country in which I know no one and don't speak the language!" I scream.

"I know," he says. "I'm really sorry. But please, I need you to help me."

I breathe deeply to suppress my internal squall and let the silence instead speak between us. Finally, I hear his voice again, humbled and softer now.

"I'm so depressed," he says. "What's happening with you and Dad is killing me. I can't get away from it. The only time I feel good is when I'm high."

I suck my breath in. This is the worst possible response he could have given me. All I hear is blame for a situation I didn't cause and an acknowledgement of the obvious fact that I can't make it better. Fixing things has always been one of my most important roles as a mother: problems with friends, problems at school, problems sleeping or eating or with health – fix, fix, fix. Without my maternal superpower, I am unrecognizable to him and to myself. But is our separation the cause of his ruin or is it an easy excuse? I am incensed, but I refuse to be the only one carrying the burden of responsibility.

When I get home an hour later, I chug the remains of an open bottle of white wine straight from the bottle and get to work, calling the airline – which I learn is now closed for Shabbat – and the mothers of the other boys. I am usually the take-charge mother, the one who easily manages logistics, and I'm attempting to do so now but without grace or presence of mind. The other mothers beseech me to calm down, reminding me that the boys are safe and there's no need to panic. I don't know how to relay the root of my hysteria, that my beautiful family is crumbling before my eyes and I am powerless to stop it. Getting him home from Israel? That's the easy part, requiring phone calls and money. Getting him out of this vast pit of unhappiness? No phone calls or handfuls of money will help.

I text #3 to tell him I have to cancel our weekend plans as I will be returning to the city to receive Hudson, who will arrive at 5am on Sunday. As angry as I've been at Michael these past months, it's got nothing on the fury I've turned toward myself. I have been foolishly pouring time and effort into rebuilding my life. What right did I have to turn any of my attention away from my kids?

I believed I might have a relationship? Find love again? What a joke. I need to be a mother right now, nothing more and nothing less. The idea that I thought I might be entitled to my own personal life is at best laughable and at worst tragically unrealistic.

#3 calls me immediately. He says that in his limited experience with teenage boys, smoking weed is quite common and that the extenuating circumstance of his being in a foreign country makes it more complicated, but not necessarily a more heinous offense. I explain that Hudson has been in trouble at school before for this same reason and that I am terrified we are on our way down a slippery, dangerous slope. Being a single mother to an angry teenage boy who despises me for being the parent he is stuck with feels way beyond my pay grade.

"I'm sorry that I have to cancel. I suspect I'm more trouble than I'm worth. We can reschedule, I hope, but if you don't want to, I get it," I say, so afraid of rejection that I try to beat him to the punch.

"I have an idea," he says brightly. "What if I meet you in the city? My friend has an apartment I can stay in."

"You would drive into the city to see me?" I ask, moved and astonished.

"Yes, why not? I want to see you and a night in the city will be fun."

I'm not sure how to respond. I am scared that I am failing in my most important role – as a mother. But now that I've had a taste of what it feels like to be seen as a woman again, I'm reluctant to turn my back on it. Is it ever going to be possible to be both, an attentive mother and a woman with a fulfilling romantic relationship? My going on a date will not have a direct impact on Hudson, since he will be on an airplane anyway, but I am afraid that acting on my own needs will inadvertently take away from him in ways I can't yet fathom while rewarding me, when what I deserve is punishment for falling down on the job and allowing Hudson's predicament to even exist. Regardless, I accept #3's generous offer, hoping I can sneak in this one last hurrah before settling in for the long haul on my own again.

CHAPTER 9

Comfort Zone

I was a month shy of five years old when my father died. My mother had subsequently refused to go anywhere without me and my sister, worrying that we would be further traumatized by her leaving us for even one evening, so she toted us along on dates friends arranged for her. I recall curling into a booth at a Japanese restaurant with my sister while my mother and Larry got acquainted, her soulful blue eyes flickering back and forth from her date to her children. She brought us coloring books and invisible ink pads, and if we were well-behaved, saucer-sized black and white cookies from Zaro's Bakery, leading me to believe that her dating life was a fortunate turn of events for me personally. The first man she conceded to go alone on a date with was reluctantly invited inside our apartment to await the arrival of our always-late grandmother, who was to babysit.

She had warned him that we might ignore him, that we weren't used to having men in the apartment with us, but within minutes, we had marched out our ample collection of stuffed animals to put on a play for him and sobbed when our grandmother showed up and they left for their adult-only date. We had given our immediate approval, which was the incentive my mother needed to take us downtown a few weeks later to jump on his waterbed while they packed up his studio apartment so that he could move in with us. Even as she moved on in her romantic life with her soon-to-be husband, I understood implicitly that we would always come first: it was the ultimate act of maternal devotion, attending to her needs only after ours were managed.

In books and movies I run through in my memory, it seems women who move on from their spouse's death or from divorce are often able to seamlessly fold their new husbands into the mix – after a bumpy start, the dust settles and the kids accept it as a given that their mother has moved on. Sometimes the dust endlessly floats through space and the kids hate their stepfathers forever, but this rarely stops the mother.

Why does this challenge have me flummoxed when other women seem to manage it without such intense turmoil and inner strife? My kids aren't rebelling against anyone at this point and they're not the ones throwing up roadblocks – I am. I cannot wrap my head around how logistically this is supposed to work. If I am to continue to be a good mother in the way I perceive good mothers to be, it means abrogating myself outside of my maternal duties. But the experiences of the past few weeks – flirting with men, talking to them, having sex, imagining the possibilities – has unleashed a previously forbidden side of myself I am unwilling to bottle back up. I am torn between what I have always believed a good mother to represent – complete devotion – and what I now think I need to be a complete person, which includes, but is not limited to, being a good mother.

*

The day I return to the city is cool and gloomy with relentless rain. I drive two hours with windshield wipers methodically thumping from side to side, and all the produce I bought at local farm stands tucked in the seat beside me so that I can prepare the dinner I had planned for #3. He texts me throughout the day. The heavy downpours are slowing traffic to a halt and his ETA keeps getting later and later. He has his dog with him and has to make frequent stops to let her out. I feel guilty that I'm the reason for this disastrous trip, and when he finally arrives well into the evening after countless delays, it feels decidedly anticlimactic. I wait for him under an umbrella in front of his friend's apartment building, ready to apologize for everything from the weather to the traffic to the difficulty of parking in the city. I see him emerge from his car before he spots me and I am struck by how out of place he looks here, a country boy in the city. I am enamored of him in his bucolic milieu, but here, in my hometown, he looks out of his element, as if he might be consumed whole by the carefully styled bearded hipsters and lithe women pushing thousand-dollar strollers.

We have to walk his dog before we can leave her at his friend's apartment. The dog is not used to concrete city streets and #3 asks if there is a grassy area where she could be more comfortable, so I lead them a few blocks west to a park along the Hudson River.

I keep a safe distance from him, my arms folded tightly in front of me as we walk, nervous that I will run into people I know. I feel guilty all over again that this man has come hours out of his way to see me only to find me stiff and aloof, but seeing him out of context and on my home turf has made me unexpectedly ill at ease. It doesn't feel like play-acting as it does upstate – this is my actual life, lending an air of gravity to what had been fantastical and safely anonymous until now.

When we reach my apartment an hour later, I realize this is the first man I've had to my home. I feel exposed in my newly renovated apartment with its shimmery purple velvet sofa, Japanese heated toilet seat and Subzero refrigerator. I say I like to keep things simple, but simplicity is not what is on display here and I feel like my other side, my fancier self, has been unceremoniously unveiled. I have been immersed in an arcadian country life this summer, but the truth is that while I feel genuine contentment and peace there, delighting in my garden and spectacular sunsets and abundant farm stands, I also embrace and feel at home in my busier – and more extravagant – life here in the city.

As the night progresses, I slowly thaw but I am off my game and it is clear to me that he can feel it too. We each pull back the blankets on opposite sides of the king-size bed and climb in carefully. I am apologetic, explaining that I am anxious about Hudson's imminent return and also that I had not imagined it would feel this strange to have another man in my bed. We set an alarm for five in the morning, which is when Hudson's plane lands and thus signals that it's time for him to hightail it out of here. I sleep fitfully, ill at ease that Michael's side of the bed is filled with a foreign male body and nervous that if we oversleep, Hudson – who is being driven home from the airport by his friend's parents – will walk in on us. When he kisses me goodbye perfunctorily in the pre-dawn darkness of the early morning, I am relieved that he is gone and lonelier than ever.

*

Over the next few days, my attention shifts away from myself to my brooding teenage boy. Whether I approach him gently or angrily, he is guarded and wary of me. I beg him to talk to me or Daisy or a therapist or a friend, anything to expel what appears to be eating him alive and what he is using drugs to attempt to contain. My friends Jen and Rebecca, who experienced their parents' divorces when they were teenagers, text him to share that they understand how he feels, to try to normalize his feelings, but he doesn't respond to them. I am in despair and all I can do is remind him that I love him wholly and unconditionally, and will do anything I can to support him. It's not enough – I need Michael to help us through this. The frustration at knowing I can't access that help exasperates me, making me feel hopeless.

In the meantime, I had become accustomed to frequent text exchanges with #3, but now there is only a flat static hum. I don't want this past weekend to stop us dead in our tracks; even though it's only been a couple of weeks since we met, I already miss the witty banter we had so effortlessly established. I call him for some small bit of reassurance, but he is circumspect. I remember this sinking feeling from my teens, that moment of knowing a boy's interest in me was receding. Bigger than my disappointment about him in particular is the overarching fear that I will not be able to pull off what increasingly feels like a magic trick: being a present and available mother while also being present and available to a man who is not my husband. One role automatically negates the other, making her disappear. I am a mother, and the woman in me becomes invisible; I am a woman, and the mother cannot successfully do her job. One-night stands I am mastering – anything more feels firmly, preposterously out of reach.

CHAPTER 10

Mama Bear

Michael arrives upstate to pick up Georgia for the weekend and when he passes Hudson in the house, Hudson ignores him, walking by him as if he's a piece of furniture he has to skirt around. The scene is heartbreaking and infuriating to witness. I don't know exactly what Michael should be doing differently, but I feel certain that in his shoes I would camp outside Hudson's room night and day until he was forced to acknowledge me. He is confident that Hudson will eventually come back to him, but I share none of his optimism. Hudson is famous in our family for his stubbornness and loyalty, neither of which will work in Michael's favor any time soon.

I am determined to come up with activities to keep Hudson busy and engaged with me, so I entice him with a trip to the Catskill Mountains, where there is a river with rapids and tubing. Where he is athletic and adventurous, I am fearful and cautious. I'm scared of the rapids and of getting wet in icy water, but I put on my game face. We ride in a rickety yellow schoolbus to a location twenty minutes away from the shack, where we pick up our tubes. There are no guides on this adventure – I've already signed my life away on a stack of waivers – so when the bus dumps us at a spot upriver, I know that we are expected to make our way back on our own in individual tubes that look like old tires. I see people walking along the road, having emerged from the river shivering and muddy, and the guys next to us on the bus are talking about people who have died in rapids. I don't realize that my breathing has become shallow until Hudson whispers, "Are you sure you want to do this, Mom?"

"Oh yes, I'm fine, it'll be great," I say through gritted teeth, and he laughs because we both know that I am petrified. We collect our equipment and head toward the water, where he patiently suggests that I step to the side and let everyone else go ahead of us since it will take a long time for me to take all the baby steps I need to become immersed. Smiling, I set my tube in the water and hop right in, immediately drifting away while he stands on the river bank watching me, stunned. I am freezing, scared and uncomfortable, but I want him to see that I am strong and brave too. I am far from fearless. In fact, I have many, many fears, lists I could stay up all night writing, classifying those that are paralytic (ziplines, mice, getting water up my nose), to those that just freak me out (mayonnaise), to those I could work up the courage to face down if I was so inspired to (like this very moment). I may proceed with a whimper, not boldly like he does and like I wish I could, but I am doing it all the same. I am emboldened by the fact that I am already living through some of my worst fears and surviving, sometimes even with grace, so stepping out of my comfort zone? That's my home now. It was easy to bow out of activities that daunted me while I was married because I felt then that I didn't need to prove anything to anyone, but now, I am first and foremost proving to myself, and secondarily to my kids, that I am tougher and have a stronger backbone than it may have previously appeared.

While Hudson watches me and I gloat in the glory of my lion-heart, I crash into a pile of rocks. My tube tips over, my leg scrapes against the rough edge of the rocks and I flip under the icy water. It pierces me like nothing I have ever felt before – bracing and bone-chilling – but I understand immediately that that's all it is, cold. I have bigger fish to fry, as I emerge sputtering and coughing. I have to hold onto the rocks with one hand and secure the tube with the other so that neither I nor it are propelled forward down-stream without each other, but I am panicked and stuck in place as the water is coming too rapidly for me to right myself. Suddenly Hudson appears next to me in his tube and he's not laughing, which means he's worried.

"Mom, I'm holding the tube steady for you, let go of the rocks and pull yourself into it."

"No, I can't let go, I'm too scared."

"I've got it, I promise. Just move quickly."

I do as I'm told, gracelessly hurling my body forward and landing awkwardly across the tube on my stomach. He holds my tube next to his while I roll over to rearrange myself as we are pushed away together by the water.

"Do you want to get out?" he asks.

"Get out?" I respond indignantly. "We just started."

"Oh, OK, I just thought maybe falling under would be enough for you," he says. "We can stop now. I'd still be proud of you for trying."

"Nope, let's go. I've got this."

For the next couple of hours, we drift together and apart downstream. There are a few relaxing moments in which we gently bob along while I catch my breath and prepare for the next set of rapids. Miraculously, I do not fall out again, though I have enough heart-stopping close calls to feel I am facing down a fierce element. When I see big arrows spray-painted on the side of a bridge, I am surprised to realize we are at the end of the course and have to pull our tubes ashore. I am cold, muddy and a bit worse for the wear, but I made it to the finish line.

"I'm proud of you, Mom. I didn't think you'd be able to do it," he says. "And this water is freezing, even for me."

I am aglow with pride.

We climb up the hill to reach the road back. A couple on the path ahead of us shush us and point to a tree in the woods about ten feet away, in which a mother bear is up in the branches with her four cubs. Silently, we watch in awe until enough people come up the path that the bear gets nervous and climbs down the tree. We are not sure what to do, slowly back away or stand motionless, but she turns away from us disinterestedly and lazily makes her way to the water while her babies jump down and frantically scurry to catch up with her.

I think of our past few months together, me and my own baby bears, the fervent love I feel for them, the exceedingly bumpy road we have travelled together, the way they are always at my heels, knowing I will do everything in my power to lead them in the right direction. The words I said to Hudson hours ago as we set off on our adventure come back to me: I've got this, and in this one moment, I do. I fiercely love this boy, and I am newly resolute that I will help him get through this painful chapter. In the days to come, he will start calling me "Mama Bear" and I will think back to this moment with feelings that flood me with pride, warmth and hopefulness.

CHAPTER 11

Busted

Alex, my one close friend upstate, texts me with a confession: she worked up the courage to approach a man she's had her eye on for me at her gym. He's fit, very cute and friendly, and she would go for him herself if she wasn't married, but since she is, she's determined to live vicariously through me. After confirming his single status, she did an admirably hard sell of me until he gave her his number and suggested that I get in touch. I demur, telling her I'm too stressed about Hudson and sad about messing up my chance with #3, feeling in general blah and overwhelmed. She responds that it's too early in the game for me to feel so overwhelmed and that all I should do right now is dip my toes in dating waters and have fun.

Alex's coaxing spurs me on. She's right – I can't be in a real relationship right now, so I should take whatever opportunities present themselves to keep myself distracted and feeling good in the moment without worrying about what comes next. I text him before I lose the little nerve I have. Alex has told me nothing about him aside from the fact that he's got an alluring six-pack, a bunch of kids, and is from a local family who own the orchard where I buy fruit and cider doughnuts. He responds with a suggestion that we meet for brunch on Sunday of the upcoming weekend. He gives me a choice of two restaurants; one is a café I frequently go to with my parents, so I opt for the other one in a newly renovated inn where I am unlikely to know anyone.

I've been wary of running into people I know when I'm out on dates, not wanting to have to explain myself. With the exception of my close friends and family, I have managed to contain the news about my marriage, which is surprising as I am usually an open book. The weight of the situation is too heavy for me, threatening to crush me every time I have to disclose it. This new state of affairs, the one in which I'm a single woman on the prowl, is too big for me to explain too, albeit in a different way. Instead of threatening to topple me as my separation has, this new state is like a lump of clay waiting to be colored and shaped. I am still malleable, not ready or willing to commit to any one mold yet. If I am spotted on dates by people I know, I fear I will be pulled out of the character I'm playing and return to the Laura they know again, not the one I am trying on for size. Inside I know I have the same core values, the same love for my family and friends, the same silly sense of humor, the same love for the color pink and vintage glassware and the *NYTimes* crossword puzzle, but my life's circumstances have changed – turned upside down, actually – so being exactly the same person is just no longer possible.

*

The next morning, I leave the house to meet the guy from Alex's gym while Hudson is still asleep. The air is heavy and I don't want to wear anything close to my body, so I opt for the same shorts and tank top from my date with #3, and a pair of flip-flops. I arrive a few minutes early and stand hesitantly on the porch, pondering whether to get a table indoors or out. A man bounds up the steps with a wide grin, glances at me and says confidently, "Laura." I am confused as this man looks like a boy, clean-cut and wearing cargo shorts and basketball sneakers. He embraces me in a tight, warm hug, immediately putting me at ease. We agree that the air outside is sticky, so we find a table inside against the window. He peppers me with questions about my newly single life, listening attentively while his beautiful aqua blue eyes bore into me.

"Dating is surprisingly fun," I say gaily. "Maybe because it's still new to me. In fact, this is the first blind date I've ever been on in my entire life."

"You're doing great," he says laughing, and then his voice becomes more serious when he asks me for how long I have been separated. I confess that it is relatively new, only six months, and that I just recently started dating.

"Were you in the process of separating for a long time?"

"No," I say, shaking my head. "It was very sudden."

He nods his head thoughtfully and gives me a knowing look. This is a question that I am frequently asked, particularly by other women, and I understand but I also resent it. Saying it was sudden is clearly a euphemism for admitting that one of us had an affair, which instantly satisfies everyone who wants a reasonable explanation as to how a 27-year relationship met a sudden demise. There are equal parts curiosity and self-preservation in the question, akin to asking someone with cancer if they smoked. What's the difference, I always want to ask. Whether or not you can trace the origin of my diseased marriage is irrelevant, because either way now I'm here. Would it make a difference if I had had more time to prepare for its end, or is it intolerable to not have someone or something to blame?

He excuses himself to use the restroom, possibly fleeing after having witnessed an uncomfortable series of emotions ranging from sadness to anger cross my face in a matter of seconds. When he returns, he leans forward over the table toward me, sighs deeply, puts a hand over mine and says, "Listen, I've been in your shoes. It gets easier over time, but the shock has to wear off. You seem like a really nice person and I'm sure you didn't deserve whatever it is that happened to you."

I nod my head but don't say anything. A quick onset of tears has become a frequent occurrence in my life as of late, but I refuse to let them emerge on a first date. My awkward pause is saved by two older men who get up from the table next to ours and nod to us as they prepare to leave.

"Hey," #4 smiles at them, his eyes twinkling mischievously. "This is our first date. How are we doing?"

"Wow, first date huh? I never would have known. I'd say the date is going very well," one of the men says. "But if anything takes a turn, give me her number?"

We laugh and I am at ease again, smiling as I watch the men walk out the door, holding it gallantly for an incoming couple. My smile is short-lived; unbelievably, that incoming couple is my mom and my dad. I freeze in alarm and after a moment slink down into my seat.

"Oh my God," I whisper. "My parents just walked in."

"Oh great, let's say hi," he says in a loud voice, twisting his body to see them.

"No!" I practically shriek. "Please turn around immediately. Don't draw attention to us! They don't know that I'm dating yet."

He is laughing but I break into a cold sweat like I'm a teenager on the couch with my boyfriend, having just been busted by my parents.

"OK, listen, they're going to the bakery, probably to buy bread and then leave. Just give me a little cover here, I'm going to block myself with your body so they can't see me. I'll tell you when you can move. I know I seem nutty but I'm not ready to have this conversation with them yet."

I am practically begging him.

"OK then," he says carefully. "You sure you don't want to just say hi?"

"Please," I say. "Carry on. As you were saying…"

I'm barely listening to him as I track the movements of my parents. I see they've got the bread now, but it has started raining torrentially and they're looking out the window with concerned expressions; then my father sits on an empty stool while my mother approaches the hostess. My worst fear: they're waiting for a table to open up. It seems like my father is looking right at me, but he doesn't register seeing me. Is he playing it cool? When the waitress clears the table next to ours and the hostess gestures to my mother, I know that I have no choice but to out myself. I apologize to #4 and say that I have to excuse myself, alone, and to please stay put.

I am so anxious as I arise that I do not realize my flip-flop has gotten caught on the leg of my chair and I fly forward as the chair tumbles backward. #4 quickly reaches out to stop me from falling flat on my face. This date has turned into a horrendous sitcom – surely even the clumsy Phoebe from *Friends* would deal with this situation with more grace. Too humiliated to even thank him, I make a beeline for my parents.

"Hi," I say breathlessly, leaning toward them.

"Laura, hello!" my mother says happily, leaning in to peck me on my cheek. "How funny! Who are you here with?"

"Well, kind of funny actually, I'm here on a blind date," I say with a grimace.

"Already?" my mother asks in a loud, indignant voice, while my father looks on silently with a bemused smile.

"That's helpful, thanks Mom – Alex set me up with someone she insisted I meet, she said I should start getting out so I'm trying. This is super awkward and I want to die," I blurt out in one rambling, breathy sentence.

"OK, OK," she says. "Don't panic."

"Listen, they're clearing off the table next to us and you cannot under any circumstances sit there or anywhere else where you can see me. And don't come over and say hello or even look over at us. Please."

"OK, calm down, Laura. Go sit. We won't look," she says reassuringly.

I am already playing through the conversation I know will take place from this encounter later today.

I make my way back to my seat, gulp down a glass of water as delicately as possible, and return to the business of attempting charm. As soon as I see that my parents are seated on the other side of the wall, I relax. To their credit, they don't even glance in my direction. #4 kindly asks me if I am OK.

"Yes, great. This is not a conversation I'm ready to have yet with my mom, but here we are. I don't want to have to explain myself," I say.

"Why do you have to?" he asks with genuine curiosity.

"Excellent question. I always feel like I have to answer to someone. It doesn't seem to matter how old I get, I still want my mom to feel I'm doing the right thing," I say.

"Why would your being on a date suggest to her that you're doing something wrong?" he asks.

"She thinks it's too soon, maybe that I'm acting rashly, that I'm not thinking clearly yet. I wish I cared less," I say wistfully.

#4 looks down at his watch and remarks that we've been sitting for over two hours and should relinquish our table. When the bill comes, he pulls out a crisp $100 bill as I reach behind me for my bag, which he firmly waves away. I thank him, grateful for his generosity and that we have successfully navigated the date to its conclusion.

It is still raining when we exit, so we carefully walk down the slick steps and run under the porch for cover. I wonder if I will ever get used to this awkward dance of saying goodbye. We strategize how we will get to our cars without getting soaked and finally, when we are out of things to say, he gives me a hug and says it was great to meet me. The hug lasts long enough that I can smell the clean scent of soap on his body and feel how solid his muscles are under his thin shirt. I linger, breathing him in, and when I pull away our faces stay close so that he can lean in for a kiss. I wrap my arms around his neck, pulling him toward me, and he kisses me again; when we pull away we realize we are standing on full display next to the kitchen windows, where there are at least eight people working.

"I think we've given them a pretty good show," he says and kisses me again. My eyes are open now and I am watching every pair of legs as they come down the staircase in front of us, terrified the legs will belong to my parents.

"Can we scoot over to the side where we're less conspicuous?" I ask and we shuffle over. I fully feel like a teenager now, as if over thirty years haven't passed since I was having sex in my parents' basement and praying I wouldn't be caught.

"So, do you have children underfoot at home today?" I ask, getting my mojo back.

"I do not," he says. "Would you like to come over?"

I nod eagerly and we dash through the teeming rain for our cars so that I can follow him home.

On the drive over, I call Lauren.

"How did it go? Did you like him? Tell me everything," she says.

"It's still going, but I ran into my parents and it was extremely uncomfortable. I'm following him to his house now."

"I love you," she says, laughing. "You seem so sweet and innocent but you always get the job done."

I promise to call her later so she knows I'm safe and sound, then pull into a long driveway until I reach a large ranch-style house set back from the road, half suburban, half country, with a pool in the backyard.

#4 holds the front door open for me and two dogs, of course, come bounding over. They are pugs, small (thankfully), cute and making snorting noises. I'm more than a little delighted when he shoos them out of the house and closes the door behind them. I'm making progress: a dog in the room to a dog outside the room to dogs outside the house. He takes me through the house, a combination of a bachelor pad and a family home, as if it can't quite decide what it wants to be, and that is probably true depending on who is inhabiting it at any given moment. His bedroom is in an open lofty area with a king-size bed, its plain brown comforter covered in dog hair.

We stand near the bed, quiet now that the house tour is over. He kisses me as I pull my shirt over my head and kick off my shorts so that I am standing in my lingerie. He unbuttons his shirt and I am intrigued by how taut and muscular his arms, shoulders and chest are. I've never been with a man so brawny and hairless and I love the way his skin feels, smooth and warm. He presses himself against me until I back up and sit on the edge of the bed. Apologizing that he wasn't expecting company today, he pulls back the hair-covered blanket to expose sheets that look rumpled but clean enough if I'm not being fussy, which right now, I'm definitely not. I take note that this is the third man in a matter of weeks who has excused the conditions of his home because he wasn't anticipating having a guest over. I seem to push ahead even as my dates are ready to kiss and say goodbye; it's never enough for me.

He climbs on top of me, stroking my body and working his way down until his mouth is between my legs. Then he looks up at me, a boyish grin lighting up his face.

"You take good care of yourself," he says.

At this I smile: I do take care of myself. If there's one benefit to the swell of anger raging inside of me, it's that I work out like I'm on fire and sweat is the only thing that can douse it. The more rage I get out through heavy exercise, the less likely I am to expel it later through ugly, impassioned text missives to Michael. When he bought me my own Peloton bike a year earlier, he could not have known how much it would actually come to help him too.

#4 reaches for a condom that he must have placed discreetly under a pillow at some point, and I watch him unfurl it onto his penis. I feel decidedly awkward during this part of a sexual encounter – am I supposed to help with the condom or watch him put it on or avert my eyes? There is something that makes a man look so vulnerable when he is handling himself and I think I should stay out of it altogether but maybe that's considered rude or unfriendly?

Our bodies glisten with sweat – even though the rain has cooled the air outside, it's stuffy and close in here without air conditioning – and we slide against each other, which one could interpret as hot and sexy or just unseemly. I'm choosing to go with hot and sexy, that this is what lust looks like. He is inside me for only a few moments when we both come, but without skipping a beat, he peels off the condom, tosses it on the floor and we keep going, new condoms appearing every so often, seemingly out of thin air. He is at once aggressively manly and appealingly tender, touching me gently but insistently.

There seems to be no beginning or ending to this sex, just a middle chapter that stretches on. He is six years younger than me and his virility is matched by my insatiable curiosity and thrill at being desired. Of the four men I've slept with since I've started this journey, this is the most physically satisfying sex I've had. He laughs with enthusiasm when I sigh deeply and tell him in a grave voice that I really love sex. He seems to know exactly how and where to touch me, and I can't get enough of his hard, sleek body. It's as if I'm being cracked open again and again; it's not explosive so much as a feeling of being totally present in my body and with his. It feels good to be wanted, to want, to be appreciated, to know that I am quenching someone's thirst, to know my body is capable of both giving and receiving, to match his vigor with my own.

When we have finally expended our sexual energy, we lie wrapped around each other. As much as I am shocked to discover how much I love touching and being touched, I am surprised by how nourishing I find this part, this calm after the storm. I feel completely enveloped as our hearts return to their regular rhythms and we lie, exhausted but sated, in the aftermath of the intimacy we have shared. *Why*, I wonder, *do I feel I could stay in this spot for hours but when I was married, instead of reveling in the physical connection, I ran from it?* Within seconds of having sex, I was already rolling back to curl in a ball on my side of the bed, so relieved that this obligation could be checked off my list and I could go back in my corner to be left alone. I usually orgasmed and I enjoyed sex once I mustered up the energy, but I could take it or leave it – and the affection that came with it I recoiled from, believing myself to be a physically unaffectionate person. The desire I have now to be touched – not just sexually, but any kind of physical connection is potent and primal and proving wrong everything I thought I understood about myself and my physical needs. If I crave being touched, hugged and held, and if my sexual desires and curiosity are endlessly piqued, why wasn't that a part of my life with the man I shared my bed with for 27 years?

I allow myself a few minutes to soak up this feeling of warmth and then, much as I hate to extricate myself, tell him I have to go home as I know Hudson is probably wondering where I am. He tells me to stay put, that he will get something with which I can clean myself.

He returns a minute later with a warm washcloth and when I reach for it, he says, "No, let me." He gently cleans between my legs, taking care to clean my bikini line and between my lips. I am struck by how tender he is and by how intimate this feels. I had always thought intercourse was the most intimate thing two people could share but I am learning that sex can be physical without being profound and that moments like this take intimacy to a decidedly new level.

I am wobbly going down the stairs and have to reach for the bannister to steady myself. In the kitchen he hands me a tall glass of water, which I inhale. He laughs watching me, saying that he's spent as well. *Is there a prize for wearing this robust man out?* He walks me to my car, though in truth I am practically strutting. Standing barefoot and bare-chested in the driveway, he watches me as I turn around to pull out. Right before I pull away from the house, he calls out "Wait!" and then jogs over to my open window, where he leans in to give me a boyish grin and one last kiss goodbye before I am on the road again.

*

I brace myself later in the day for a phone call from my mother, but it doesn't come. By the next day, her silence is making me nervous as I know she's building a case in her mind and soon I will get one of her famous speeches that my sister Jennifer and I call her "I've been thinking" sermons. Finally, two days later, the call comes. I debate not answering but I know I have to get this over with.

"Hi Mom," I say.

"Listen, Laura, I've been thinking," she starts. "It's fine, you don't have to explain yourself. I'm just worried about your dating, that this could be held against you in some way if you get divorced."

"That would be kind of ironic, no?" I ask.

"I don't know, I'm not a lawyer, I just think you should check with someone," she says.

"OK," I say, relieved that this is the only objection she voices. When I call a lawyer friend and learn that I could sleep with a different man every day and it won't legally be held against me, I consider that all the approval I need.

CHAPTER 12

This Must Be Bad

When I tell friends that Michael and I have separated, they want an explanation. It makes little sense to anyone, aside from the friend who stunned me when he bluntly announced his surprise that we had actually made it this long. We bickered within the range of what I thought was expected and normal for a long-married couple, we loved and often adored each other, we had just moved into our "forever" home, we traveled and loved spending time together with our kids. We often poked fun at each other's peculiarities (the animalistic way he tore into his grapefruit standing over the sink every morning, the way I chewed apples like a horse). I was proud of his professional success – and of having been by his side as he built it – and I still delighted in his ability to be playful, optimistic, and sometimes flat-out zany. For decades, he had been my perfect counterbalance: an embracer of change and the unknown when I resisted both, and able to find the glass half-full when I seemed only to find it half-empty. In exchange, I had given him freedom to come and go as he worked long and unpredictable hours, showing unwavering faith and support in all his endeavors. Most importantly, after his having bounced around countless New York City apartments as the only child of divorced, bohemian parents, I had made him a home, one that looked and smelled and felt like a warmly shared space in which a loving family lived.

My closest friends are astounded. Some friends who are slightly less close comment, "You never know what goes on behind closed doors." This hits me like a slap in the face, as if we had been putting on a front the whole time, as if who we really were as a couple was different from who we appeared to be. I understand that these friends want to believe there was a sinister story unfolding at home so that this event could make some sort of sense, but I am as shocked as they are, so how can I offer reasonable explanations? How can I reassure them that their own marriages won't fall prey to this trauma too? I had always been the advice columnist of our group, the one friends had referred to as "Dear Laura", ready and able to dispense advice and resources. If this could happen to me, it seemed reasonable to assume that it could happen to any of them too.

I have been selective with whom I have shared my tale of woe but still, word spreads. One day I run into an acquaintance who has been battling cancer. She has lost her lustrous, cascading curls and now a colorful silk scarf frames her face. I tell her that I am inspired by her, the way she bounces through the world with such bravery and positivity; she tells me that I do the same for her. I want her to know that I don't think we are in the same camp, that there is a difference between my heartbroken status and her fight-for-her-life status, that my courage pales in comparison to hers.

"To be honest, Laura, I would say it's pretty even. I don't know how I would survive being in your shoes."

I am dumbfounded. Sure, it's a nightmare to have an unfaithful husband, but I cannot believe that someone would prefer to fight a life-threatening illness. When I mention this to a close friend who recovered from cancer years earlier, she surprises me by not agreeing with me.

"I get it," she says. "When you're sick, you strategize to attack it. You turn to experts to make decisions. In your situation, there's no clear path. You may have tons of love and support from friends but at the end of the day, none of them can tell you what to do. The unknown is more terrifying to a lot of people than something known and scary."

This must be bad, I think to myself. I have at times tried to convince myself that men (and women too, but mostly men, let's be honest) have been having extramarital affairs since the beginning of time, and that since it happens all the time, maybe it's not as big a deal as I'm making it. If I can put it into historical context, I will be fine. Of course it doesn't feel fine at all, but sometimes I can convincingly rationalize to myself that this is nothing but a bump. Now people around me are validating the worst and scariest of what I feel: that this is just as bad, if not even more calamitous, than I had thought.

When I confide in friends, they inevitably ask, how did you find out? It amazes me that no matter how compassionate they are, and knowing this will evoke painful memories for me, they have to know. I understand and have reverse sympathy. They need to believe there was a fatal error I made, or something inherently wrong with

Michael, anything to verify their own immunity. I am annoyed that their need to know trumps their wanting to protect me from having to relive the story, but I comply with an answer anyway.

This is the story I tell.

For weeks, maybe months, I had a nagging sense that something was wrong with Michael. In our 27 years together, he had usually been the first to apologize, asking within minutes of an argument, "Can we be friends again?" He did not hold grudges and moved on from personal and business disagreements with admirable speed. When I realized one day that he didn't come to me anymore asking if we could move on, that time seemed to only make him angrier at me after even the most trivial argument, I was alarmed. I tried to gently probe, asking why he was upset with me so much of the time. He insisted that he wasn't, that he had hit a stressful patch at work and didn't want to add to my daily stress by sharing it with me.

"You know how it goes with work stuff," he said with a knowing look, and I nodded my head. I did know. He had owned his own business since the end of graduate school, so I was well-acquainted with the ups and downs of entrepreneurial life, how we could be drawing from our line of credit one month and then the next flying away for a family vacation. I dropped the subject.

One evening, a few days later, he forgot to pick Georgia up from her afterschool class. I was furious at him, upset that Georgia had been left alone with the building's handyman after everyone else had left and she was still waiting to be picked up. When Michael arrived home later, he defended himself before I could even formulate words from my rage.

"Before you start harping about this, tell me when I have ever done this before," he seethed.

"You haven't, but you're late to pick her up all the time," I said tersely.

"But when have I ever forgotten?" he asked.

"You've never forgotten because I've never given you the chance to. I didn't remind you today because I thought you could handle it on your own and look at what happened."

He was livid, all but foaming at the mouth, and slammed his fork down on the kitchen counter. A small piece of white marble flew up into the air.

"You just chipped the counter," I calmly stated.

"Good. Now every time you see this chip you can remember what an unbearable nag you are and maybe you'll think twice before you open your mouth to complain again," he shouted and stormed out of the room.

Daisy had been quietly doing homework on the couch in the living room, and her eyes caught mine in horror.

"What's wrong with him?" she asked.

"He feels guilty about forgetting Georgia and he's very stressed at work."

A few minutes later, she piped up again, "Mom, do you think Dad could be having an affair?"

"What? No!" I said, laughing. "Dad can barely keep track of us, how on earth would he keep track of a secret lover? You've been watching too much TV."

*

The next morning, Michael was even colder and more hostile. I called him into the family room where I was working through a pile of mail and asked if we could talk before he left for the day. He stared hard at me and inhaled deeply, then turned and dramatically closed the double doors to the room so we could speak privately.

"Here's the thing," he said, pausing as if to make an announcement. "I'm not happy with you."

His words hung heavily in the charged air between us. His demeanor was stiff and formal, so unlike his usually bouncy and high-spirited way of moving through his days that I wanted to laugh and say OK, enough of this charade, let's be friends. But strangely, he didn't so much as crack a small smile.

"I don't understand," I said, shaking my head.

"We barely communicate and spend zero time together unless the kids are involved. I'm not happy," he said again. I suggested that was an easy fix and we should try to spend more time together. He let out a deep sigh, shaking his head.

"Laura, you don't get it. If I had to grade our relationship right now, I would give us a C. That's how bad it is."

I grimaced and tried to joke that I was pretty sure a B was more in order, but I could see his frustration increase with my inability to digest what he was trying to impress upon me.

"I don't have time to deal with this right now. Work is a disaster and I have to get to the office. We need to deal with this, but not now."

With that, he flung the doors of the room open and within moments was gone from the apartment.

I sat immobilized at my desk. What he had said to me felt unfair and out of left field. Happy? Who had said anything about our being entitled to happiness all the time? We were busy and didn't have much time to connect, it was true. But he was suggesting we were at some sort of a crisis and I was perplexed. Our lives felt chaotic – three kids in three different schools, two homes, a business to run – compounded by a busy fall touring colleges with Daisy and helping to care for my normally healthy mother who had slipped weeks earlier, shattering her wrist and kneecap only days after being diagnosed with breast cancer. Why couldn't he see that we needed to wait until our plates cleared and then hit the reset button? We had frequently discussed that this time in our lives with our kids at home was precious and fleeting and that we would have countless years alone together in the future – why so much rancor about it all of a sudden? As far as I could see, happiness as an overarching goal was momentarily irrelevant. We needed to get through his business plight, my mother's health crisis, support Daisy through her senior year of high school, and in general live our lives with a little less angst. Happy? How about we strive not to totally fall apart?

Over the next few weeks, I tried a new approach with Michael to force a reintroduction of happiness into our home. During the day, I commuted uptown to accompany my mother to doctor appointments and cook meals for her, squeezing in my responsibilities as PTA president at Daisy's school and racing back downtown in time to pick Georgia up from school. When Michael came home from work, I greeted him cheerfully and asked if I could heat up dinner for him. I offered glasses of wine and inquired about his day, and when the kids needed homework help or it was time to put Georgia to bed, I did it all without glancing his way to see if he might help. Every few days I asked him if he could find time to talk to me, but he said he was consumed with work and I didn't press it – I wanted to show him that I could be supportive and loving and not the nag he had accused me of being.

On Valentine's Day, I arrived home from the gym to find Daisy eating a late breakfast at the counter next to a vase of flowers nestled in a delivery box from the florist. I frowned at them, asking her where they had come from. She shrugged, saying they had just been delivered and she assumed they were from Michael. The flowers looked sculptural, overly precious and arranged too deliberately. I riffled through the tissue paper in the box, looking for a card, but there wasn't one. I texted Michael, asking if he had sent me flowers, and he replied that he had, that they were from a new flower shop near his office that was owned by the woman who used to arrange flowers for Barack Obama when he was in the White House.

"What a strange choice," I muttered out loud. "These are so fancy."

"Mom!" Daisy reprimanded me. "That's so rude! Dad sends you flowers for Valentine's Day and you complain that you don't like them?"

"Sorry, I know how I sound ungrateful. It's just... Dad knows I like cheap bodega flowers, these are too fussy. He's never once sent me flowers before and knows I wouldn't want him to spend so much money on something like this. It's just so out of character," I said, perplexed, as she gave me a look of consternation.

Later, Michael burst through the door with his signature enthusiasm, calling out for the kids to come, that he had special gifts from Cupid for each of them. When he was done passing out treats, he told me to close my eyes and hold out my hands. When I opened my eyes, I saw a cellophane bag with a label from the overpriced gourmet market near his office, its contents an array of pink and red M&M's. I furrowed my eyebrows and frowned.

"Michael, I just stopped eating sugar. Remember? It's all I've talked about the past few days, how I'm trying to eat healthier, how tortured I am without my sugary treats at night?" I asked.

"Yes, I know," he said matter-of-factly. "These are for when you eat sugar again."

"But I'm not going to eat it again. The point is I stopped eating it. Why would you give this to me? It's like you're mocking me, openly predicting I will fail at this, instead of perhaps showing a little support," I said angrily.

Daisy shot me a look of dismay, incredulous at my lack of gratitude for the second time that day.

"So don't eat it. Give it to the kids, I'm sure they'll be happy to have it," he said.

"Do you ever listen to me? I'm just wondering. When I talk, do you hear me?" I asked.

His insistent cheerfulness started to fade and all three kids turned to scold me for being so cranky and unappreciative. I knew I sounded like a petulant child; I hated myself for it and for how the kids were looking disdainfully at me, but I was alarmed. We knew each other so well, and these gifts were puzzling to me; it was so obvious I would not like them.

Then the kids' school break arrived. Mid-winter recess in February, aka the absolute coldest, dreariest time of the year. Daisy headed to Boston to visit her friends and I took Hudson and Georgia to our house upstate. Michael joined us on Friday, the last day of the break. He called me when he went to pick up Hudson at the ski mountain to let me know that our son was injured with what appeared to be a broken hand.

I let out a long, angry sigh. This kid's skiing was the bane of my existence – he was passionate and talented, but every season we weathered broken bones or concussions. Michael applauded his fearlessness while all I could see in it was more trips to orthopedic surgeons and an open checkbook. I blamed Michael for encouraging this and was further angry that I had to be the one to figure out what to do with every accident.

When they arrived home later with Hudson's broken hand in a cast, I had warm bowls of chicken tortilla soup waiting for them. As we ate dinner, I tried to catch Michael's eye, but he wouldn't look at me. I kept my eyes on him as he stared down at his bowl of soup resolutely. As strained as things had become between us, this felt egregiously harsh, as if he couldn't bear the sight of me. It was at that moment that the gravity of what he had been trying to tell me weeks earlier clicked and I realized with growing alarm that something in our home had gone terribly awry.

After dinner, Michael said he was exhausted and would put Georgia to sleep in our bed and go to sleep with her. I eyed his phone on the counter; I understood at that moment that I would have to scroll through it that night for a clue as to what was happening. I offered to charge it in the kitchen for him, but he grabbed the phone and closed our bedroom door behind him. If he refused to share the real reason behind his unhappiness, I would dig for it myself. I felt like I had just walked through a doorway to another planet – this was my family, my home, my marriage, my forever, my safe ground I walked on no matter what was whirling around in the world outside, and yet suddenly there was a chasm in the ground. I could sense it, but I couldn't find its source; I was terrified that when I did, I would plunge through it.

I cleaned the kitchen, then tiptoed into our bedroom and took his phone from his nightstand. My heart pounded as I walked to the chair at our desk off the hallway and sank down onto it. I easily opened his phone since he and I used the same passwords. I had no idea what I was looking for, so I read his texts, wading through hundreds of business-related texts and finding only one text of note. I didn't recognize the sender; when I googled him, I saw that he was a therapist. Why wouldn't Michael tell me if he was seeing a therapist?

I then skimmed through hundreds of emails, still coming up empty-handed. I was starting to feel foolish about my paranoia and guilty that I was invading his privacy, but I knew something was amiss and I wasn't going to know exactly what it was unless I found it out on my own: Michael had closed himself to me.

I went into his Notes folder and in a bit of technological wizardry I didn't know I was capable of, figured out there were notes in the virtual trash bin that could be opened. I found a letter he had written to someone to whom he had given a watch – not just any watch, but the first watch his father had ever given him. It was a loving letter but not proof of anything. It could have been a note to Hudson, though it was odd that neither of them had mentioned it to me. Stumped, I sat idly, staring at the phone screen, grimacing at my suspicious mind but also enormously relieved.

I was about to turn his phone off and quietly return it to its spot on his nightstand when an app caught my eye – I had used WhatsApp to communicate with friends in other countries, but I didn't know Michael used it. I clicked on it, but it was locked. I entered the passwords we usually used. Still locked. My stomach dropped as I instantly understood that what I was looking for was in here. I frantically entered passwords until an error message popped up saying I had tried too many times and was now locked out. This password was all that was standing between my bewilderment and the clues I needed to make sense of the state of my marriage. Was it portentous or a gift that I was locked out? I could go to sleep right now and in the morning ask Michael about it, or press a little harder about why he was so mad at me if I couldn't bring myself to confess I had searched his phone. I could stop the ground from opening beneath me by setting the phone down now and calling it a night.

I clicked on the OK button to close the app when it unexpectedly opened and I was in. I had been sitting with the phone for two hours. I noted the time, 11:30, and the last text Michael had sent was at 9pm to a female friend, saying he was going to sleep – and here are the words I read as my life as I had known it ceased to exist – he wished it was with her. I felt sheer panic as my finger scrolled back through their conversation. Words leapt off the screen at me in fragments I couldn't piece together: "I can't live my life in secret anymore". "My mother is onto us".

"I stand to lose everything". "Tell my wife". "Soulmate". "Love". "Divorce".

I knew that once I closed WhatsApp, I would never be able to access it again, but I couldn't get out fast enough. I felt like I had been sucker-punched. Words in the texts were flying at me and gutting me; like passing a car accident and simultaneously wanting to look and avert one's eyes, I could not stop the image of those words even after I squeezed my eyes shut. In a stupor, I stumbled breathlessly back into the bedroom I had walked out of with the phone what now felt like a lifetime ago.

"Michael," I said sharply, shaking his shoulder and putting my mouth close to his ear, not wanting to awaken Georgia, sleeping so angelically on my side of the bed, hands folded across her chest. "Wake up."

"What's wrong?" he asked, his eyes flying open with fear.

Shaking, I held his phone aloft.

"What?" he asked again.

"I know everything," I said, my hand clutching the phone and waving it in front of him.

"I don't know what you mean," he said.

"Michael, this would be laughable if it wasn't so horrific. You always say I'm the best detective. You should have known that eventually I would figure it out."

"Figure what out?"

"Your affair. I know it all. I know you're in love with her and want to leave me. I know, I know," I said, as my voice began to reach a tone of hysteria.

Michael took a deep breath and sighed angrily as he threw the blankets off and followed me out of the room so we wouldn't disturb Georgia. We went downstairs to our cozy family room, a name that seemed like a cruel joke to me now.

"It's not what you think. You're acting crazy," he said, shaking his head in disgust.

"Michael, the worst thing you can do is lie to me. If you have any love left for me, you'll tell me the truth."

"There's nothing to tell. You're being ridiculous. It was a fantasy. We didn't act on it," he said.

"I don't believe you. I'm begging you to tell me the truth."

"You don't understand what you read, it was out of context," he said. "I'm telling you the truth."

"Can you at least admit that you crossed a line in your friendship with her? That whether or not you physically crossed a line, you crossed a line emotionally?"

"OK, I crossed a line emotionally. But that's it."

"How many others have there been?" I asked, my mind lurching back through time, remembering countless business trips and late dinners and missed phone calls.

"None!" he insisted indignantly.

"I can't do this with you," I said. "I know what I read. Until you're ready to come clean, I will not talk to you. If you won't respect me by telling me the truth, I'll have enough respect for myself not to listen to your lies."

With that, I walked back upstairs, my alarm growing with each step that I took without him trying to stop me or offer reasonable explanations. What surreal nightmare had I become ensnared in? Could I go to bed now and pretend this didn't happen in the morning?

I walked straight into our bathroom, which I locked behind me as I went through my night-time washing rituals. My life was exploding in pieces around me, but I was damned if I wasn't going to floss and brush my teeth. By the time I came out, Michael was back on his side of the bed and I nudged Georgia into the middle so I could climb into my side. I lay there for what felt like hours, my heart pounding and my mind racing. *This is our bed*, I thought, *and this is our child between us. This is our home, this is my husband, our son is asleep upstairs.* What, really, had changed? All the physical pieces of our life were exactly the same, but now I was a foreigner in it. When I could no longer bear to hear him breathing across the bed from me, I tucked the blankets carefully around Georgia and slipped across the hall to her room, where I curled up in her canopy bed, her soft yellow blanket tucked under my chin.

At the break of dawn, Michael came into the room.

"Can I lie with you?" he asked.

I wordlessly scooted over to the edge of the bed, pushing aside Georgia's collection of stuffed animals to make room for him.

"Can I hold you?" he asked.

"No. Don't touch me. And don't stay unless you're ready to tell me the truth."

"This isn't helpful, Laura. You don't need details," he said.

"You don't get to decide anymore what I need. How long has this been going on? The truth Michael, please, I'm begging you. The truth."

I wondered if this was what insanity felt like, the evidence of his affair on spectacular display in front of me and yet he was saying there was nothing there.

"This is not productive. If I tell you I had sex with her, that's all you'll focus on," he said.

"The sex is the least of it at this point. You fell in love with her! I need to understand how this happened. I feel like I'm going insane second-guessing my memories of our life together. And I know what I read, so your denials are making me feel like I'm losing grip with reality. Please, please, how long?"

"I don't know. A few months," he said unsurely.

"A few months? OK, it's February. Around Christmas? Thanksgiving?"

"Around Thanksgiving," he said.

"So when my mom fell and was in a wheelchair and I was upset and in overdrive trying to help her, you started having an affair?" I asked incredulously.

"I guess so, yes," he admitted reluctantly.

"So when your mother was dying I took care of her, and when my mother needed help, you were busy falling in love with another woman? I need you to get out of here right now. I can't take anymore," I said, nausea rising inside of me.

"It's over, Laura. It's over. We ended our relationship last week. I was trying to figure out how to tell you, that's why I was seeing the therapist whose text you found," he said.

"Your relationship?" I choked out. "Do you hear yourself?"

"But it's over now," he said. "And I want to be with you. I love you. I know that now."

"You texted her last night saying you wished you were sleeping next to her. If that's how you talk now that it's over, I'm terrified to know what you said when you were together," I said, weeping.

"It's over, Laura. I'm telling you the truth," he said.

"You'll have to forgive me if I no longer believe your version of the truth. Get out, please. I'm begging you. I need to be alone," I said, tears dampening Georgia's blanket. Quietly and slowly, he rolled out of the bed and closed the door behind him.

The size and scope of this information was too great for me to process. When I closed my eyes, I pictured myself falling through space, away from the soft cushion of the life I had known and toward – well, toward what exactly? In my mind I was just falling, but slowly, drifting through a vast grey space. What do you do when you find out your husband of 22 years, your best friend of 27 years, the father of your children, the man you have made far-off retirement plans with and fantasized about being grandparents with – what do you do when overnight, this man ceases to exist?

I texted Jessica, who is an early riser, praying she would be awake. I needed to share this news, to see if I put the words out there if someone might set the record straight and tell me this was impossible and could absolutely not be happening.

"Jess, I can't call you," I wrote. "But I need you. It's an emergency. Michael's been having an affair. I don't know what to do."

She wrote me back immediately and offered to get in a car and drive upstate, but I didn't want her to come running to save me, I wanted her to make this nightmare go away.

"But I don't understand. You've always said Michael is so in love with me, that he seems to love me more than I do him. How could this be happening? It makes no sense," I wrote.

"I don't know Laura. I'm so sorry," she wrote back.

"Please make this go away."

"I would do anything to make that happen. I'm sick for you," she wrote as my panic swelled.

In too great a state of disbelief to comprehend the enormity of this news, I could only stare in horror at the phone's screen, willing Jessica to write back with an explanation that did not – that could not – come.

CHAPTER 13

The Only Way Out Is Through

That austere, dismal February day Michael confirmed his affair passed in a haze as I shuffled between Georgia's bed, the bathroom, and my own bed. I texted my friend Erika and asked her to call me. She told me later that she had been in the middle of making pancakes with her daughter when she got my text but immediately called her husband Tony to take over, knowing that something was wrong as I was not a friend who normally sent out SOS messages. It still pains me to picture the scene – her sun-drenched suburban kitchen, Tony taking the bowl from her hands so she could tend to me, who would never know that kind of domestic ease with my own husband again. She'd known Michael as long as I had, since she and I had been roommates throughout college; she also knew me better than just about anyone, my other half ever since middle school. She said she was devastated for me, but not totally surprised, that Michael had always been hard to fill up, barely finishing one renovation before looking to move again, or planning the next vacation when we were already on one. She had long felt it was the same with the love I gave him: never enough.

I was stunned. I had convinced myself that this was mostly my fault – I wasn't sexual enough, I wasn't kind enough, I didn't adore him the way he adored me, I had insisted we marry too young, I had wanted babies right away, I hated moving and resented it every time we did, I complained about his weight. I complained about the way he ate grapefruit, I complained about his snoring, I complained when he took a second cup of coffee and didn't leave enough in the pot for me. If there was an emptiness inside of him that was simply unfillable then we were both damaged goods who shared in the corruption of our marriage. That thought didn't soothe me so much as temporarily quell the self-loathing that had begun in earnest: an iota of reassurance that was a mere drop in the bucket of my anguish.

Sick with grief, I was unable to eat or drink; my breath was shallow, my eyes were puffy and red, my skin pale and clammy. I had no idea what to do next. I felt like a caged animal in my bedroom, unable to leave for fear of having to face Michael or explain myself to the kids, but crawling out of my skin alone. Erika called back a few hours later to tell me that she was getting in her car to drive upstate and would arrive by dinner. She instructed me to shower and drive to a nearby restaurant. I protested, unable to fathom taking the steps even to change my clothes, but she was adamant that I could and must do it. I was reminded of a time she came to visit me in the city when Michael and I had rented our first apartment after graduating from college. When she left to return home to the suburban town we had grown up in together,

I stood on the corner and cried as her taxi pulled away. I was homesick, found the city overwhelming, and missed her being glued to my side. I felt homesick for her again and longed for a part of my past I could still rely on.

Hudson was confused that I had been in bed sick all day and was now going out to dinner, but I came up with vague excuses, stuffed a wad of tissues in my purse and drove to the restaurant. When Erika came, I wept. When I picked my head up and met her sympathetic gaze, I wept some more. She urged me to take a few bites of the food I had ordered but I pushed it around my plate, afraid I would vomit. When she reminded me that I could not take care of the kids if I didn't take care of myself, I forced a few bites down. I explained that I had asked Michael to leave, at least for a week, to give me time to digest this, but that he wouldn't, that he planned to stay in the family room. Erika agreed that it was only fair to give me space right now.

"He refuses," I said. "He won't stay with a friend either, he says that's demoralizing. I was looking up cheap hotel options when you came."

"Laura, stop. You've done everything for him for years. He's a grown man and can find a place to stay on his own. You can't solve his problems right now," she told me.

"OK, but if I don't solve this he'll stay and I can't tolerate that," I said.

"You're going to have to take a step back and let him handle this by himself. All you have to do now is take care of yourself and the kids. Stand your ground and focus on what you need to get through a terrible situation he created. You didn't do this, he did. And he has to clean it up. If you need space, he can at least give you that."

When I arrived home, I was relieved to see my bed empty and Georgia's door closed; Michael had had the decency to give me privacy for the night. When I awoke in the morning after a fitful sleep, I staggered down the hall to the kitchen to find him typing on his laptop at the table.

"Oh, hey," he said, cheerfully. "So here's what I'm thinking. I'm writing you a letter. I'm going to write you a letter every day to tell you how I'm feeling so that I can be totally honest with you."

"What? Why? How is that going to help me?"

"You said you wanted the truth, so I'm going to give it to you and share my feelings with you on a daily basis."

"No, please don't," I cried out. "I don't want to know what you're thinking. It's a moot point now."

"This could be the best thing that's ever happened to us," he said with an incessant chipperness. "I see this as an opportunity for us to improve our marriage and reinvent what we once had!"

"Wow, Michael. Look at me, I'm a wreck," I sobbed. "I can't eat, I can't sleep, I can't stop crying. The rug has been pulled out from under me and I'm still falling. I am questioning everything about our lives together since we first met. You've always been an optimist but to call this an opportunity? The best thing that could ever happen to us? That's delusional. You have destroyed me," I said, and with that, put my head down on the table and convulsed with sobs.

When I picked my head up, he looked at me with something between compassion and pity and asked, "What can I do to help you through this?"

"You can leave. You can find a place to stay. If you want me to consider giving our marriage a chance, you have to give me space. In the meantime, I have to clean the house and pack up to go home. Apparently, life just keeps going," I said, "even when your heart feels like it might give out any second." With that, I shuffled away in my slippers, pulling my bathrobe tightly around my body, which already, in just the past 36 hours, felt diminished.

I paused before I passed out of his sight and turned back to look at him, saying, "One question I have to ask."

He looked at me so expectantly, even hopefully, that I almost felt bad for him.

"Those flowers you sent me on Valentine's Day... Did you send the same ones to her too?" I asked.

His face fell and I sucked in my breath, despondent, understanding the meaning of his silence.

*

We returned, as scheduled, to the city that evening. I huddled next to Georgia in the backseat, unable to bear any physical proximity to Michael. He lied and told the kids he had meetings upstate over the week so would be dropping us off and then driving right back up. The kids were confused, asking what kind of business meetings he could possibly have upstate. He offered a feeble explanation and when we got home packed a small suitcase to take with him. It was a bitterly cold February night, but warm and cozy in our beautiful new home, and the kids and I were talking in front of the fireplace when he came in to say goodbye. Watching my partner of 27 years wheel his suitcase out of our home and our family made me feel equal parts contempt and pity for him, but absolute agony for myself. I was witnessing one of the saddest moments of my life, representing our failures as individuals and a couple, and the end of my dream of having a loving, stable nuclear family. How was it possible that all the essentials he needed to exist could be zipped up in that one black carry-on size piece of luggage? We had a four-bedroom house filled with family photos and books and artwork procured over the years at school auctions and vintage shops, small sculptures of buddhas we bought 25 years ago in Thailand, stuffed llamas from our trip to Peru, his grandmother's china and my grandparents' silver, but all he needed to go forward was folded into a 22-inch bag?

My grandmother had suffered the loss of her mother as a young child, my mother had been abandoned by her father at only a few years old, and my father had died when I was not yet in kindergarten, but I had always felt certain that I would break my family's curse. I was not just grieving now for my own loss but for the family history I would not successfully redirect after all. Why had I so wholeheartedly embraced the fairy-tale notion of a happily ever after when I had so little evidence aside from schmaltzy television shows that such a thing existed? Why had it never occurred to me that my marriage could come to a screeching halt if I didn't consistently keep my foot on the pedal? I had believed myself to be impervious to becoming a divorce statistic, above something as cliché as an affair. What did I know of this life if my most basic understanding of its essential elements had been wrong all along? I pictured a Jenga tower with my relationship with Michael at the very bottom, every other wood piece balancing on that base – my family, my past, my future, my sense of self. How was I to stay in one piece now?

Watching my husband kiss our kids goodbye and then hearing the front door slam shut, I fought hard to control my reaction so the kids would not suspect anything awry. Soon I would have to come up with an explanation, but for now I had to get through my first night alone.

I moved through the next days in a stupor, getting the kids off to school and then collapsing in tears. I cried to friends, I cried alone, I cried in the bathroom with the shower running when the kids got home from school, I cried in the pantry as I attempted to throw together meals for the kids. Twice a day I dropped CBD oil on my tongue that Erika had sent to help calm me. Jessica made an emergency appointment with a therapist she found for me, whose face looked so pained as I choked out my story that I cried even harder; after two sessions, when I realized she didn't seem able to help me make a plan for how to move forward, I stopped seeing her. I was so lost that I felt I needed a cartographer, not a therapist.

By Tuesday night, the kids were onto me. After I put Georgia to sleep, Daisy and Hudson approached me as a unified force, startling me with their intensity on getting to the truth.

"Mom, where's Dad?" Hudson asked, fixing his gray eyes on mine.

"Upstate. Meetings," I responded.

"That doesn't make sense," Hudson said. "What's really going on?"

I took a deep breath and sat on the sofa. I had not planned this conversation, assuming I had at least a few days before I had to tackle it.

"OK, guys, I'm sorry. I wanted to gather myself before talking to you. You know how Dad and I have been fighting a lot lately?" I asked.

"No," said Daisy, resolutely.

"OK, well you know how we've been having a hard time with each other lately?"

She shook her head again.

"OK, well we have been, which I had thought was pretty noticeable and we decided that we need some time apart, temporarily, to try to fix things between us," I said.

"Are you getting divorced?" Hudson asked, panic rising in his voice.

"No, but we're separating. We need some time apart," I said. What I wouldn't have given to be airlifted out of this disaster zone, the agonized and confused expressions on my children's faces. Was it too late to backpedal and assure them we would be in tiptop form in a week and not to worry?

"One of you is having an affair," said Daisy, suddenly and pointedly. "There is no other possible explanation for this. It's too quick. Why isn't Dad here talking to us too?"

I had already decided that I wouldn't lie to the older kids if they asked. I recalled having been cornered like this years earlier when the kids demanded to know if Michael and I were Santa, and the Easter Bunny and the Tooth Fairy and Cupid and Petal, their special summer fairy, knowing that the second I confirmed it the sweet, innocent chapter of their childhoods that I had so assiduously protected would come to a swift conclusion. Now I was going to close yet another chapter with the information that their parents were not indomitable and that the safety of the family life they had known and relied on was gone, just like that. My silence spoke volumes before I could summon the courage to respond.

"Oh my God, Mom. Just tell us," Daisy cried.

"It wasn't me," I said quietly.

Mayhem ensued. If I had thought my life had already fallen apart, this moment proved to me that I was in fact just in the introductory phase. The panicked reactions of my kids were devastating on a whole new level than I had yet experienced. Daisy sobbed, Hudson quietly raged. They asked me questions I could not answer about what had happened and what would happen next. Daisy called Michael, who could barely hear her as he was pulled over on the side of the road with a flat tire, and screamed at him until she exhausted herself and hung up. Watching my kids suffer this way was brutal, the fury I felt at Michael all-consuming.

My friend Sarah came to my rescue, offering her mother's pied-à-terre around the corner for Michael to stay in for a few weeks to give us a chance to regroup. He was angry that I wouldn't let him return home, but now even if I could bear it, I had the additional rage of the children to manage. Daisy was like an erupting volcano, her fury and grief a molten lava that could burn anyone in her path. Michael and I had given her a happy family and he had single-handedly taken it away, and now she understood that trust – even in her parents – was conditional. Hudson's reaction was much scarier in its silence, as he retreated into himself, becoming impenetrable and taciturn. He met Michael at a diner a few days after learning of the affair to tell him that if we divorced, he would stay with me and that he wanted no further contact with his father. He did not tell me this – he did not tell me anything – but Michael had reported it to me as evidence that if anyone was now responsible for the breakup of our family, it was me, in shutting him out of our home.

The worst was yet to come, as I still had to break it to sweet little Georgia. The dread I felt was palpable. This was the one child of ours who would lose her belief in her parents as an indestructible unit before she would lose her belief in magic, and I wondered if as an adult she would be able to recall our ever having been together. On Saturday morning, as she happily yammered away in my bed, I told her that I needed to share some difficult news with her.

"You know how Daddy has been away this week? We're having a hard time getting along and we think if we spend some time apart it might help, so he's going to stay somewhere else for a few weeks," I said.

"How many weeks is a few weeks?" she asked.

"I don't really know, maybe three weeks?"

"In three weeks, he'll come home?" she pressed.

"In three weeks, we'll see if that's been enough time apart for us to stop being upset with each other," I said.

Georgia curled up in a tight ball, pulled my blanket over her head and wept. I wrapped myself around her and silently cursed Michael again. That our kids should feel this kind of pain was devastating to me, but that their own father had caused it was intolerable. If I could ever forgive him for having an affair, would I ever be able to forgive him for hurting our kids like this? An image came to me from my childhood, my lying curled up in my narrow bed 43 years earlier, my own mother wrapped around me after telling me that my father had died. There had been a before and an after in my childhood and now I was passing this sad legacy on to my daughter, only two years older than I had been when I first ran headlong into loss and grief. I had so desperately wanted a cohesive, traditional, forever family, and now I had to face not only that I wasn't going to get it after all but also that this outcome had not been inevitable as death had been for my father: Michael had had a choice and he had willingly forsaken us.

*

Every day after that felt like a lifetime. I woke up in darkness with my heart racing, and lay still and stupefied until it was time to see Hudson off to school. I would coach myself out of bed, feeling nothing but dread for the day ahead, by telling myself: put one foot down, then the next, then start moving. Looking forward to my first cup of coffee had always been all the motivation I needed to get up, but now the smell of coffee turned my stomach and I thought ruefully of all the mornings Michael and I debated how that day's brew was as the kids made fun of us for having the same conversation every day. During the day I spent hours talking to friends or sitting alone at home, thinking and crying. I stopped reading the newspapers that piled up in front of my door and tried to keep reading books, my most cherished activity, but I could not track the words across the page, let alone digest their meaning. I found a new therapist, someone my friend Libby connected me to after I started crying in the lobby outside our girls' ballet class, unable to make small talk anymore. The therapist asked what I was looking for in my sessions with her and I replied unhesitatingly, "Clarity. I am lost at sea right now, and if I don't find my direction soon I am afraid I will be lost forever."

Gone were the lovingly prepared dinners Michael had praised me for, replaced by piles of tortilla chips with cheese I melted over the top and boxed macaroni and cheese I served to the kids with mumbled apologies. I could not imagine a time this misery would end, but Jessica had shared with me the quote "The only way out is through" and I repeated it to myself dozens of times a day, holding onto it like a lifeline. I was in deep right now, but I had to believe there would someday be an out. By the end of the day, I was emotionally spent, but the kids were in constant need of comforting and counseling so I would go from room to room listening or offering soothing words or accepting misplaced blame that had nowhere else to go until I was finally free to fall exhausted into my own bed.

CHAPTER 14

Almost There

The last winter weeks blurred together as spring break approached. Somehow I had managed to make it through each seemingly endless day, and now I decided to splurge on a room at a ski lodge in Vermont so Hudson could ski while I entertained Georgia at the indoor water park. I bought Daisy a plane ticket for her 18th birthday to visit her friend in California and give her a break from our turmoil. In the taxi on the way to the doctor's office to have the cast removed from Hudson's hand the week before our trip, a video clip came on, showing a young couple getting engaged on a quiet pier in the city. I scoffed noisily, disparaging the couple for their inability to see the inevitably grim and broken future that awaited them. I had been trying so hard to keep my anger in check, just days earlier weeping on the phone with Erika as I told her I was terrified that my once easy-going demeanor had been permanently expunged, wholly replaced by bitterness. I was not lacking self-awareness, and yet I could not seem to stop myself, resentment seeping out of my pores over the way in which I had been so egregiously wronged. Hudson eyed me mournfully, then looked out the window, away from me. I could accept that I was now openly dismissive of romance and commitment, but I was horrified to be passing that along to my kids, especially Daisy and Hudson, who were around the age I was when I first started to have sexual experiences.

Maybe they'll do better than I did, I thought, understanding that I had to try harder to keep that option intact for them.

At the doctor's office, the cast came off, but with instructions not to ski for a while. I saw Hudson's eyes well with tears.

"Listen," I said to the doctor, "I'm a big rule follower, but Hudson has ADHD and the lack of activity is making him depressed, on top of which we're going through a family crisis that would knock any kid out, so I'm confessing to you that I'm going to let him ski this weekend. I'm letting you know that I hear your medical advice but I'm not going to follow it and it's not because I don't have a ton of respect for you."

Her eyes met mine without judgment and she nodded understandingly as she directed Hudson not to be a total daredevil just yet. I could have flung myself at her, I was so grateful for her compassion.

When she left the room, Hudson whispered a thank-you to me. I put my hand on his shoulder, giving it a gentle squeeze, connecting us for just a moment.

Hudson, Georgia and I were determined to stay in good spirits on our road trip to Vermont. Hudson was thoughtful and attentive, carrying bags and helping Georgia, and I was moved as I witnessed their deep connection to one another. I reminded him that I valued his help but he needn't be the man of the house, that I was still the parent and quite capable despite the current circumstances. I was proud of him for jumping out of the car to get our luggage and holding Georgia's hand as we crossed streets, but I wanted him to feel like a kid and I did not want him to worry about me.

We checked into the hotel and were given a room with floor-to-ceiling windows overlooking the water park. Although over the years we had gone on day trips to amusement parks, Michael was adamantly opposed to kid-centered vacations. The novelty of this current situation was not lost on them. Even trips to Disney had been one-day affairs, and we would screech out of the parking lot at the end of the day to go to whatever hip hotel Michael had chosen for us. Now, they marveled at all they could do here over the next three days. Georgia's planned itinerary would require my participation – water rides, an arcade, ice skating, rock climbing – and while it was hard for me to decide which amongst these was my least favorite activity, my only goal was to keep her so busy and happy that she wouldn't remember her father was not with us.

Hudson left early the next morning to ski while Georgia and I changed into bathing suits. She stopped suddenly and climbed back into bed, watching the scene at the water park warily from our windows.

"I don't feel well. My stomach hurts," she said. "I don't want to go down there."

I surveyed the scene below, moms and dads toting kids around, holding their hands and catching them at the bottoms of slides.

"Georgia, are you sad that we're here without Daddy?" I asked.

Her big blue eyes welled with tears that she fought to restrain. I climbed back into bed with her, reaching for her. She pressed her face against my chest, which I could feel get slick with her copious tears.

These sudden about-faces in mood had become frequent since our separation – when we had gone out for dumplings and her face had changed, taking in the completeness of the family next to us and the missing piece of our own; when we watched her perform in a show at school and she realized that Michael and I weren't sitting together; when we celebrated Hudson's 15th birthday and then Daisy's 18th and Michael wasn't with us. No explanation for his absence was adequate for her, and why should it have been? He had stolen a huge chunk of her childhood innocence and I was enraged and heartbroken every time I faced the fallout of it. As I soothed her, I plotted long, vicious texts I would send to him later, accusing him of not loving his children enough to consider consequences while having his affair, of fracturing his family and decimating their happy mother to a sniveling heap, of sullying our pristine family by recreating his own broken home, of traumatizing me by returning me to the scene of my own childhood in which my father had been taken from me too soon. Every tear the kids shed I reported to him immediately, so that I could vent my anger and hit him over the head with blame. His unwillingness to stand still and accept the blows – his insistence that we move forward, not back; that I look inward to share my part in it – only served to make my rampages even more intense. The damage I was doing to myself was just as severe, as after I had worked myself into heated rages during which I felt victimized and wronged, it wasn't easy to be calm and present for the kids. The bitterness building in me was to be my ruin, but understanding that only made it worse as I felt powerless against its crushing weight.

Georgia and I waited until Hudson returned from skiing so that we could ice skate together. It had been years since I had been on skates and I was scared of falling and dreaded even the idea of being cold. Hudson offered to take Georgia so that I could have a break, but I knew they wanted me to skate with them. Michael was agile and athletic, so it had always been reasonable for me to cede physical activities to him: skiing, ice skating, skateboarding, biking, swimming, tennis – these had all been his domain, but now I had to find a way to make all domains my own.

At the rink, I stacked three milk crates on top of each other to use for balance as I got my bearings. After a few slow loops around, the kids insisted I give up the babyish crates and skate on my own. They each took one of my hands and promised not to whip me around at full speed to amuse themselves. When I felt steady, I let go of their hands. The rink was nearly empty and I picked up speed with each lap around, spinning faster and faster, leaving Georgia behind with Hudson. I felt free, singing and smiling and watching my kids from a distance as they set up an obstacle course. *Here I am*, I thought. I hadn't wanted to be here, was terrified to be on my own, scared of moving fast and feeling uncomfortably cold – but I was not only here, I actually felt a sense of inner peace and something I might even call happiness surge through me. *Just keep doing this*, I thought, *face the things you are scared of, put on a brave face for your kids, let yourself be present in joyful moments without panicking over what comes next, and you might actually find your way through.*

*

On our last day in Vermont, Georgia and I checked out of the hotel and went to a bowling alley while we waited for Hudson to finish skiing. We had just laced up our bowling shoes when my cell phone rang. A stern voice asked if I was the mother of Hudson Williams. My heart sank. It was ski patrol, informing me that he had suffered a head injury and blacked out, and they needed to know how quickly I could get there.

Georgia and I kicked off our bowling shoes and raced up the hill in our car. I was so panicked when I reached the ski lodge that Georgia had to point me in the right direction. We ran into the medic's office, flying in to see Hudson lying on a board, his neck immobilized in a brace.

"I'm sorry, Mama," he whispered.

"What is the one thing I asked you not to do before you left this morning?" I asked, a sob catching itself in my throat.

"A back flip," he said.

"And how did you hurt yourself?" I asked pointlessly; the guilty look in his eyes told me everything I needed to know.

The emergency medical technician pulled me aside to tell me that although he was now lucid and could state his name, Hudson did not know what year it was or who the President was. She gave me a choice between the local ER or the trauma center an hour away.

Opting for the trauma center, I was given directions so that I could meet the ambulance there. I didn't want to leave Hudson alone in the ambulance, but couldn't leave Georgia behind either. The ambulance driver caught my hand as she saw me hesitate, promising that she would take care of him until he got to the hospital. When I still could not seem to make a move to leave without him, she upped her promise, saying that she would treat him like he was her own son. Oh, the kindness of strangers, and all I could do was whisper an insufficient thank-you to her.

Georgia and I headed north on the highway. Snow started falling and cars slowed down as I cursed and wove my way around them. Pulling up to the hospital entrance, I saw an ambulance near the side door and assumed it was Hudson's, but when I went tearing inside, the receptionist told me he hadn't arrived yet. I insisted that she was mistaken and not looking for the right child, explaining that I had just driven through a snowstorm and hit traffic and there was no way I beat the ambulance. With a withering look, she instructed me to sit down until he arrived.

I paced the waiting room with Georgia at my side until my name was finally called ten minutes later. We burst through the doors to the room they directed me to and the sight inside stopped me in my tracks: a team of six doctors and nurses were lifting Hudson onto a table and there was a flurry of activity around him, oxygen masks and IV lines. I put my hands on Georgia's shoulders and turned her to face me so that she would not see her beloved big brother in a scary state like this.

I stood frozen by the door until they had settled Hudson onto the examining table, and then cautiously approached the doctor who seemed to be in charge, asking her to please check his legs right away, that I hadn't seen him move them yet. I held my breath waiting, and when his toes started moving, I collapsed in the chair next to Georgia. Hours later, after a series of X-rays and MRIs, a brain bleed was ruled out and we were reassured it was just a concussion. Shakily but gratefully, we left the hospital. It was 9pm and I wanted to start the drive back home. I mapped out two hours on local roads and saw we could stop at a motel for the night at that point. The skies and roads had cleared and we set off.

Within an hour, both kids were sound asleep and thus could not hear the stream of curses emerge from my mouth as a sudden blizzard blew snow in every direction. The roads were pitch-black and curvy, snow coming down in white twisting sheets. I drove 25mph, leaning forward in my seat as far as I could. Georgia woke up and started asking a litany of questions: where are we, is this safe, can we stop for the night, are there any snacks in here?

"Georgia!" I yelled. "Stop talking. I have to focus."

I saw a sign indicating that in ten miles there was a gas station and a motel. *Hallelujah*, I thought, and crept along the road, counting down every mile. When we at last pulled off the highway, the gas station was closed and the only difference I could see between this motel and the one in *Psycho* was that this one was called Lee's. There was no sign of life, just a few dim lightbulbs over weathered doors and broken screens.

"Mommy, do you want to stay here?" Georgia asked with trepidation.

"No, we can't stay here. It's creepy and it looks deserted anyway."

Back on the road, slipping along in a blaze of white, it was now 1am and my eyes were fluttering. I was exhausted, terrified, and saw no end to this journey from hell. Every twenty minutes my mother would call, demanding an update on our whereabouts, and I would calm her down only to panic myself. On and on we went this way as I searched my GPS for the nearest motel and reassured Georgia with a false cheerfulness that we would be at a warm, clean motel very soon.

When we pulled off the highway thirty minutes later into the motel parking lot, I laughed bitterly when I saw that it was not just closed but actually boarded up. I put my head down on the steering wheel and started pounding it with my fists.

"Mommy, do you wish now that we had stayed at Lee's Motel?" Georgia asked so sincerely that I started laughing, possibly a tad maniacally.

"No, I don't wish that. Well, maybe just a little I wish that. I'm going to find a place to turn around and we'll continue our search or else we'll nap in the car."

Up ahead I saw lights, and my heart swelled. When I got closer, I saw that it was a small hotel and through the lobby windows I could see a man standing at the front desk. I felt like I had just discovered life on Mars. *If this hotel is fully booked*, I thought, *then I give up, the universe can take us and spit us back out into the night and I will tell my kids that I'm sorry, but I've got nothing left.* Luckily for us, they had a room as warm and clean as the one I had promised to Georgia, and so we were given a reprieve for yet another day.

CHAPTER 15

Breaking Point

Michael and I had limited our contact to once a week in couples' therapy as our therapist had worried about our ability to communicate with each other without her mediation. I felt certain that therapy was doing us more harm than good. In our therapist's presence, we lashed out at each other viciously and she couldn't rein us in. I was feeling beaten down and shouldering what felt like excessive blame. She had started our therapy by declaring that we would not play the roles of victim and villain.

"You just gave him an out," I cried. "I *am* the victim and he *is* the villain. Someone has to accept responsibility and it's not going to be me."

"I'm not condoning his affair, Laura," she said. "But we won't get far if we can't dig deeper than that."

She was determined to get to the underlying causes of the affair, what had been broken in our marriage to give the affair room to grow, but I felt that until he first acknowledged how damaging the affair was, we were dead in the water. I expected him to be contrite, but he was furious at me. He expected me to want to understand why the affair had happened, but I couldn't face that there was a whole underworld happening beneath the surface of our life of which I had been blissfully unaware. Every week in therapy, he would rattle off all the ways we had been going off course for years and I would sit stupefied, wondering what rock I had been living under, and feeling more and more of my reality slipping away. So now my future wasn't going to be what I had expected, but even my past was being savagely edited and rewritten? That meant all I had was my present, which was filled with bitterness, anger and hate – I was reaching my breaking point.

*

One morning, Georgia woke up in my bed, where she had been sleeping since Michael's departure, and asked, "Is six weeks a long time?" I launched into a long, rambling answer about how it would depend on the context, how long she had already been waiting and how excited she was for what was coming. She gave me a confused look, making it clear that my abstract answer was not in line with the topic at hand, and tried again.

"Daddy's been gone for six weeks. Is that long enough for you to make up with him?"

"Oh, Georgia," I said, deflating. "I thought it would be, but it's not. I don't know how much longer it's going to take."

"But you said three weeks, so how much longer?" she asked, her voice rising in panic. "How much time will be enough time?"

"I'm so sorry. I wish I could make this go away, but I can't. I don't have an amount of time to give you, but Daddy and I both love you so much and will do anything we can to make this easier for you," I said.

"Easier would be if Daddy could come back home," she said, sobbing, as I held her. Silently, to myself, I agreed. That certainly would be easier, and for the thousandth time since our separation had begun, I wished I could blink and make this all disappear.

*

In May, at the three-month mark of our separation, I saw no end in sight to my ambivalence about my marriage. I was still seeing my own therapist once a week, and she helped me accept that a clear path was not going to be in my sightline anytime soon. It was with this in mind that I texted Michael and asked him to find a one-year lease on an apartment, explaining that the pressure of a deadline for him to move back home had become unbearable. Our therapist had told us when we first started seeing her that the longer couples stayed separated the lower the chance they would ever reunite, but I could take or leave our marriage at this point. Friends asked for updates, wanting to know what I thought would happen, and I would give them 50:50 odds, some days feeling sure we were done and others unable to wrap my head around a future without him. I still could not bring myself to look at him, but letting go of our future together was intolerable. For most of our adult lives we had been one unit; I could not fathom our being divided without it killing me. Already I was having to allow our past to take new shapes and colors, but to obliterate our future?

In couples' therapy one day, I silently raged as Michael explained why he could not completely cut this other woman out of his life.

"She's not a bad person, Laura," he said as my eyes almost fell out of my head in disbelief.

"Michael, I'm going to caution you from defending her," the therapist said.

I realized it was the first time she was seeing the situation from my perspective instead of trying to make me acknowledge how my shortcomings had led to our demise.

"I can't do this anymore," I announced abruptly. "I come in here hopeful every week, just to get flogged. I go home a little more broken every time. Then I work up the courage to come back only to have what little self-respect I still have beaten to a pulp. Michael, your loyalty is to this woman, not me, and I'm suffering. You have to acknowledge the extent of the damage you've done. If you can't, then we're done."

Both he and the therapist were silent.

That week I found a new family therapist who I felt would advocate for both of us, not just him, and asked Michael to switch to her. She was soft-spoken and started our first session by leading a deep breathing exercise. It helped. When we spoke to each other, we did so with self-restraint. When we veered away from the subject we were discussing to assign blame or make snide remarks to each other, she would gently steer us back. She made a list of the upcoming events we couldn't figure out how to navigate so that we could make plans for them: Daisy's prom, her graduation, our summer in the country. She was like a magician, putting a spell on us so that we could speak respectfully and kindly. One day she asked me to look directly at Michael when I was talking to him as until then, I had addressed him while looking at her or out the window – I hadn't looked him in the eye in months. I said I would try, took a deep breath and stared at him. He looked like a stranger to me, that deep connection we had for so many years simply nonexistent. The thousands of words we could once have communicated with just our eyes had gone silent. I had held out hope that when I finally looked into his eyes, we would magnetically connect to each other again; instead, the lack of recognition blindsided me all over again.

"He's taken everything from me," I cried. "I don't know him anymore, I don't recognize myself, I've lost the peace of mind and ease with which I used to walk through the world. I used to think to myself at random moments of the day, I'm happy, I love my life. Now I'm terrified I'll always be sad and angry and the enormity of my emotions is eating me alive. I want my old life back," I said, and with that, covered my face with my hands and let my body heave.

"Laura, look at me," she said, after a few minutes of letting me air my grief. "I need you to look at me."

I dropped my hands from my face and raised my eyes to meet hers, taking in her serene demeanor, her silver hair, her kind eyes. She leaned forward toward me, her eyes never straying from mine.

"You are still you. You have not lost the essence of yourself. I see you. I see who you are. There's no old life and new life, there's just you. Don't ever give anyone the power to take you away from yourself. You will always know who you are, no one can change that."

"OK," I said, sniffling and holding her steady gaze. "What if I'm so lost that I can't remember who I am or find myself in here? What if I'm actually lost forever?"

"No, it's not possible. Right here, Laura," she said, pressing her hand to her heart and leaning forward even further in her seat, "you are here. Look inside. You're too strong to have disappeared. Find yourself, embrace yourself, that's the part no one can ever take from you, that will always be there for you. You know who you are."

Slowly, I nodded my head, as if she had just re-introduced me to myself. I was wounded, but I wasn't dead. I had fallen, badly, and had convinced myself that I would never be the same again, but somewhere amidst the wreckage, whatever it was that made me a mother and a daughter and a friend, that was still there. It was possible that whatever had made me a wife was gone forever, but that was only a part of who I was. Its absence would not kill me: it would hurt, it would redefine parts of me, but it would not destroy me if I didn't allow it to.

*

On Mother's Day, I took a spin class that the instructor peppered with feel-good quotes about motherhood. I took a lot of spin classes so I was accustomed to these motivational tidbits and I was apathetic to them. Yes, I showed up, yes, I was doing my best and that was good enough, blah blah blah, but really, let's be honest, I was here to fight age and gravity.

"When life deals you a tough hand, don't ask why. Don't bother yourself with why me? Why *not* you? Because you can handle it, that's why. You've hit hundreds of walls in your life, but you're powerful and you're resilient and you've got this, that's why you. Because you can."

I nodded along and by the time she was done I had to restrain myself from shouting out, "Yes, I can! Yes, I do! I've got this." These last months had been tumultuous, showing me the best in friends and strangers and sometimes the worst in people who loved me the most, the weakest and the strongest parts of myself. Time and time again I had fallen apart but I had picked myself back up just as many times. I thought of all the kindnesses friends had shown me and the generosity of people I knew only minimally who took time to acknowledge my sadness and humbly extended support: the super from my old building who offered to come over and repair anything that needed fixing, the hairdresser who told me to pop in when I had a date so she could style my hair free of charge, the kids' former nursery school teacher who saw me at a coffee bar wiping away tears and pressed a tiny handmade doll into my hands, then silently walked away. My friends and family had been devoted and generous: Georgia's teacher, my friend Karen, who had her come in before school started because she knew mornings were tough for her, bringing her a croissant and her favorite Earl Grey tea; my brother, who flew in from LA to sleep on my couch within days of Michael leaving so that I wouldn't be alone, despite two snowstorms that made him have to cancel and reschedule; my friends who fed me countless meals and dropped off the kids' favorite treats with such volume that you could get a sugar rush just walking by the pantry; my friend Jen who took me out to dinner with her husband to show me that I still had a place with them, that they wanted me whether or not I was part of a couple; the friend of a friend who took me out for lunch and bravely shared her own story to help me understand that I was not alone; my friend Heidi who sent me powerful books that had helped her through difficult times; my stepsister Lori who had scooped up Georgia from the hospital in Vermont while I waited for Hudson's test results and took her out for sushi. As much pain as I felt, I had so much love to counterbalance it – I was grateful for every bit of it.

I had always been an optimistic person and I felt sad for myself now without feeling sorry for myself. All the time, I wondered why me? I didn't mean it in a 'woe is me' way, I meant literally, why me? What had happened in the trajectory of our lives together that allowed this to happen to our marriage? Is it that we were so young when we met? That we settled down without experiencing enough of other people and the world? Were we doomed with our tumultuous childhoods – the early divorce of Michael's parents and their unconventional lifestyles, the death of my father when I was so young and my mother's subsequent remarriage? Was it the recent deaths of Michael's parents, forcing him to stare down his own mortality and then flee from it with a woman almost half his age?

I had never stopped to ask myself during the many amiable years of my marriage, why am I so lucky? What have I done to deserve this beautiful life when other people suffer? If I didn't question why I had been fortunate, I refused to now question why it seemed my fortune had changed. I accepted that it had but that it was temporary, and that all of the things in my life that were still going strong proved that in fact my fortune was shifting but was not completely upended. I was still raging at how Michael had betrayed me and wounded our children, but I realized I wasn't broken, that he had not destroyed me, that in fact I had everything I needed inside myself.

When I was a child and upset or angry, my mother used to offer platitudes like "Life isn't fair" or "Life will go on". The simplicity of these statements, their deficiency of advice or a plan of action, were a source of frustration to me. Now I sighed ruefully as I thought of those conversations, because it was so true, this most basic of facts: life isn't fair and yet, life indeed does go on. My life overall had been more than fair – it had been downright generous actually, giving me much more than it had taken from me. So when friends ask what happened to me and Michael, the unsatisfying answer is that nothing happened and everything happened – life had happened in all of its beauty and ugliness, its love and its misery, its community and its terrible loneliness – and that I was determined that my life, the life I had known and loved and was grateful for, would go on.

CHAPTER 16

Cookie Crumbs

Those grim winter days seem safely in the past as I revel in the lush days of mid-August. I have always loved summer, the season when I am most alive – the shedding of layers, the heat soaking through my body and thawing my bones, which in all other seasons creak with a cold chill, the flowers and fruit and sand and thunderstorms and overgrown richness of the landscape. The storm that has been agitating my family has not yet passed, nor do I feel confident that it will pass anytime soon or maybe ever. Back in early summer I did not have the energy to plant a garden as I usually did and the barren plots of dirt, now filled with weeds instead of fragrant herbs and colorful pansies, rebuke me every time I pass by. I do not have the wherewithal to stock my house with an abundance of freshly picked cherries and peaches from orchards I have always loved to meander through, and I apathetically watch birds devour every last blueberry from my bushes without even attempting my annual battle against them. My biggest home repair – trying to fix the relationship between Michael and the two of our three kids who still refuse contact with him – is dead in the water. Still, even though I have no cause to, I feel stirrings of hope and find that a mere iota of optimism after a punishing winter goes a long way. I regard myself as a delicate flower bud and imagine myself emerging from the soil after a long, cruel winter as something miraculous and precious. I am fragile, but even the coldest frost can't stop me from poking my head through the soil. The fact of this gives me a sense of bravura I have never recognized in myself before now.

Most of my attention is dedicated to preparing for Daisy's impending departure for college. She has made it clear that having Michael present on her move-in day will make her more anxious than she already is. I long for a partner for this milestone – someone to smile at as we bask in the glow of a job well done, someone to hold me steady as I walk away and let her go – but I am on my own.

This is not the way it was supposed to be, I think to myself for the umpteenth time, mournful that the milestones we had envisioned spending together are now my sole domain.

We drive home to the city for a few days to finish packing, and on the way the build-up of pressure and sadness and anxiety about all the ways in which our family has changed and is about to again with Daisy's departure explosively ruptures and spews venom and heartbreak. It is coming from all three of us in the car in equal measure: me, Daisy and Hudson (lucky Georgia has dodged a bullet by staying upstate with my parents). We are like live wires of emotion and I have to pull the car over at a rest stop to keep us from combusting on the highway. Daisy is mad at Hudson for being aloof and sullen; Hudson is mad at Daisy for escaping us and abandoning him; both of them are furious at me that I can't glue our family back together but even worse, they pity me; and all of us are enraged at the person causing this maelstrom who is not in the car with us. I fold in half, resting my head on the steering wheel and weeping as I have never wept before, primal sobs wracking my body. Sadness I can manage, but this anger – toxic fumes of anger from all of us – suffocates me. Daisy wordlessly places napkins scrounged from the glove compartment on my lap; when I finally pick my head up, I see Hudson in the rear-view mirror looking at me with hostility and contempt.

"The anger at me and at each other has to stop," I say quietly but firmly, holding his gaze in the mirror. "I can handle your sadness and will listen to you cry all day everyday if that's what it takes, but I can't be a punching bag anymore. If you're testing to see how far you can push before I break, please know you're getting very close. If you hate living with me, you are free to go live with Dad. That's your alternative."

Daisy and Hudson are silent as I pull back onto the highway.

When we arrive in the city, we scatter like strangers. I go for a walk to clear my head and find myself immobilized on the sidewalk, watching people pass by, coming and going in all directions. When did everyone in this city get so beautiful, I wonder. I seem never to have noticed what an attractive, fit species New Yorkers are. Suddenly I perceive every woman who passes me as competition and I am crestfallen to recognize that I am no match for their vibrancy. How does anyone stand out here? My newfound sexual prowess and confidence drain out of me, leaving nothing but a small dirty puddle in the gutter. The two ways I have for decades identified myself – as a loving wife and dedicated mother – are on shaky ground, while my brand new way of identifying myself as a desirable woman now simply vanishes, leaving me with the uncomfortable understanding that I can no longer rely on the self I thought I was. I register that my successes with numbers one through four were completely situational, that my small victories on the amateur fields led me to foolishly believe that I was ready for the big leagues; while I thought I had been gaining a deeper understanding of myself I was actually slowly losing what tenuous understanding of myself I did have.

I picture myself almost twenty years ago, standing on the corner outside a bakery on the Upper West Side. I had been trying and failing to get pregnant and had fallen into a deep depression, despondent that friends around me blinked and got pregnant while I seemed destined for barrenness. A therapist suggested I do a simple activity that made me feel happy, and I told her my greatest happiness was found in cleaning my apartment on a Sunday morning after Michael left for work, then going to the bakery for three Italian bakery cookies and a cup of coffee, which I would slowly savor as I paged through piles of manuscripts for work. My therapist had told me to go do it then, to bring a simple pleasure back into my life, to remind myself what happiness felt like.

Ever the diligent student, I had done as she instructed. I vacuumed our apartment, polished the dining and wooden end tables, scrubbed the ten linoleum squares that made up our kitchen and bathroom, and left the tiny apartment in its gleaming glory to walk around the corner to the bakery. Once I reached it though,

I stopped outside the door leading inside, immobilized as I watched other customers stroll in and out. I could see the glass case of cookies through the window and I felt nothing so much as bafflement: this once made me happy? These crumbling, garishly colored cookies? Jockeying for a spot in line with all the couples pushing overloaded baby strollers? I desperately wanted to be a mother, I wanted to coo over a baby with Michael, saying she has my eyes but your smile, I wanted to know what it meant to feel a life growing inside of me – and these cookies were supposed to bring me some modicum of joy? I didn't want the crumbs, I wanted the whole bakery. I was disgusted with myself, a simpleton who had been fooled by such a mundane pleasure in the past.

Now, standing here on the sidewalk, I have that same feeling of bewilderment. I had thought happiness was still within my grasp and an emotion that I understood – men were mine for the taking just like those cookies had been, lined up on their trays, waiting to be chosen and packed up for home. But I don't have the fire in me to compete with these strutting women who dominate the streets of my hometown. I suddenly feel used up and spit out, my eyes swollen from my meltdown in the car, my curly hair puffing up in the humidity, my skin coated in a toxic layer of acridness that I am certain will repel anyone who comes near me.

I feel, finally, defeated.

Slowly, I walk back home, letting Daisy know I can help her finish her errands if she wants and texting Hudson a long note that has been purged of the rage I felt just an hour ago. I tell him I love him unconditionally, am sorry I lost my temper and know we will get through this together. If I can only retrieve one part of my former self, it'll be to mother the hell out of my kids – that's the one job at which I absolutely will not allow myself to fail.

To their credit, the kids get their emotions under control and our reunification spurs me along. Back upstate, every night leading up to her departure, I cook one of Daisy's favorite meals and then excuse myself to wipe away a sudden onslaught of tears while the kids murmur to each other, "Is she seriously crying again?" Daisy and I have always been deeply connected to each other, and she is the child of mine who bursts through the door at the end of the day spilling out an endless series of stories. We are already down one loud and buoyant family member, and her departure will take us from what was just recently five inhabitants to three. The night before she is to leave, Hudson surprises me by packing Daisy's astounding volume of belongings into the car trunk while I'm in the pool with Georgia. This help was a peace offering, and I stand dripping in my bathing suit while he proudly shows me that he got every last pillow and bin of food shoved in there.

I have not had time to see #3 or #4, but both men still text me most days to say hi – a pleasant surprise given how sure I was that #3 had decided I came with too much baggage. After a period of lying low, we seem to have found our way back to the easy repartee we had established so quickly early on, and of course I am determined to stay in touch with #4, hoping for a repeat opportunity of mind-blowing sex. All that I want to share with Michael right now I share with them instead, expressing concern with how all of her belongings will be transported to her room and how I am terrible at goodbyes even when it's just a normal "See you later!"

I recall the first time Michael and I drove Daisy to sleepaway camp when she was just eight years old. I started crying as we drove up the dirt road to the camp and he sternly reprimanded me, "Get it together, Laura. You can cry all you want after we drop her but for now it's your job to send her off, not fall apart."

I knew that he was right, and it wasn't until I gave her a hug and quickly walked away with my head down that I realized Michael was not walking next to me. Glancing behind me, I saw him on his knees in the grass, eye level with Daisy, saying "OK, just one more hug" many times more than once. I walked back and gently took hold of his elbow, saying, "It's time to leave now, Michael." I had felt like a confident parent then, doing my part to gracefully separate from my oldest child; I was both moved and annoyed by his inability to do the same.

Here I am eleven years later, ready to repeat the scene and launch this child into the world, but now I need to be brave without any support as I am very much alone. Texting #3 and #4 about this monumental event is wholly inadequate – they don't know her, they hardly even know me. #3 has told me sweetly that he could show up in the parking lot with a school hat on and pretend he's part of a move-in committee, and #4 has said that he's going to wrap me in a long hug and keep me there a while the next time he sees me. The morning we are to leave, they both text to wish me luck. It breaks my heart that from Michael I do not hear even a small peep, as if he's given up on us.

CHAPTER 17

Easy Access

Mission College Drop-off accomplished, I am gifted a small, precious window of time when the kids go to my parents' house for the night. I contemplate what to do: settle in with a glass of wine and a book I won't be able to focus on, or attempt to conjure up that bold vixen who tells strange men that she is available, ready and able. *One foot in front of the other*, I remind myself, *just keep moving forward*. I had felt thoroughly defeated days ago, but now I'm trying to view it as a temporary trouncing, like losing to my sister at Big Boggle when I had been the family winner since childhood, or ceding the "Who can hold the longest plank?" contest to Hudson after I had been undefeated for years. I didn't as a result of those losses abruptly stop playing Boggle or say I'll never do a plank again. Those sleek women on the city streets may have unwittingly held up an unflattering mirror to me last week, but that can't mean I'm supposed to quietly retreat. Before I lose momentum, I text #3 and #4 that I have some free time. I have not told either of them that I'm actively dating other people, which makes me feel sneaky and dishonest, but I am unclear as to how to establish dating parameters. Is it assumed that you're dating other people until you clarify with each other that you're not, or is it assumed that you're not dating other people until you clarify that you indeed are? It feels a little late in the game now to bring this up so instead I swallow the discomfort and proceed to throw myself into their orbits, hoping at least one of them will want me and give me a chance to get my head back in the game. Both men respond, so with a fair amount of anxiety I book #4 for late afternoon into evening and book #3 for later in the night.

When #4 opens the door to his house for me later that day, he is wearing a plush green bathrobe loosely belted around his waist, his skin and hair still damp from the shower. He opens his arms and I step inside them; wordlessly we stand like that, with the pugs running circles around us and the front door open, for longer than I think I've ever hugged anyone before. I rest my head against his chest, he presses his body against mine, and I feel like I might be having a spiritual breakthrough, so strong is my reaction to being touched. Why have I never liked to be hugged before? This is amazing, like someone is holding my heart just so it can beat with a little more ease, the warmth of his body spreading into mine. I have so much to learn about intimacy, I am like an infant learning language. I thought I was unaffectionate and didn't like being touched – Michael always used to marvel at how affectionate I was with our kids when I seemed to physically recoil from everyone else around me – but I do like it, in fact I feel a kind of unexpected peace and comfort wash over me.

As #4 hugs me, I can feel him growing hard against me. We

don't attempt small talk, he simply takes my hand and together we walk up the stairs to his room. He nods toward the bed, telling me he washed his bedding in anticipation of my arrival. I love that he considered this, overcoming his bachelor ways to present me with a clean duvet. He takes his robe off and underneath it his body ripples with finely tuned muscles that thrill me all over again. I am wearing a maxi dress with a halter top that miraculously does not require a bra, so I simply roll it from the top all the way down my body, revealing that all I have on underneath is a pale pink lace thong, which I step out of.

"Cool dress," he says.

"Easy access," I say.

"You've had a tough couple of weeks," he says. "You need some TLC. Roll over."

I do as instructed, settling on my stomach and hoping my bare ass is smooth and not sporting the unsightly bumpy rashes I often get from the Peloton bike that is otherwise keeping my ass in tip-top shape. He straddles my legs while his strong hands knead my shoulders and work their way down my back. A good massage may be the only physical pleasure that I still think is better than sex, and I allow my body to sink down under the pressure of his hands. He takes his time, rubbing and pressing my muscles all the way down to my feet and then working his way back up again, the movements turning into strokes as his hands arrive between my legs. He teases me, touching my upper thighs and getting close to my lips and then pulling away again. My breath turns shallow, and finally, when I think I may come just like this, I wriggle myself forward until I can flip over and then tell him that I need him inside of me right away. When he enters me, I dig my nails into his butt cheeks, pulling him into me as deeply as he can go, and I sigh with gratitude that my urgent need to be filled up has been met. We come together and I am in awe that we can get our timing just right.

He slides to the side of me and we lie holding each other.

"Thank you," I whisper. "I really needed that."

We are quiet for a few minutes, neither fully awake nor asleep, and then a Cure song from the '80s comes on the radio, which I say I love, and soon we have gone into our phones to play each other some of our most beloved '80s songs, from Yaz and Bon Jovi and The Clash and R.E.M. We talk about school dances and our college days, our families and the challenges of being a single parent. My mouth drops open when he tells me that on nights he has his kids, he feeds them packets of ramen noodles or boxes of Kraft mac and cheese. I tell him I know he can do better and promise to send him some simple, no-fail recipes. As the sky outside begins to fade, he asks if I'm hungry but assures me he's not offering anything from his understocked pantry. I pause and look down at his penis, which is soft against his thigh, and pause as I ponder it. The skin along the shaft is smooth and looks like a hood and I startle to realize this is the first uncircumcised penis I have ever seen. It reminds me of a turtle inside its shell and when I now touch it, running the edge of my nail along the shaft, it hardens until it has emerged from its shell. I am too shy to do what I really want, which is to tell him this is my first close-up with an uncircumcised penis, and to more closely examine it, so I settle for another round of sex and then agree we can go eat dinner.

He asks if I want to take a shower; I guess the washcloth clean-up was a first-time customer special only. Remembering that I am going right from him to #3 and scrubbing myself clean of one man before I see the next seems like the polite thing to do, I head to his daughter's bathroom to use her shower while he gets into the shower in his bathroom.

We drive into town for dinner, to a restaurant that he insists has the best steak, and we stand in the dimly lit hallway to the dining room as we wait for the host to set a table. We gaze at each other with playful smiles; he looks to his left and then to his right and seeing no one coming, leans across the hallway to give me a quick kiss.

When we sit at the small table, he takes the candle, vase and the salt and pepper shakers from the center of the table, moving each object one at a time to the table next to ours, and then reaches across the now-empty space for my hands, which he holds. There is something boyish and endearing about him, his gestures intentional and confident.

"Oh, I almost forgot!" I say excitedly. "There's a weekend in September when I have the whole weekend free. Maybe you can arrange not to have your kids that weekend and we can do something?"

"Sure, great," he says.

"Hang on, let me see which weekend it is," I say, scrolling through the calendar on my phone. When I give him the dates, he nods but doesn't note it in his own calendar.

"OK, we'll figure it out," he says.

On the walk back to his car after dinner, I text #3 to tell him I am running late and will head over soon. #4 drives me back to his house, opens the front door and we head inside. I assume I am back inside for a quickie before I head out and I gather my long sundress in my hands and start climbing the staircase.

"Oh sweetie, no," he says, stopping me dead in my tracks. "I'm sorry, but it's late and I have to be up early."

Luckily I am still facing forward and he is behind me, so he cannot see me wince in embarrassment at my overly forward misstep. His addressing me as "sweetie" is the worst part – condescending, like I'm a child trying to stay up past her bedtime.

"Oh, OK, no problem, sorry, I just assumed," I say, hastily thanking him for dinner before making my exit. Something between us just turned but I cannot figure out what exactly or why, and I'm distracted anyway by trying to assuage myself of the guilt I feel as I set my GPS to guide me the half-hour drive to #3's house.

Am I going to now sleep with #3 too? Is that obligatory? Two men inside me within hours of each other? I don't feel dirty exactly – I mean, I did shower, after all, using copious amounts of #4's daughter's coconut body wash – but I do feel deceitful. I'm "all honesty all the time", but I certainly can't tell this kind, gentle man who I've been texting all day long for the past few weeks how bottomless I really am, how deep my need is right now that it can't be met by just one man. *What is too much?* I wonder. Is this empowering or an indication that I'm unfillable, that the hole inside of me is so vast that I could throw more men into the mix and it would be like tossing Band-Aids at a life-threatening injury?

I let myself in through the screen door and find #3 in his kitchen, cleaning up after a late dinner. I sit at the counter and we talk while his cats jump on the counter only to get gently nudged off, over and over again. He tells me about his day and a meeting he had with a client. I feel a twinge of sadness at the feeling of cozy domesticity this scene elicits, two adults catching up at the end of their day. I feel the ache of not having a partner anymore, the only person in my life who would care whether or not the washing machine was fixed or that I had received a phone call from Daisy that afternoon telling me she had made her first two friends at school. My head is spinning – from the passionate sex I just had with #4 to the romantic dinner date to the stinging rejection when we got back to his house to my sitting here with such ease in #3's kitchen. I feel mercurial, like I'm fostering different personalities to see which one I will ultimately adopt. With #4, I'm the six-years-older MILF who can't get enough, with #3, I'm the patient end-of-day sounding board, and underlying both of these personas is the memory of the devoted wife I was to my husband, who theoretically I could still go back to if I could find him. I hear a voice urging me to keep going, leap forward, don't look back, pedal faster, have more sex, learn more, explore more, discover more – more, more, more – and then another voice yelling a command to stop and retreat, don't abandon the life you know, decamp for safer pastures. If I could clarify whether I am losing or finding myself, I would find the key to the door I am meant to unlock.

"I'm so tired," I say suddenly.

#3, wiping down the counter, pauses to glance at me and invites me to sleep over. I nod my head in assent.

Upstairs in the narrow bathroom, he loans me toiletries and

together we brush our teeth with his natural toothpaste that makes me wish I had a powerful dose of chemical mouthwash, moving around each other in an intimate dance that feels familiar even though it's our first time doing it. In his bed, naked beneath a cotton sheet, a window fan gently blowing on us, we kiss. I know that I could tell him I'm bone-tired and he would graciously accept it, that the pressure to have sex with him is self-inflicted. I love the physicality of having sex, the way my body tingles and shivers, but I also love how it makes me feel grounded afterwards, how the sharing of intense energy connects me with whomever I happen to be having sex – even if the connection ends the minute we put our clothes back on. Tonight I will get to hold onto that feeling all night since I am sleeping here, so I rally and then drift off to sleep to the whirring of the fan and beyond it the rush of the river. The scene would be pretty close to perfect if not for the cats who jump on the bed throughout the night with the regularity of a cuckoo clock, climbing on top of me to let me know that my presence is not appreciated. In the morning, we rise at dawn, both exhausted after a fitful night. I shower while he shaves in front of the bathroom mirror and we hurriedly dress and say goodbye, as he heads off to a meeting and I go in search of coffee that will be strong enough to wake me up.

*

I have always thought that my birthday, which falls over Labor Day weekend, is perfectly placed on the calendar, that I am lucky to celebrate another year of my life in synchronicity with summer getting one last hurrah. Usually we are away on our annual summer vacation in Cape Cod and I wake up to handmade cards and gifts from Michael and the kids: rocks and seashells that have been painted, small gifts wrapped in aluminum foil, breakfasts in bed that the kids eat themselves while I sip from a mug of coffee. Michael would let me sleep late and in the afternoon would corral the kids so that I could have an hour or two to read on the beach by myself, and later, as the sun set, we would eat lobsters and drink cheap white wine at a no-frills clam shack. Summer got a proper send-off while I got another year added to my age, awash in the love of the family I had created.

This year, as I turn 48 years old, there will be no family holiday. Daisy is away at school and holidays are from the last era of our family life, but Hudson and Georgia pull through. Hudson gives me a deck of playing cards with a note on the front that says "52 things I love about you", and every card contains a note scrawled in Sharpie: you laugh at all of my jokes, you laugh at all of your own jokes, you make me food when I'm hungry and even when I think I'm not hungry, you let me play my music in the car, you always listen to me, you are strong, I know how much you love me. It is the best gift I've ever received, and I embarrass him and worry Georgia when I start crying as I flip through the deck.

This is enough, I think to myself, *more than enough*.

My parents arrive later, bearing a cooler filled with food my mother has cooked for me: an Asian shrimp salad with mint and lime juice, a poached salmon with thin lemon slices lining the top, fresh bread and bright red tomatoes from her garden. For dessert, in another cooler, are four pints of ice cream they procured from my favorite farm stand. There is enough food here for at least a dozen people, but there's just the five of us. I know my mother is worried about me – her forced cheer is determined not to let in one sad thought of the way things used to be on my birthday – and I am matching her efforts with my own so that she doesn't have to worry. Like two laughing Elmo dolls with fresh batteries, we are intent on keeping spirits high. The truth is that I'm OK, we could afford to take it down a notch. I'm wistful and more than a little reflective, but grateful for this abundance of love, my mother's delicious food, the fact that I'm 48 and still have my parents here celebrating with me and my children who, without any parental guidance, still figured out how to make my morning special. All of the firsts have been challenging to navigate – my first holidays without Michael, my first summer without Michael, my first birthday without Michael – but I am inundated with the recognition of all the ways in which my life is rich. I am assessing how much I have and am startled to realize that my glass is half-full and not half-empty. All those years of Michael haranguing me, "What's right, Laura? You only ever say what's wrong!" and here I am, finally seeing as if for the first time: I've lost Michael, but in doing so, I've drained my glass and then filled it.

Hudson tells me after dessert that he will babysit Georgia so I can go out. I text #4, hoping he will treat me to eye-popping birthday sex, but a text comes back saying that much as he would love to celebrate with me, he is busy. I text #3, who has dinner plans with friends but will meet me for a drink afterwards. I am already well into my glass of rosé at a restaurant bar when he arrives, kissing me hello. We stay for an hour and then he gallantly pays for my birthday drink and walks me to my car. I am leaving for the city in a couple of days; I will be back here and there on weekends but our summer romance is going to have to be redefined.

"Can we talk about a serious subject before you go?" he asks, leading me to a bench. "I'm in my 50s and I've never been married. I don't want to find myself in my 60s still saying the same thing. I wasted too much time on a relationship that I should have ended years ago and I can't afford to make that same mistake again, to casually see where things go if the cards are stacked against it going in the direction I want."

I nod my head, understanding that he has a clear goal, envious of his clarity.

"I really like you," he continues. "You're smart, funny, beautiful, and I never get tired of talking to you. But I'm worried you might be the right person at the wrong time. You can't even put my name in your phone because you're scared your kids will see it, so it's hard to imagine this is going to work out for me in my time frame. I have to protect myself."

"That's honest and fair," I say. "But it's also sad. I can't give you any more than this right now and I'm not giving you much. I hope you know that it's not because I don't want to. I really like you and I'll be sorry not to see you again."

"I wish we had met a year or two from now," he says.

I take his hand and rest my head on his shoulder. We sit quietly for a few minutes.

"I'm going to be up here in a few weeks without the kids, so if you want to keep the door open and still see each other when we have the chance, we can try doing it that way and see how it goes. If something better comes along, go for it," I say.

"Well, I'm not looking for something better," he says.

"Something more consistent, but not necessarily better, how's that?" I ask.

He walks me to my car and kisses me goodbye, tapping gently on the car hood after he closes the door for me. My heart sinks as I drive away. I care about him enough that I want him to find what he's looking for, and I am dispirited that it won't be me.

CHAPTER 18

Green Hulk Sauce

I have always thrived on routine, so every year I welcome early September back-to-school days with wide open arms. I throw myself into the rhythm of the kids' school days as energetically as they resist it, rising in the dark to rouse Hudson for his commute to school, then sitting in the quiet kitchen with the newspaper and coffee until it's time to awaken Georgia, who is like a teenager with her penchant for sleeping late and has to be harassed out of my bed, where she ends up every night. Some mornings after Hudson leaves, instead of sitting in the kitchen, I slip into Daisy's bedroom and lie on her bed, pressing my face against her pale pink ruffled pillowcases, gazing at the framed prints of ballerinas lining the walls, the bulletin board covered with the smiling faces of her friends. I miss her acutely and have to remind myself that she is very much alive and well, just not a resident in our home at the moment.

I hear from #3 daily, and reading texts about the antics of all his furry friends makes me smile. One day he texts me that he thinks we should try talking on the phone more often, making use of my privacy when the kids are in school. I call him right away, but within minutes I'm standing at the gate to the schoolyard picking Georgia up from school and the din from the crowd of parents and nannies drowns out his voice and I shout out that I will try again the next day and hang up.

My big weekend is approaching – and by "big" I mean that I have Friday night until Sunday afternoon kid-free – and I try to pin him down to make plans. He is vague about his schedule and finally writes a heartfelt text that he doesn't think he should see me, that it's unwise for him to invest further time and feelings in me when it seems unlikely that he will get what he wants out of this relationship. He wants a wife – not me as his wife, but not me if I don't have the potential to someday be a wife. He says I should call him if I want to discuss it, but I don't. I thank him for being straightforward and kind, tell him I have loved our time together and I hope he soon finds the lucky woman he can commit to. I feel a pang of disappointment and loss that takes me by surprise. Though we didn't see much of each other, we had forged a strong connection and it had been reassuring to know there was someone out there who was keeping track of me, who felt invested in me. Will I ever meet another man as gentle and decent as this one? Truthfully, it seems unlikely, but aside from abandoning my life here in the city, tantalizing as that may seem, the writing on the wall is pretty clear: it's time to move on.

#4 has been equally dodgy about making plans for my free weekend, though he and I have only been in touch sporadically. Finally, I text him that I am anxious to cement plans so that I can maximize this rare opportunity of kid-free time, and he texts me back that he is sorry but it's his family's busy season at the orchard and he has to help.

"I enjoy spending time with you, but I don't want to chase after someone who doesn't want to be chased by me. I know you're busy, but I feel like you're blowing me off and I would rather you just say so straight out so I stop suggesting we make plans. No hard feelings, I just want to be clear," I text him. Later in the afternoon, my phone rings and I am surprised to see that it is him as we have never before spoken on the phone. I am walking in the door with Georgia after school, and I take the phone into my shower stall and close the glass door behind me for privacy.

"Yeah, so hey listen, I got your text and I don't want you to feel like I'm blowing you off. I really like being with you, it's just that it felt like it was getting serious too quickly," he says.

I am thoroughly perplexed; given that we have only texted a handful of times since I left and have never spoken on the phone before now, I can't figure out how he and I have such opposing perspectives. I also want to laugh, as I was just rejected by one man for my inability to be serious with him and now I'm being rejected by another for being too serious. What am I not getting here? "Serious" in my experience has meant cohabitation, marriage, kids, a mortgage, and going to the same dentist. In the 27 years I've been off the market, has "serious" come to mean something else entirely that you can achieve in three dates or less?

"I think you're an amazing person going through an incredibly difficult time and I want to be here for you," he says.

"OK, ummmm, that's nice, though I don't completely understand what you're saying. You want to slow things down?" I ask, even though I don't know how much slower we can go. Even highways have a minimum speed you have to maintain.

"I want to be a friend to you, I want you to know that I'm here for you, but I don't think we should see each other this weekend," he says.

"Ah, OK, I see. Well, I appreciate your honesty and your empathy for my situation. And it's been lovely getting to know you. Maybe our paths will cross again someday," I say, trying to figure out how to gracefully end this awkward phone call.

"I really want to stay in touch, you know, as friends," he says.

"OK, as friends, got it," I say. "Well, you have my number, you know where to find me."

"Hey, remember you said you had some easy recipes you could give me? I need to get some variety in my cooking, everything I make is so plain," he says.

"Recipes?" I ask incredulously, seeing my reflection in the glass of the shower door, the line between my eyebrows now deeply creased.

"Yes, remember when you told me you had cooking tips for me?" he asks.

I start laughing to myself. *This is just perfect*, I think, *you don't want to have sex with me anymore, you don't want to hold my hand across the table from me in a restaurant or write me texts about how you will wrap yourself around me when you see me – you want recipes.* Now I am laughing harder, not just to myself, and every time I start to respond, I laugh just a bit louder. Georgia shouts for me from the other side of the bathroom door, wondering why

I'm in the bathroom by myself, laughing like a hyena, and I call out to her to give me one more minute.

"Sorry about that, something struck me as funny," I say. "Yeah sure, I would be happy to send you some recipes. I have to run now, take care." I hang up the phone and immediately text Alex to let her know that she can stop congratulating herself for her stellar matchmaking skills now that #4 has given me the heave-ho and also that her days of having sex with him vicariously are over.

I feel thoroughly deflated now, with a free weekend looming ahead and pools of rejection to wallow in. I'm also embarrassed, worrying that I gave off the impression that I wanted more than I actually did. It comes back to me in a flash, the way his face was momentarily streaked with apprehension when I had suggested at dinner that he block my free weekend in his calendar so that we could spend it together. I cringe, thinking of the way he took this as my wanting to pin him down – which I did, but not because I had wanted him so badly as much as I wanted a sure thing in my calendar. I recall getting back to his house that night and heading upstairs when he stopped me with a curt "sweetie" as if I had overstepped the mark. He must have been anxious to get rid of me, worrying that I wanted more from him than he would be willing to give. Looking back, I can see how I seemed at that moment: desperate.

I consider this perspective. I've made progress and I'm proud of the sexual confidence that I am gaining, the newfound comfort with my body, knowledge of what it can do and what it responds to and my openness to talking about sex and all its accompanying feelings. But my dating acumen, knowing how to read cues from men, understanding the delicate dance of what is not enough and what is too much – in this area I feel mortifyingly sophomoric. That said, I am far from desperate, because desperation connotes a sense of hopelessness. I may be lonely, I may be sexually insatiable, my unseemly heartache may still be on public display, but my chin is up, I know my worth and I'm confident that I can attract men. I'm not confident that I can keep them, but I don't want to right now anyway. One foot in front of the other as now it's time to find #5 – but first, I close out #4, texting him a recipe for a versatile green herb sauce that months from now he will randomly thank me for, texting me that he calls it his Green Hulk sauce and makes it all the time, thinking of me when he does.

CHAPTER 19

'Help Wanted'

When I was in my 20s, I bore witness to my girlfriends running on dating treadmills, trying to find men with whom they could hopefully settle down. It was an unenviable task, one in which they often seemed to be running in place. I had repeatedly thanked my lucky stars that I had met Michael when we were college students, enabling me to bypass the anxiety and challenges that my friends seemed to be enduring (note: ironically, every one of these friends is still married to the husband she eventually found). Before Michael, I had met one boyfriend at a summer job and the other at a fraternity party. They just happened, I didn't have to put up a billboard with photos showing my face and body from every angle to see if they were worthy enough to capture a man's attention.

Friends keep floating the idea of online dating past me, but I steadfastly refuse. I picture a man zooming into my photos to see the size of my breasts or wrinkles on my face without being drawn to a characteristic that you can only witness in real life, like the way I am quick to laugh or how I talk with my hands excitedly. I want a man to be attracted to me for something other than my physical appearance; I want to be attracted to a man for deeper reasons too. It's not clear to me how that could possibly happen by looking at two-dimensional photos. Thus far, I've managed to meet men by going to bars, or agreeing to a blind date, all of which has served me well by giving me the illusion, albeit an admittedly false one, that I just happened upon these men – not that I was actively looking for them. Taking my quest online seems akin to posting a 'Help Wanted' sign.

So when Karen brings her daughter over to play with Georgia one afternoon and I complain that I am soon to be kid-free for a couple of days but dateless and she suggests I take my search online, I am indignant, insisting that those apps are just hook-up sites.

"And your problem with that is…?" she asks, eyebrows raised.

"Fair enough. But I can't make myself public like that. What if Michael is on one of these apps and sees my profile? Or a dad from school? Or a teacher from one of the kids' schools? I can't," I say. "It would be embarrassing. It seems pathetic, like I can't find a date on my own."

"You've got bigger fish to fry than worrying about being embarrassed. You've already proven that you can find a date on your own, but you have limited time and this is how people date now. No offense, Laura, but you haven't dated since the last century. Do you want to be chaste or do you want to be back out there?" she asks.

"Back out there?" I say as more of a question than a statement.

"Right. So come on, let's make you a profile on Tinder. It'll be fun," she says.

"Fine, let's make the profile and when I'm ready I'll make it live or whatever you do with it," I say. "But I'm not promising when that'll be."

As the girls run in and out of the kitchen to get snacks, Karen and I uncork a bottle of rosé and get to work. She scrolls through photos on my phone, choosing one in which I'm dressed up at a bar mitzvah and looking playful, with a lot of bare skin showing, my face half in and half out of the frame. In the next one she picks, I am dressed in a fitted tank top with my hair pulled back in a messy ponytail and my hand atop a Nutribullet, which I had been demonstrating for Jessica. She likes that I look natural in it. Finally, she clicks on a photo of my profile, my head thrown back in laughter, another bare shoulder shrugging toward the camera, also taken by Jessica. I realize that many of my favorite photos of myself have been taken by Jessica, who always manages to capture me mid-laugh, as if she anticipated it coming and had the camera ready just in time. For the umpteenth time since my marriage went on the fritz, I think to myself: *I must have done something right in my life to have dedicated girlfriends like these.*

Satisfied with the array of photos she's chosen, she turns to filling out my biographical information.

"OK," she says, typing with fervor. "You're 48, you live downtown in New York City, you have three children, you graduated from Washington University, you're a freelancer."

"A freelancer? As in freelance plumber, baker, tutor, doctor, housekeeper, personal shopper, short order cook, life coach, chauffeur, gal Friday, psychologist?" I ask, listing off the roles I fill in my real-life job as stay-home mother, but she's already typed in "freelancer" and has moved on to the age of the men with whom I hope to match.

"Oh, hmmm, I think we should go for broad options, young to old. Some men love a cougar. Why not try, right?" I ask.

"OK, 20something?" she asks.

"Gross, no, not so young they could be my children. 35 baseline. And up to late 50s."

We move on to location next, and I instruct her that the men have to be close by and thus geographically desirable.

"OK, anything else? Religion, race, height preferences?"

"No, just normal and nice," I say.

"Those aren't options here," she tells me. "Can I please make this live? You look good, it's a nice profile, you're going to get tons of hits."

"Hits from all the crazies. Leave it for me to look at later, I need to work up the courage," I say.

"Fine, just don't wait too long. Your big weekend is coming!"

*

After I put Georgia to sleep that night, I log into my new Tinder account to review my profile. I study the images as if seeing myself for the first time, trying to evaluate myself as a potential suitor might. I look tanned, happy, relaxed, like I'm always up for a big laugh and a good time. My curly hair, a bit wild, indicates that I'm not buttoned-up or afraid to look like the most natural version of myself. My strapless clothing shows that I'm comfortable with my body. Those things are true about me, I'm not purporting to be someone I'm not. This may be a superficial and one-sided presentation of myself, but it's not false advertising. I'm showing my teeth – white enough and straight enough; I'm showing my body – petite, strong and healthy; I'm showing my nails – manicured and brightly colored. In other words, there shouldn't be any surprises when a man meets me in person, nothing that I'm squirreling away and hoping he won't notice when I'm alive in front of him. And if Michael does see my profile then it means he's on Tinder too. I do the thing that I've been doing over and over again for the past few months: I take a leap of faith. I click the button to make my profile public for anyone on Tinder to see.

A few hours later, lying in bed with Georgia pressing her warm feet against me as she sleeps, I stare at my phone and wonder how I survived the monotony of my life pre-Tinder. Tinder contains a vast sea of men, so many of them with such odd profile pictures that when I find the occasional one that doesn't reek of inappropriateness, I click the heart button just to show solidarity, like hey, my normal sees your normal and thinks we might be able to make some normal magic together. It doesn't matter if I find the person attractive, I just care that he seems like a person I could know in my current life. If it looks like a mug shot, swipe left – if you can't smile for this one picture, I worry. Sitting in your car with your seatbelt on, swipe left – come on, live a little! There have to be more creative backdrops for a selfie. Lying in bed shirtless, swipe left, don't be so obvious. Oh, even better, take a pic of yourself in front of a mirror with nothing but briefs on, swipe, swipe, swipe! All of your photos are ones in which you're posing with other women, swipe left – that raises suspicion, are you hinting at an open marriage? You're posing with your kids, swipe left – don't drag your kids into this sordid place. You're posing with your dog in every photo, swipe left – I've been down this road, I see your dog for the jealous lover she really is. You never part your lips when you smile, swipe left, what are you hiding? An overgrowth of facial hair, body completely covered in tattoos, you're holding a gun, you only show one photo of yourself and ten of sunsets, you're dressed up in an elaborate costume, you show your body but never your head, your head but never your body, you say you're forty but look like a teenager, you say you're forty but look like a grandpa?

Despite this, I am amused and delighted. I live in a densely populated city, so the quantity of people to potentially match with seems limitless. Sure, I have to swipe left 100 times before I earn the privilege of clicking on a heart, but there are certainly educated, sporty, fit hearts to be had and when I click one and am instantly rewarded with hearts flying at me and "It's a Match" popping across my screen in bold letters, I feel a moment's worth of *well, look at that, my work here is already done.* Like Pavlov's dogs, I am so roped in by instant gratification that I cannot stop looking and swiping and clicking.

When I wake up in the morning, I have a new reason to open my eyes: to check my Tinder action! There have been so many matches that now I can afford to get a little cocky, double-checking men's profile pictures and thinking, *no, surely this one was a mistake, I would never click on a man wearing a fitted muscle shirt at his gym or someone arrogantly winking into the camera.* But there are enough that seem promising and some have sent messages that are cheeky and charming, like "Hey Laura, you have lovely pics... just curious, how many 'little black dresses' do you have :)" or "Hi Laura, you didn't write anything about yourself, but you have very sweet dimples".

I write back short answers with questions thrown in to attempt a conversation, "Why thank you, nice to meet you on here, looks like you travel a lot, where have you gone recently that you've loved?" or "You seem to be on the move a lot, what's your favorite neighborhood to explore?" I feel silly and am forcing a whole lot of chipper-ness, but I have nothing to lose and I am enchanted by the anonymity the site provides (though it turns out that I will someday randomly run into people I've exchanged messages with on Tinder, and after figuring out the connection, I will feel wholly exposed and most decidedly *un*-anonymous). I learn quickly about myself that I am a sucker for doctors, which is no surprise – I've always loved their authority and in truth, I've had crushes on many of them throughout my life, even convincing myself that some have been in love with me too (the most devastating being the doctor who joked that my allergic reaction to my wedding band was perhaps an allergic reaction to my husband, which I took as a veiled suggestion that I should consider him instead, until Jessica broke it to me that this doctor was gay and often spotted around the Village with a parrot on his shoulder). Ditto for firemen – if you're part of the FDNY, I've probably clicked on your profile first out of respect and second because you're probably young and hot. I also confirm that I am, true to being my mother's daughter, an educational snob: if you have an Ivy League School attached to your bio, I am definitely pretending those close-mouthed smiles are you being coy and not having some strange tooth situation. And finally, I have to face that I am more shallow than I thought: a defined six-pack lets me forgive any man who posts a bathing suit shot of himself – unless he is visibly erect, in which case even the six-pack can't save him.

Conversational flirtations begin in earnest. There is a middle-school English teacher with a degree from Penn who seems funny and wry, with a close-cropped beard and friendly eyes. He asks me what kind of freelance work I do (thanks a lot, Karen) and when I reply that I am really a stay-home PTA mom, he writes back, "PTA! That's hot." This should give me pause but does not until later, when during an otherwise pleasant conversation, he asks me what I'm wearing and if I could dress up for him as a PTA mom. I ask with befuddlement why I would dress up as something that I in fact already am and when he replies, "Because I've been a very bad boy," I promptly learn how to unmatch with someone.

The kind and considerate businessman who raced home from work to coach his daughter's soccer team? We are trying to nail down a date to get together when he tells me he needs to run something by me before we meet in person and that he hopes it won't scare me away. "I'm intrigued," I write back to him, code for "I'm terrified." He responds that he had been married for many years to a woman who did not enjoy oral sex and that he needs to know not only that I am open to it but also that I will allow him to spend uninterrupted hours exploring my pussy with his tongue. After dropping my phone and washing my hands, I politely decline, letting him know that while I am indeed open to oral sex,

I cannot say what I would want or for how long in advance of it actually happening and thus would not want to waste the precious time he could spend with another woman's pussy. He writes back that he is disappointed as I seem so great, and am I certain?

Indeed, I am.

The gorgeous, 30something bachelor with the perfect teeth and killer six-pack? He asks if I've ever had sex with a married man and I answer that I would NEVER not EVER have sex with another woman's husband because that DESTROYS lives and causes heartache and misery, and why would I want to be with a man so selfish and deceptive? Suffice to say, I did not hear from him again.

The chiseled, bald dad-of-two who loves to cook, does yoga, reads voraciously and does the *NYTimes* crossword puzzle every day? He needs to know before he meets me what my feelings are on anal sex. "My feelings are," I respond, "that as much as I appreciate your candor, I am preserving intimate conversations like this for men with whom I'm actually intimate, so I suspect we are not a good match." Another unmatch and moment in which I ask myself, how do men move the conversation from favorite novels or restaurants to the details of the kind of sex they are hoping to have with such dizzying speed? I'm pretty easy to get into bed and in fact will probably get to the bed faster than you, but still, certain niceties must be met. I can't commit to having anal sex or oral sex or any kind of sex with you before I even see you in person because what if I don't want to? Would I be obliged by some kind of Tinder code of conduct?

However, because I am applying myself to this process like the conscientious worker bee I've always been, I cast my net wide and come up with a few viable options – not many, but solid options nonetheless. And because I'm terrified to spend time alone, lest I have to listen to the voice inside me that is questioning why Michael and I have been back in the city for weeks yet neither of us has even mentioned the possibility of resuming couples' therapy, I plan not one, but four dates for the following weekend.

CHAPTER 20

Number Four (and a Half)

As a warm-up exercise, I arrange to meet a man named Kevin on a weekday afternoon. He and I had been exchanging texts on Tinder when he tersely let me know that he isn't into endless text exchanges, that if I'm interested in him we should arrange a phone call. His bio lured me in with his having attended an almost-Ivy League school and his career as a writer. On the phone, I decide to ignore his heavy Brooklyn accent tinged with a nasal quality, opting instead to focus on the fact that he is smart and funny. We set a date for me to go to the residential neighborhood where he lives in Brooklyn. He will meet me at the subway station and we can walk to a café from there. I tell him I know my way around the area and can meet him somewhere, but he says it'll be easier to pick me up at the station. I will soon learn a valuable lesson: meet on neutral ground and have a plan so you don't have to make decisions on the fly, especially when you're someone like me who often resorts to being polite first and self-protective second.

Climbing up the stairs of the subway station on a beautiful

blue-sky September day, I spot Kevin waiting at the top. He looks like his pictures – bald, gleaming head, muscular, a bit thicker and more solid than I had pictured him. He leans in for a quick hug and then points me in the direction we will walk in, which I know is where the main street is, with lots of cafés where we can perch for an hour or two. He asks if I want to grab cups of coffee that we can take to the park, which I immediately agree to – going for a walk seems less intimidating than sitting face to face.

A few blocks later, he says, "Actually, we can make coffee at my place to take to the park, my apartment is right here."

"Oh," I say, pausing. "Um, no, you don't have to bother, we can just pick it up."

"It'll just take a minute and we're here already," he says, pointing to a street-level door at the base of a brownstone.

I reluctantly agree. This is my first Tinder date and he seems so self-assured that I try to ignore the red flag being waved directly in front of me. I don't want to seem nervous or suspicious as that would be a huge turn-off, but entering his apartment seems like a frankly bad idea. I feel trapped and unsure what to do, still more concerned with how I appear than with my own safety, but I try to exude nonchalance, following him as he slides the key into the iron gate leading to the front door. Inside, the apartment is dark and drab – the natural light is dim and his room-length book-shelves are filled with bulky hardcovers, CDs and DVDs. There is an abundance of art and cumbersome sculptural objects hanging on the wall. The kitchen is an open area between the living room and the bedrooms in the back, and true to his promise, he starts filling the coffee pot and dumping scoops of coffee from a huge tub of Folgers into the filter. I hate when I recognize myself being a snob but nonetheless note the Folgers with disdain, thinking a writer in Brooklyn who insists on making his own coffee should have some artisanal blend that he makes in a special coffee filtration system only the most coffee-educated could appreciate – not Folgers in a Mr. Coffee pot. As the coffee brews, he suggests that when it's done, we take it to his backyard instead of to the park. I hesitate and then quietly agree again, admonishing myself for not saying what I want to say, which is that I feel uncomfortable and would prefer a walk in a public space. I want him to know that I recognize that I am being deceived in some way, that I'm not so gullible I don't see it, but I don't want to appear to be a mousy, timid, nervous woman. Reluctantly, I accept the coffee, which tastes bitter and stale, and follow him out the back door to the yard.

The yard is small but pretty, with an abundance of greenery and a porch swing under an awning, where we sit, gently swaying as we talk about his writing, until twenty minutes in, I confess that I am terribly uncomfortable, that I'm getting bitten up by mosquitoes, pointing to swollen red spots on my bare legs, and he leads the way back inside. This time, we sit on his couch in the living room and I ask about his vast collection of DVDs and CDs, items that don't get a lot of shelf space in most homes anymore. Only a few minutes into our having settled on the sofa, he leans toward me as I am mid-sentence and starts kissing me.

"OK," I say, pulling back slightly. "Well, that's one way to get me to stop talking."

"Can we move to my bedroom?" he asks, his coffee-laden breath too close to my face.

"Um, OK, sure. That was fast," I say, grimacing slightly. I don't really want to sleep with him, but I don't know how to get myself out of here. He has steered me here, but I have shown only hesitation, not one sign of actual resistance. I feel completely disconnected from myself, as if I am no longer here in this gloomy apartment but on the other side of the door where a brilliant blue sky shines on my real life, where I should be right now. I am scared to say no to this man – he is intense and determined, and I fear that I might have led him to this inevitable conclusion so that saying no now would brand me a tease, a blue-baller, a naïf, someone who doesn't understand the sexual dynamics between a man and a woman. I feel myself floating out of my body, much the way I do in moments of crisis with my kids when I've cradled them after falls have broken their bones or bloodied their faces, and I remain preternaturally calm, managing their physical care while not allowing in the repulsion of gushing blood or limbs that seem to be bent in the wrong direction.

Silently, I follow him to his bedroom and take my tank top and skirt off, folding them and placing them on his dresser, then lie down in my lacy bra and underwear. He strips down to his white briefs, and I see that his body is intimidatingly thick, solid and muscular. He goes down on me, and I am gone now: in my mind I am floating in a vast ocean, warm water carrying my body, sun beating down and saturating me. I don't want to be in bed with this man, and the longer I stay here, the more I am disgusted by him – and, more horribly, by myself for being here. Sex has been purely fun and joyous and liberating and toe-curling and energizing and fulfilling and transcendent these past two months, but now the ugly side of it is lashing its forked tongue at me: asymmetry of power, physical vulnerability, fear, mistrust, revulsion.

He puts on a condom and comes inside of me and then lies next to me, interrogating me about my sexual predilections. Do I like anal sex? Have I ever been with a woman? Am I interested in threesomes? What is the kinkiest thing I have ever done? I respond haltingly and do not ask him anything at all. Finally, I say that I have to get home to my kids and he strokes my upper thigh up to the curve of my hip and back down again to my waist, asking, "Can I have you one more time before you go?" The wording of his question is spot on, as that's exactly what he's doing: having me. And I am allowing it.

"Sure," I say quietly, because now I am so far gone that I suspect I will not return to my body for days. He straddles me and rolls me onto my stomach, then he enters me vaginally from behind. I lie like a ragdoll, just letting it happen. When he shudders and then collapses on top of me, I feel like all air has been pressed out of me and I wait for him to realize he is crushing me.

I deserve this, I think, *to feel breathless and powerless, because I have willingly made myself prostrate and obedient.*

Finally, he rolls off me and I wordlessly rise from the bed, taking my small pile of clothes from the dresser and heading to the bathroom, where I clean myself as best I can with toilet paper and water and put my clothes back on. He is waiting for me in the kitchen, looking like the lord of the manor, relaxing in a bathrobe, refilling his coffee cup. I say goodbye and head to the door, which he opens for me as he waves a distracted farewell, coffee cup in hand like he's sending me out on my way to work in the morning.

Number Four (and a Half)

This man, who had been so keen on meeting me at the subway station, does not offer to walk me back to the station or ask if I know where I am going. I feel cheap and know that I have given too much of myself to him – my pride and my sense of agency noiselessly handed over. I do not cry as I make my way back along the quiet leafy streets toward the subway, children brushing against me on their scooters, mothers jauntily pushing strollers toward the park to revel in the last hours of the day. I do not call any of my girlfriends to merrily spill the details of my latest sexual conquest. This afternoon of sex – dirty, animalistic, making me feel fragile – I do not want to share. For the first time in my life I feel an emotion that I've never felt before and it takes me some time to recognize: shame.

Years ago, when I worked in a corporate office, my young female colleagues and I would whisper stories of bad behavior by men in senior positions as we rolled our eyes and warned each other which male colleagues were an actual threat and must be avoided at all costs and which were annoying but harmless. There were men who would invite us out for drinks and get a little too close at the bar, heedlessly placing their hands on our legs as they leaned towards us; men who would stand near our desks to chat during the day, jingling the coins in their pockets and commenting on the way our clothes fit; men who would make snarky comments about our boyfriends or husbands, and then seem to leer as they awaited a reaction. Those situations were marked by an imbalance of power, by our valid concerns that these men could make us or break us if we didn't play the game according to their rules. The only power Kevin had over me was the power I readily gave him, as I never have to see him again if I don't want to (and I don't want to) and he has no way to influence any facet of my life. How do I justify having sex with him despite the fact that it was unequivocally clear to me and probably clear to him that I didn't want to and that it was unlikely there would be repercussions if I had decided not to?

I had sex with him because he expected me to and I feared that to rebuff his advances would be impolite, unseemly, and mark me as a foolish, unsophisticated tease of a woman. Now I feel debased, submissive and humiliated, and I fear that I have only myself to blame. Kevin did not hide what he wanted from me and I never said no, but I have to try to understand what got me here so that I never let myself get back here again. I know that my body is strong and powerful; my sexual prowess is burgeoning, drawing men in and reveling in the pleasure that I receive from them and give back. It is my sense of self that is waging a battle here: I can no longer rely on the person I have been until now to carry me forward. That person is still very much a part of me – polite, kind, funny, literate, maternal and compassionate but not so nice that I can't also be snarky or sarcastic – but that person had no compelling reason to take a hard, cold look at herself to question what she was made of or who she wanted to be. I cannot let other people decide for me what I want and what I will give of myself. Not random Tinder hook-ups, not Michael, not my friends or even my children. At the end of the day, I have to answer to my harshest critic: myself. If I treat other people humanely or disrespectfully, if I constantly prioritize my kids' wants and needs or sometimes defer their needs to my own, if I remain in the only box I have ever known or wanted for myself or find a meaningful life outside of it – it only matters that I stay true to myself. But how does a person stay true to a self she doesn't even recognize anymore?

The following week, I get a text from Kevin, asking if we can arrange another meeting. I am repelled by how transactional his language is and quickly decline, explaining that it turns out I don't enjoy having sex without some morsel of emotional connection. He doesn't respond and I delete his number from my phone. For a long time, I will look back at this event with regret that I made myself small, that I didn't use my voice, and I will refuse to assign this man a number in my list of lovers – and yet I appreciate the information that the experience gave to me. Sex is like no other act – requiring physicality and vulnerability during which we literally open ourselves to another human being – and there are countless ways to revel in the pleasure and beauty in it or conversely to be defiled by it. I had viewed sex during my marriage as mostly ho-hum and up until now in my life post-marriage it has been life-affirming and revelatory. Having intercourse with Kevin reminded me that sex can be a double-edged sword and that I need to be more careful and discerning going forward. I can have sex with whomever I want whenever I want, but it needs to be because it makes me feel good and sexy and powerful, not because it meets someone else's needs.

Like most lessons, this one was painful to learn.

CHAPTER 21

Another White Girl with Curly Hair

I stash away my experience with #4.5 and it becomes a shameful secret I carry, starting from the moment I entered a strange man's apartment – not just a man who was a stranger to me, but a man who even from our first phone call gave off a vibe I didn't wholly trust. It's not exactly like I had known #1–4 terribly well, but I did spend a few hours with each before going home with them and they had been kind, straightforward and respectful. Frankly, in each case, if anyone had been the aggressor, it was me. But I've got four dates lined up for my upcoming weekend, so I put #4.5 in a little box in my brain, use it as a wake-up call to be more prudent going forward, and forge ahead.

First up, Friday morning, I head uptown to meet Scott for coffee. He owns a swim instruction school and will meet me during a break between lessons. He warns me he will be coming from the pool and casually dressed, so I put on a pair of cut-off jean shorts and flip-flops. I spot him in the coffee bar as I enter and he looks a lot like his pictures – tall, graying but still-thick hair, a prominent nose that looks slightly askew, like it's been broken once or twice. We have only communicated by text, so his robust Long Island accent startles me. We take a seat at the counter and the banter between us comes easily. He is an engaged listener and lobs questions at me, which I appreciate as I always ask a lot of questions and it's a nice break for me not to have to carry the conversation. It turns out his swim school is just a side hustle, that his main job is as a physical education teacher to kids with special needs. It also turns out that he does not live uptown as he told me via text, but a half-hour drive away (if there's no traffic, which there always is) in Long Island. I am confused and also annoyed, as he's just become geographically undesirable.

"Is this a ruse you use to get city girls?" I ask with a laugh, though I'm on alert now – if you lie about where you live, what else might you lie about?

"No, I used to stay there a lot and then I decided to rent it out to be closer to my daughter in Long Island. Hey, has anyone ever told you that you look like that actress, what's her name?" he asks, eyebrows furrowed as he tries to recall the name.

"Sarah Jessica Parker? I get that a lot," I say.

"No, not her," he says.

"Elaine from *Seinfeld*?" I ask. "I get that a lot too."

"No, no. I was totally in love with her when I was a teenager. She was in *The Karate Kid* and *Cocktail*. Elisabeth Shue!" he calls out, finally remembering. When I shake my head no, he calls over the waiter, asking him, "Doesn't she look exactly like the actress Elisabeth Shue?"

The waiter studies me for a long moment, tilting his head and flicking his eyes from my head down my body.

"Nah," he finally says with indifference, "she just looks like another white girl with curly hair," and walks away.

"Ouch. One man thinks I'm an '80s film goddess, the other thinks I'm just another white girl," I say.

Scott pays the bill and we head outside to the muggy day. He says he is having such a great time that he doesn't want the date to end and suggests a walk to the East River. He chivalrously offers to carry my tote bag, which is weighed down with two newspapers and a hefty 620-page hardcover novel that I schlep around for subway reading. The path along the river is wide and mostly empty, giving children and dogs ample room to run. A woman walks in our direction with a large, excited dog that suddenly bounds over to me so that I stop short, startled, and back up a few steps. The dog is more playful than menacing but still, for me, intimidating. The woman does not apologize, if anything scowling at me for not greeting her dog warmly.

"See, this is what I hate about women with dogs. You don't have a dog, do you?" he asks.

I shake my head.

"She let that dog run right up to you. Not everyone wants a dog getting so close to them, but so many women with dogs just let the dogs lead them," he says.

I explain the origin of my fear, that once I was jogging on a quiet country road and a dog came charging at me. I stood still, but every time I started to edge forward, it would get closer to me, baring its teeth. Finally, I heard a voice down the road and the dog went running, but ever since then, whenever a dog comes at me like that, I get nervous.

"But why do you refer specifically to women with dogs?" I ask. "Don't you think it could just as easily be a man with a dog?"

"No," he says definitively. "Single women with dogs are like mothers with children, they think everyone loves their dogs."

"Wait, how did single women get dragged into this?" I ask. "What's the difference if the woman is single or not?"

"I would never date a woman with a dog, that's all I'm saying," he says with a bemused smile. This strikes me as an odd and arguably offensive comment, but the expression on his face indicates that he's overstating for comic effect.

He changes the subject and asks me about my involvement in the PTA, commenting that I am different from what he would expect from a PTA mom, that I look like the fantasy version of a PTA mom, not like the ones he's seen.

"Oh, I don't know about that. The PTA moms I know look a lot like me. Maybe you go to the wrong PTA meetings," I say.

We return to the spot on the river where we started our walk and turn back onto the city streets so he can walk me to the subway. A block from the river, as we wait for the light to change at a busy intersection, he turns toward me, takes off his sunglasses and leans forward to kiss me. I smile when he pulls back and nod toward the light that has changed.

"Sorry," he says, smiling. "I've been trying to find the right moment to do that since we got to the river but you didn't stop talking long enough to give me a chance. Something about that corner seemed just right."

We keep walking and when we pass by the pool where he teaches, we go inside so I can use the restroom before I get on the train.

When I emerge, he is looking down at his phone, but he lifts his head and studies me for a minute as I approach before looking back down at his phone.

"You know, you're prettier in person than in your pictures," he says.

Not for the first time today, I find his forthrightness both refreshing and disarming.

"Um, thank you?" I respond.

At the subway, he stands with his hands deep inside the pockets of his athletic shorts, shifting from foot to foot, asking if we can go on a proper date, and we make a plan for the following evening in Long Island. I'm not thrilled to have to drive to a date, but I like the idea of how anonymous I will be once I am there. He puts his hands on my hips and pulls me in for a longer kiss and then I hold up a hand to wave goodbye, skipping down the subway steps.

CHAPTER 22

Sunshine and Roses

That evening, I don a long, silky royal blue strapless dress, tie my humidified mane of hair into a loose knot at my neck, and hail a cab to meet Karl, who has reserved a table at a jazz club. I like that he took it upon himself to make a plan without any tentative back-and-forth conversation. From his texts, he seems intelligent and well-traveled with a taste for expensive restaurants. At the last minute he informs me that he's only 5'7" so if height is an issue for me, I should not feel obliged to proceed with the date. I tell him that at 5'3", I've never been in a position to complain about anyone else's height.

In the taxi, I get a text from Scott, saying he is looking forward to our date tomorrow night and asking what I'm up to. I tell him I'm on my way to meet a friend and he says he assumes I mean a date and that I don't have to be coy. I consider this progress, that now I don't have to be secretive about who I am seeing, that going on multiple dates in a short time period is what is expected of me in the online arena.

Karl is already sitting at the table when I arrive, and when he stands to greet me I notice that he's handsome, smartly dressed and, well, short. Not shorter than me, but not much taller either. I inhale a Margarita even though this bar's specialty is whiskey (I have to stick with what I know on these dates), he orders appetizers for the table and we break the ice. He's gentle and kind, has a twinkle in his eye and is clearly a history buff, as he keeps peppering our conversation with stories about ancient noblemen and bits of Russian history. I concentrate on following what he's saying – it's noisy and I'm on my second drink and the stories seem to randomly appear without context. I don't think he's showing off for me, but maybe citing historical facts is a kind of nervous tic. When I stand to use the restroom, I totter for a moment in my high heels and hold onto the edge of the table to get my bearings. In the awkward lulls of our conversation, I consumed two drinks at lightning speed.

When I return to the table, he has already paid the bill and is ready to go. I wonder if he's anxious to get this date to its end, but he walks with me toward home and on the way suggests that we should stop for dessert. I doubt we will be able to get a table at the crowded restaurant he points to, but he says he knows the host and we will get in, no problem.

Walking next to him, I note that we are eye-level, though in all fairness I'm wearing heels. Still, it feels weird to me and I realize that I've always been diminutive compared to men I've been with. If I'm being honest – even though I admit this with regret that I care – I like being the smaller one and feeling protected by a larger man at my side. I think of a friend who always dates men who are her height, with whom she can even share jeans – I shudder at the thought. I've often teased her that she likes men to be petite so she can tuck them in her pockets when she's out and about and keep them close by. I have always conformed to gender stereotypes of physicality, feeling that masculinity is defined in part by physical prowess, but I also fully embrace the concept of metrosexuality. Michael had been more interested in fashion and shopping than I had ever been, and arguments we had about spending too much money on clothes, accessories or fancy toiletries were due to his bills, not mine. I didn't like how much money he spent, but I liked that he cared about what he wore and how he looked. One friend, when I told her that Michael and I had separated, admitted to me that she had always thought he was gay. I had never even thought of that as a possibility, and laughingly told her how when we were younger and would walk the city hand in hand, I would often feel him squeeze my hand and I would know that an attractive woman was walking toward us – this was his silent and inadvertent reaction. He loved women, but he also loved Paul Smith blazers, expensive scented candles and Alexander McQueen scarves. I was comfortable with this aspect of his personality, as long as he was taller and bigger than me.

The restaurant is packed when we arrive and the host Karl said he knew does not seem to know him, so I hang back and pretend I can't hear the seating arrangements he's negotiating. We are finally sent to a lone barstool squeezed tightly between seated patrons at the bar and Karl directs me to sit while he lingers behind me. I try to turn so that I am sideways both to him and the bar and can thus talk to him, but it's too crammed. He leans over me to order another drink and desserts to share and we shout comments to each other that neither of us can hear. When we are expelled back into the street, I am relieved that we are only a few blocks from my apartment.

"You're very cool, you know that? A lot of women I go on dates with won't let me walk them home because they don't want me to know where they live. They often seem paranoid. You exude confidence," he says.

I ponder his words – is that how it's supposed to be done, am I screwing up in my self-protection department yet again and he is confusing confidence with ignorance? As we near my building, a teenage girl approaches us, her arms weighed down by a mound of long-stemmed red roses individually wrapped in plastic sleeves. I walk past her, stopping a moment later when I realize Karl is no longer next to me. I turn back to see him pull out his wallet and hand her a $5 bill, then pluck a rose from her pile to present to me. I am moved that he bought a flower from her, as it's rare I stop for anyone on the street.

"She's just a kid, out here at this hour," he says. "I always think of my daughters."

"That was nice of you," I say. "I'm always worried I'm getting hustled."

We are standing under the canopy outside my building now.

"Do you want to come up for a little while?" I ask, thinking, if you want to see confidence, I'll show you confidence.

"OK, sure, just for a little while. I have to catch an early train tomorrow to help my friend on his farm," he says.

I lead the way inside, discreetly tucking the red rose alongside me so the doorman doesn't see it. I know how these doormen gossip and I can only imagine what might be said about my having arrived home late at night in high heels with a red rose and a man who is not my husband.

Inside my apartment, I lay the rose on the counter and offer him a glass of wine, though I'm strictly drinking water now, already feeling tipsy. We sit back on the deep couch in the den and soon he is moving closer to me and leaning over to kiss me. His mouth is warm and tastes smoky from the whiskey he had been drinking. I lie back and he presses against me.

"I have a huge, lovely bed," I say. "Shall we move over to it?"

He follows me down the hall to my room. He lies back against the mountain of pillows on the made-up bed and I straddle him, opening the front fold of my dress to reveal a lace thong. He lifts my hips so that I'm kneeling and then scoots down the bed so that his head is under me, pulls my thong to the side and flicks his tongue against my clit. It's been weeks since I've been touched and I sigh with the relief of being back in the game. After a few minutes of this, I ask if he has a condom and he replies that he does, yes, but that he would rather do this instead.

"Oh," I say. "Everything OK?"

"Yes, I just… it's just our first date," he says haltingly.

"OK," I say. "I mean, that's never stopped me before but carry on."

After I come, he pulls his head back up against the pillows and smiles at me. I close the front of my dress and pull myself on top of him. I feel his stockinged feet with my bare feet, my knees against his knees, my pelvic bones pressed into his.

"You know," he says, "I can tell my friend that something has come up so you and I could spend the day together tomorrow." I shake my head, telling him that I already have plans and admit that my plans include a date with someone else. He persists, suggesting instead that we get together on Sunday when he's back in the city. I shake my head again, saying that by then Georgia will be home.

"That's OK, we can all do something together. My daughters would love your daughter, they love playing big sister," he says.

I rear my head up to look at him.

"Oh God, no way! Noooooo! I'm sorry to react so strongly. Separation of church and state. My kids don't even know that I'm dating," I say. We lie quietly for a moment and then I add, "You probably need to get going, it's late and your train leaves in a few hours."

The dark and quiet of my apartment envelop me when I leave my bedroom. I am not used to being here without at least one of my kids home and I feel like I'm in a hotel. At the front door, I put my hands on Karl's shoulders and we kiss goodbye. In my future dating app searches, I will set 5'8" as a minimum for height now that I've become aware of two important pieces of information: 1) at least two fudged inches are definitely being added to the profiles of men who are self-conscious of their stature, and 2) height, which I've never thought much about before, matters to me.

*

In the morning, I wake up to a flurry of texts. George is confirming coffee. Jeff is confirming an early afternoon drink. Scott wants to know what time I can make it to Long Island. And Karl, oh poor Karl, has written, "Good morning sunshine and roses! I can't stop thinking about you and smiling today. Thanks for an incredible night."

It's only Saturday morning. Maybe I was a tad overzealous in my eagerness once I got started on Tinder?

I text Lauren, "Help! I want to go back to sleep and wake up to Georgia in my bed. How do I get out of this?"

"You're asking the wrong person. I can't wait for details," she responds.

"Well at least what I do about sunshine and roses?"

"My God, Laura! What did you do to that man?" she asks.

"Nothing! I listened to his litany of historical facts and let him go down on me."

"You don't owe these men anything. Write him back or don't, you get to do whatever you want."

"But he's really nice, I don't want to hurt his feelings."

"OK, so tell him nicely that you can't be his sunshine and roses. Now up and at 'em. Go put on some of that rose oil I'm obsessed with."

I arrive twenty minutes early to the café where I am due to meet George so I can gulp down coffee before it's time to make small talk. George is not just a doctor, he's a surgeon, and my first shot at making my fantasy of sleeping with a doctor a reality. I sip my coffee and recall the time a year earlier when I was having such severe neck pain that I had to get cortisone shots at the base of my skull. Several shots later, when my pain hadn't receded, Michael insisted that he accompany me to my next appointment to suss

231

the doctor out himself. I could see him relax when he met the doctor, a kind and attentive man, and saw that he wasn't a shyster negligently shooting people up with cortisone. When we left the office, he remarked that if anything was ever to happen to him, I should be with this man. I had laughed and told Michael that the doctor was happily married with two little boys and he replied, "OK well someone like him then, he's the type I could see you with."

Had it occurred to me then that Michael was thinking about how I might land back on my feet after he left me, I would have been horrified, but instead I loved that he knew me so well and understood that if I hadn't shacked up with him – a quirky risk taker – I would have opted for someone who could offer steadiness, security, and maybe a free flu shot every winter.

George the surgeon arrives, dressed formally for a warm Saturday morning in a sports jacket and khakis. He is handsome, serious and hell-bent on making every point exceedingly clear. The most urgent of these points is that whenever he goes on a date, he pays, in order to avoid any awkwardness when the bill arrives. Even after I acknowledge this and joke that I promise not to so much as glance at the check when it arrives, he continues to tell me how important it is for him to have this steadfast rule. He is also adamant that he always lets his date pick the location. He will go just about anywhere but he does not want a lot of back and forth, hemming and hawing about where to go and what to do. I nod earnestly, yet still he goes on to explain the origin of this rule which involves indecisive, flighty women with no respect for time or commitment. I keep nodding, wondering if he wants me to pull out a piece of paper to take notes. Two painful hours pass this way. I don't know if I should ask for a check since I'm not allowed to pay for it, but I'm crawling out of my skin. Have I misunderstood doctors all these years, thinking their authority and omnipotence offer a safe cushion when actually they just adhere to a lot of rigid rules and impenetrable order? Finally I glance at my watch and widen my eyes as I pretend to notice the time and he gets the hint, paying the bill as I watch obediently. As we walk down the block, he asks me what I like to drink. I list my top choices: tequila, wine, Prosecco, but he wants to know specifically if I like champagne.

"Sure, I like champagne," I say.

"OK, great, let's make a plan to drink champagne together," he says, then gives me a kiss on the lips and we part.

I squeeze my eyes shut and grimace as I walk away. I have to learn how to be quicker on these dates – that's the point of coffee and not a meal – just a quick in and out. Why do I always feel like I have to make myself so available? Why do I make myself seem interested when I could save everyone a lot of time and trouble by politely rising after an hour, shaking hands and saying a noncommittal, "Bye then, nice to have met you."

With this newly formed commitment to forthrightness spurring me on, I shoot off a text to Karl, who has followed up his sunshine and roses text with a photo of himself standing in a field of sunflowers.

"Hey Karl, it was lovely to get to know you. You're a genuinely kind and sincere man. I get the feeling that you want more out of dating than I do right now. I'm early in this process and want to be casual with anyone I date, which seems incongruous with what you're looking for. Thank you for letting me see that there are good men out there," I write.

He writes back immediately, "I had a feeling when I didn't hear back from you earlier. I'm not looking for anything serious, I just like you and it's been a while since I've enjoyed being with a woman. Good luck. You have my number if you change your mind."

I feel immense relief that I have gracefully extricated myself.

*

Next up: Jeff, a lawyer who meets me in the garden of a wine bar in my neighborhood. Over glasses of Chardonnay, we talk about our kids, their schools, our backgrounds, finally resorting to the weather when our well runs dry. He tells me a story with minutes of build-up and I keep waiting for the punchline but then realize with dismay that there isn't one. When the waitress asks if we want another glass and he says sure, my heart sinks. I can usually make small talk like it's an Olympic sport, but either I've utterly exhausted myself or he's hopeless. Slowly, I drum my fingers against the iron table and eye his glass, trying to calculate how many sips it will take for it to be emptied. If he takes one sip a minute and there are 25 sips left, I'm looking at half an hour.

When he has finally drained his glass, he insists on walking me home. At the corner outside my building, I point and say, "OK, this is me" and he steps forward, puts a hand on my waist, and kisses me more passionately than I ever could have expected from our vanilla conversation. I glance around, mortified to be kissed like this in the middle of the day in a spot where I know so many people, and also perplexed because where did that come from? I'm disappointed in myself as I go inside, having already failed at nailing this new "in and out" policy I came up with a few hours ago. I need to abandon some of my perpetual politeness if I am to continue to speed date. In other words, I need to actually adhere to the speed part and stop being solicitous and attentive when I know I will not see these men again.

CHAPTER 23

Strut of Success

I silence the voice that questions why Scott wasn't honest about his address on his Tinder profile and why he seemed egregiously angry at the woman whose dog approached me during our walk, convincing myself that it will be good to go on a date outside of the city since I'm paranoid about being seen by people I know. Also, he's a firefighter – a volunteer firefighter with his local fire department – but still, close enough.

It is early evening when I pull my car up to a quiet suburban street of boxy low-rise apartment buildings, all of which look identical. Several times I drive to the top of the cul-de-sac and then U-turn before giving up and texting Scott that I am outside but can find neither his building nor a parking space. A few minutes later, I spot him walking on a path, sporty and robust in a T-shirt and gym shorts, making me feel conspicuously overdressed in a short, ruffly navy blue dress belted at the waist and a pair of high-wedge sandals. He comes right to the driver's side and opens my door, asking if I want him to drive to find a parking spot. I slide out of the car and run around to the other side. He seems put out at having to rescue me.

Inside, his apartment is simple and tidy but devoid of character. A jumbo flat screen television is the highlight of the living room, with a few framed photos of him and his daughter scattered around. There are two small bedrooms flanking the main room, and the one that belongs to his daughter is homey and sweet, with stuffed animals on the pink comforter and posters on the wall. I am moved that this room has been given such attention to detail, especially when the rest of the place has a just-moved-in feel.

He offers me a glass of wine and we sit on the beige L-shaped sofa. The television is on but muted, and I can see the local news flickering. He seems distracted by the TV, his eyes darting over every few minutes to follow the news stories, but he makes no move to turn it off. He asks me what I want to do for the evening and I tell him that he gets to decide since we are on his turf. He decides to take me for a drive in his convertible down to the water, where there is a bar he likes. First, he has to change his clothes.

He goes into his bedroom but leaves the door open, and I can see him pull his T-shirt over his head before turning the corner toward the closet. I think back to my first night of sex, with #1, how I nervously took off all my clothes while he was in the bathroom, and I wonder again if this is a cue. Am I supposed to follow him to his room? Did he want me to, but not want to say it for fear of being too forward? If he didn't want me to, wouldn't he have closed his door? I set my glass of wine on a sports magazine on the coffee table and walk quietly to his bedroom, where I lean against the doorway, watching him get dressed. He has put on a pair of jeans and is buttoning a purple-and-white checked Oxford shirt. When he sees me watching him, he asks if his outfit looks OK.

"Yes, it looks quite good," I respond, a smile slowly forming. "But maybe don't go through all the trouble of buttoning it."

He comes to the doorway and faces me, coyly asking, "Oh no? What should I do with it?"

"Let me see what's underneath it," I say, my fingers already undoing the top button. When I finish with the bottom button, I let my hand linger on his stomach. His ab muscles are rock-hard, his six-pack defined and angular. He stands still, watching me eye him, not making a move closer to me but not moving away either.

"I think we should have sex before we leave," I state matter-of-factly.

"Oh really?" he says, laughing. "You can't wait, huh?"

"Of course I can wait," I say. "I just don't want to."

I put my hands on his shoulders so that I can push the shirt down his arms and off. He has the firefighter body of my dreams, each muscle distinct and firm without being excessively bulky. I unsnap the narrow belt cinching my dress in and then pull down the flimsy straps so that I can shimmy out of it. I have at long last replaced my unwieldy strapless bra with a black lace bandeau, which has laughable support but is way sexier and I don't have to hide it away before it's seen. He seems hesitant, so I stand motionless in my bra and black lace thong, daring him to turn away. He doesn't.

Sex with him is quick and physical, like a sprint that leaves you breathless and not totally sure what just happened but nonetheless glad you ran. We have barely caught our breath when he pats my thigh and says we should go out before it gets too late. Within minutes, we are dressed again and he hands me a baseball hat to contain my hair while we drive in his sporty little convertible. I decline it and instead take my cotton scarf and wrap it around my head, attempting a chic Audrey Hepburn look, but I guess ending up more like a Russian grandma with a babushka because he frowns, shakes his head and offers me the hat a second time.

The bar he takes me to is packed, clearly the town's hotspot. We find an open barstool on the deck overlooking the water. Scott gets me a Margarita and stands next to me, moving around as he speaks. He is a man who does not like to sit still and it's easy to picture the athletic, energetic teenage boy he must have been. He is easy to talk to – though we have very little in common, he is curious to know what makes me tick and what my post-marriage life has been like. As we talk, his hand rests on my thigh along the hem of my dress and then his fingers slip under the hem and inch their way up further toward my inner thigh. Neither of us skips a beat in our conversation or changes expression. His index finger pulls aside the elastic edge of my panties and presses against my clit, and still we talk without interruption. When his finger slides inside me, my eyes dart to the side where a large group of millennials is gathered next to us. They are all too busy with each other to pay attention to the handsy middle-aged couple in their midst, but also I realize with surprise that I really don't care if someone does see. Not only do I feel completely anonymous here, I care less about how I seem than how I really am, and how I am is present in this moment with a man's eyes locked on mine and his

239

finger warm and pulsing inside of me. Of course, later when I find out that this is the town where some of Daisy's camp friends live and that they frequent this bar, I will feel less cavalier and more relieved that I remained anonymous, but at this moment the danger feels fresh and exciting. When he suggests that it's too late at night for me to drive back to the city and I should spend the night, I cock my head to the side to mull the option over, pretending that I hadn't thrown a pair of glasses and clean underwear into my bag just in case this option arose.

Back at his apartment, he offers me a T-shirt to sleep in but I decline it and strip down to my underwear to lie in bed next to him. We have sex – quick again, given that he got me started an hour ago at the bar, but intense and deeply satisfying – and then I hear his breathing change as he falls asleep. I lie awake, hearing the metallic tapping of water from the air conditioner from the apartment above drip onto his air conditioner. It is amazing how jarring and noisy just one drop of water can be when it hits metal from a distance of ten feet, and I try to relax to the pattern of drips so that I can fall asleep, but there's no rhyme or reason to it so I remain frustrated and very much awake. #5 gently snores next to me and I think of kicking him as I would have kicked Michael, but we aren't anywhere near the point in which I am free to nudge him so I listen to the drips and the snores, the tapping and the breathing, and wonder if I will ever get used to sleeping with another man again. When the sun finally spills through the slats of the blinds in the morning, I rise exhausted while Scott bounces out of bed, hurrying to get ready for a race he's running with his firemen buddies.

"Walk of shame," he says as he walks me, outfitted back in my skimpy ruffled dress and high heeled sandals, to my car.

"Strut of success," I counter back, shooting him a coquettish smile.

We start talking every day after that, kicking the day off with sunshine emoji texts and catching up over phone calls as he drives home from work. Sometimes he calls late at night as I lie in bed reading, and he almost always makes me laugh. He enjoys provoking me so that I work myself up into heated, impassioned arguments about everything from politics to childrearing and then he back-pedals his staunch stance, teasing me that it's easy and fun to get me riled up. Once a week he goes to fire training classes and I hang onto all the details of what he has to carry while battling smoke and intense heat, and how many of the other volunteers couldn't make it to the end as he did. Eventually he confesses that he's never actually fought a real fire, that the local fire department doesn't get a lot of action aside from cats stuck in trees and kids locked in bathrooms, but even that information only mildly re-duces his virile masculinity in my eyes.

It is challenging for us to find time to see each other as the physical distance and our schedules with our kids get in the way, so we make do with quick weekday visits that thrill with their speed and surprise. He texts that he has an hour free at lunchtime and then rides his bike miles from where he teaches uptown to find me waiting for him in my apartment in varying states of undress, or he texts as he drives into the city to tell me that he doesn't have to be at work until 10, and I drop Georgia at school and then find him sitting on the steps of the building next to mine waiting for me as I turn the corner back to my building.

The sex we have is always hasty, intense, and toe-curling. One muggy day he comes into my apartment dripping with sweat from the bike ride to get downtown. I invite him into the shower, where he lifts me up and holds me as I wrap my legs around his waist; in the glass box of my shower with steam and water pouring down on us he presses me against the marble wall and I think, *aha, so this is what it means to get fucked.* We are barely dry from the shower when his damp, sweaty clothes go back on and he is pedaling his bike to get uptown to the class he has to teach.

I continue to meet men for coffee or cocktails that I connect with on dating apps. I've moved on from Tinder, which feels messy and slipshod and seems to display an inordinate number of shirt-less, heavily tattooed men lying on their beds, leering at the camera. The quality of men on Hinge seems slightly higher – emphasis on the word 'slightly' – and forces users to write enough words that I can at least tell if they're literate or funny or too intensely looking for a long-term relationship.

One evening as I'm frying chicken cutlets for dinner, #5 calls on his way home to say hi and to tell me that he's no longer comfortable with my going on dates with other men.

"Where is this coming from?" I ask. "When we started seeing each other a few weeks ago, I was upfront with you about my need for openness and you laughed it off, like of course that's how it'll be."

"I know I said that, but I really like you and we're seeing each other enough that I don't see why you need to see other men too. This should be enough. If it's not, then we shouldn't see each other anymore."

I am not sure what to say, flattered on the one hand that he likes me enough to want me all to himself, but rankled by being given an ultimatum. I quickly hang up, telling him I have to finish cooking dinner and need some time to think, and immediately text Lauren that I need help ASAP. She writes back that she's at a school meeting and can't talk.

"I'm in a state of panic," I write to her. "#5 says he doesn't want to see me anymore unless I am exclusive with him! I have a date Friday that I don't want to cancel and I don't want to be monogamous and I don't want someone else calling the shots."

"So tell him that's not what you want and move on," she writes.

"But I like him. And the sex is amazing," I write.

She reminds me that this is not a marriage proposal, that it's not binding, but for me at this moment it may as well be, that's how serious it feels.

"Then say you can't be exclusive."

"No," I write back, defiantly.

"Then give it a try? Remember, you owe him nothing. If it works for you, great. If it doesn't, walk away. I have to go now, I'm getting dirty looks from the teacher."

I call #5 after the kids go to sleep and accept his marriage proposal – I mean, exclusivity ultimatum. On a rational level, I recognize how absurd it is that his request is causing me to feel genuine panic. Something as quaint as going steady should not make me feel like I am entering a long and intense state of commitment, but I have been so intent on maintaining control of my dating situation that the idea I am allowing someone else to force my hand into a decision I would not make on my own is throwing me for a significant loop. The truth is, although I tell #5 that I have cancelled my date with another man who is inconveniently also named Scott, I have not. I feel tremendous angst that I have lied, my heart racing and keeping me awake for much of the night, but I can neither bring myself to cancel the date nor tell #5 about it. I would rather lie than allow someone else to construct the walls of a box around me. It may be the biggest act of rebellion in my otherwise follow-the-dotted-lines path in life. When Scott #2 cancels on me at the last minute on Friday afternoon, I do not reschedule, relieved that I don't have to continue to lie, and also that I haven't let someone else make this decision for me.

CHAPTER 24

Every Five Minutes

For months, my friends have been keeping me occupied on Saturday nights when Georgia is with Michael, taking me out to scream Alanis Morissette songs at karaoke bars or glam it up at fancy Upper East Side hotel lounges or sing show tunes around pianos at kitschy dive bars. Although I throw cash at the bill when it arrives, these friends always put the money back in my purse, saying let us do this for you, it's all we can do, please let us. Now, it's time for these friends to get back to their own lives and husbands and for me to start finding my way on my own on Saturday nights. I don't want to lie to Hudson as to my whereabouts, so I brace myself to confess to him that I'm dating.

Late Saturday afternoon, I pop my head into his room, where I find him lying in bed with the lights off, watching a movie on his laptop.

"What are you doing tonight? Hitting the town with the ladies?" he asks.

"No, they're all busy tonight. Actually," I say, taking a deep breath, then pausing for too long. He turns away from the screen to look at me. "Actually, I have to talk to you for a minute." I climb up the ladder to his loft bed and perch at the edge.

"Am I in trouble?" he asks.

"No, no, nothing like that. It's just...oh boy, this is awkward. I'm dating. I want you to know. I have a date tonight. He lives in Long Island. So, I'm going to Long Island. On the train. For my date," I sputter out.

"OK, Mama Bear, live your life," he says, turning his eyes back to his computer screen. I ask him to look at me and he complies, his expressive gray eyes turning up to me.

"It's time for me to get myself back out there. It doesn't mean Dad and I are getting divorced. I just need to figure stuff out. It's very weird for me to be dating and even weirder for me to be talking to you about it. I don't want to sneak around and lie to you, but I also don't want to upset you," I say.

"You do you, Mom. I want you to be happy," he says.

I choke out a thank you, knowing his words are genuine but also worrying that I am the cause of his being in this dark room in the middle of a bright day. His eyes back at the screen, I am summarily dismissed.

*

When I get off the train in Long Island, I see #5 waiting for me at the station, leaning against his car, eating peanuts from a red plastic cup that he filled at the firehouse. It is still light out and warm, so he drives me to a trail he likes to walk in the woods. His pace is quick and I seem always to be a few feet behind him, pausing to look up at birds or down at tree trunks to inspect overgrown mushrooms.

"I bet you're the kind of person who takes her kids on nature walks and stops to look at every bug and flower," he says.

"Oh, I definitely am," I say. "And I bet you're not?"

He laughs, which is answer enough.

I am disappointed that as we walk, he does not reach for my hand or stop to give me even a quick kiss – anything to acknowledge my physical presence. For years, I have pushed Michael's hands away from me because they always seemed to be coming at me, grabbing and tapping and rubbing, so persistent and needy, but now that he's gone, I crave being touched. I want to feel the warmth of skin, the pressure of a body against my own.

After the walk, we go home to change our clothes. I take mine off and walk around the apartment naked, getting a glass of water and digging in my tote bag for a more evening-worthy outfit.

"I like how comfortable you are with your body," he says, watching me. "I like how you walk around with no clothes on and feel no need to cover up. But, one question: have you ever thought about shaving all the hair from your pussy?" he asks.

"Well, no, I haven't," I say. "I mean, there's just a small patch of hair anyway, it's pretty well-trimmed."

"I think it's hot when women have no pubic hair," he says.

"Really?" I ask, wrinkling my nose. "I think it looks prepubescent. I've never understood how men find that sexy."

"It just is," he says. "Would you think about shaving it all off?"

"No, I wouldn't. I want to look like a woman, not a little girl," I say.

He approaches me, saying, "Oh you definitely look like a woman," and then kisses me until I've backed up against the wall, where he spins me around so that my breasts are pressed against it and he enters me from behind. He wraps his arm around my waist to hold me in place and I let out a yelp of pain as he penetrates me too forcefully, but then we settle into a rhythm. I come quickly and then he does. Immediately, I can feel his semen dripping down my leg and look down to see it making a small puddle on the floor. When he walks away, I grab a paper towel to clean the floor and then join him to rinse off in the shower. We stopped using condoms when I agreed to be exclusive with him.

He wants to see if any of his friends are hanging around the firehouse and asks if I mind stopping by before we go to the bar he is taking me to. Inside, he shows me his fire jacket hanging on a hook, his name in bold yellow letters on the back.

"Now *that* is sexy," I say. "Are there cameras in here?"

This would be a real adventure, having sex in one of the gleaming red fire trucks parked in the huge garage.

"What do you have in mind?" he asks with a chuckle.

I raise my eyebrows at him and smile but then change my mind, imagining the scandalous fire-house sex tape that they'll be all too happy to show on the local news.

He takes me upstairs where there is a bar and a few grizzled, pot-bellied older men nursing bottles of beer, watching a basketball game. They don't so much as glance at me when #5 shouts out a general hello, as if this is a secret boys' clubhouse where girls are not allowed. He walks around the bar to grab a beer but then sees the refrigerator is locked, so mutters something to himself and says we can go. This whole scene is jarring and deflating to me – is this the crew that would come for me right now if there was a fire in my home? Where are the red-blooded, muscular fire-fighters? And why exactly are we here, to get free beer and refill the plastic cup with peanuts?

Our next stop is a bar in town that is having an Oktoberfest celebration. It's impossible to talk over the band and the large groups of friends that pile in, but there's fun people-watching, and the band is playing music we know from the '80s, so we sway to the music, singing along. I feel him press against me from behind, his hand sweeping my hair to the side, his breath hot on my neck as he whispers to me, "I like you, Laura." This one small sentence feels like a victory, as I find it difficult to figure out what he's thinking. I smile but don't say anything back and he whispers, again, this time more urgently, "I really like you." And then that's it, he releases my hair and steps back from me and the moment passes.

The next morning, I text him to thank him for taking me out and add that I've noticed he doesn't touch me unless we're having sex. I am not saying what I really want to say, which is that it bothers me. I want the intimacy that comes with holding hands or a quick midday kiss, not just when we are having sex – anything to make tangible the physical connection between us. A moment later, he texts me back and I can feel the anger in his words, "If you have a problem, pick up the phone and call me, don't text me."

"It's not a problem," I explain, "simply an observation."

"Sounds a lot like criticism," he writes.

I don't like how defensive he is, but he's right. It is indeed a criticism: he uses my body for sexual pleasure but not as a repository for his affection. Am I being greedy, wanting more than is offered to me, recognizing my needs and asking him to change his normal behavior to fulfill them?

I call him, knowing this will quickly spiral out of control via text, and when he answers his voice is gruff. I apologize that my comment was unintentionally provocative, perplexed by how strong his reaction is.

"Don't text me something like that and then act innocent," he spits out.

"It's not that big a deal. Some people are touchy and some aren't. I noticed yesterday that you're not. That's all," I say, sorry I said anything at all but also uncomfortable, unsure if my honesty came out aggressively or if he's unable to accept even these small bits of feedback. Isn't this how a relationship works, back and forth? Maybe I misunderstood and this is not a relationship at all, just two people killing time.

"When should I have touched you?" he asks.

"Like when we were walking in the woods, I tried to hold your hand a couple of times, but you moved away or dropped my hand very quickly. I wish you were more affectionate, but if that's not you, it's not you. It does bother me a little but I was trying to understand it more than I was criticizing you. Let's move on," I say.

"It's funny you bring this up, Laura. I have to say, I was really surprised the first time we had sex by how quickly you moved. I was put off by it, if we're being honest," he says.

I think back to our first time together, how I had followed him into his bedroom and announced that I thought we should have sex before going out. I am taken aback, seeing now that what I had thought was a sexy, bold play was interpreted by him as aggressive and unseemly. It's not that my sexual desire is so strong, though it certainly is, more that I feel like I have to get the first time knocked out and crossed off the list – I just have to make sure it happens. I'm no longer clear if that's because it's what I want or simply part of the persona I think I am supposed to inhabit.

*

That week, I make the dreaded annual pilgrimage to my gynecologist for a check-up and Pap smear. Sitting in the waiting room, I feel old and dried up in the midst of so much new life swelling and pulsing around me. This is a busy obstetrics and gynecology practice and I remind myself to find a new practice that offers just gynecology services and not obstetrics. There is nothing that can make you feel more depleted and deflated, emptied and flattened out and alone than sitting in a waiting room teeming with beautiful women literally bursting with life, who are being attended to by doting husbands. I stare at them openly, willing them to measure their abundance and plentitude against my brittle heart and hollow womb. *My God, am I angry!* I recognize the feeling of emptiness, and it's not new, as my years of birthing are well behind me, but now that not just birthing but also marriage is behind me, I'm furious and resentful. *Why should you get the golden ring*, I wonder, *and you and you and you*, as I look from one woman to the next, *when I lost mine?*

The doctor bustles into the room where I am sitting on an exam table wrapped in a pale yellow robe. Without taking her eyes off the chart she's reading, she asks me how I am.

"I'm fine," I say sharply.

She looks up at me then and asks if anything in my health has changed that she should know about.

"Well, yes actually, quite a bit has changed. My husband and I separated and I've been dating a lot and sleeping with a lot of men. So that's new."

She puts the chart on the counter and sits down on her rolling stool, eyeing me and asking how long I was married. She contemplates my answer and then asks, "How does a marriage just end after that many years together? My friends and I were talking about this recently, trying to figure out how one extricates oneself after so much time together."

"Oh it's easy, you cheat on your spouse and reveal that you were never who your spouse thought you were to begin with," I say matter-of-factly.

Her eyes widen and she says, "I would kill him."

"Maybe. It's hard to predict what you would do until it happens to you. I don't want to kill him, I just want him to disappear forever. It's not for the weak, sustaining this," I say shrugging, my voice tight.

"OK, and tell me what you've been up to. You're having sex, are you using condoms?" she asks.

"Yes, for the most part. I'm not going to lie and tell you I've used a condom every time, and now that I'm exclusive with one man, we aren't using condoms."

She jots down notes in my chart and says she will do a full STD screening just to be on the safe side. I suggest that while she's at it, she also check for a UTI as I think I may have one.

"I'll run a test, but in the meantime I'm going to start you on an antibiotic so it doesn't get worse. I'm sure you do have one with the amount of sexual activity you're having," she says.

She is direct and forthright, which is fine, but is she judging me?

As I walk home after the appointment, I call #5. He asks me how it was and I tell him I'm fine minus an infection. I barely have the words out before he announces definitively that the infection is not from him because he doesn't have any diseases.

"Neither do I. It's an infection. Women get them all the time. I don't even know for sure if I have one. Anyway, thanks for your concern," I say sarcastically.

A few days later, he calls as I leave the nail salon with freshly painted bright pink fingernails, asking me my plans for the evening since Georgia is with Michael. When I tell him that I am going to dinner with my friend Danny, an old college friend, he sounds dejected.

"I'm disappointed. I was going to come downtown and surprise you, take you out," he says.

I thank him, but since I've had these plans for a while I don't offer to change them.

"I find it a little odd that you're having dinner with a man I've never heard about and that you didn't tell me sooner," he says.

It's not odd at all as I have a lot of friends he doesn't know about yet, but he continues, "I don't believe that men and women can be platonic friends because it's impossible to be attracted to someone as a friend and not eventually be curious about what else could be there."

"Is this one of those moments in which you're arguing with me for argument's sake or are you serious?" I say.

He replies immediately that he is serious and reiterates that he doesn't like that I have these dinner plans.

"Oh wow. Listen, I'm not someone who gets jealous easily and I've never been with a man who gets jealous, and I don't like that I feel defensive when all I'm doing is having dinner with a very old friend," I say.

"I'm not jealous at all," he says. "I'm calling you out on the fact that this is not just a friend."

"I don't think this is going to work between us," I say, coldly and abruptly. "It feels like we are fundamentally too different to be together."

"I'm hurt," he says quietly. "I really like you."

Neither of us says anything for a long, awkward moment.

"Let me come downtown and take you to dinner," he says. "Tell your friend you'll see him another night. I had a nice surprise planned for you."

"No," I say firmly. "I'm not changing my plans. If you don't trust me, I don't want to see you again."

"I'm sorry," he says evenly. "I get hot-headed sometimes. I do trust you. Give me another chance?"

I tell him that I'm too frustrated to talk further and hang up the phone.

*

The next day, I have to acknowledge that the relentless itchy sensation I feel is likely a yeast infection. Back to the gynecologist I go, tail between my legs. My regular doctor is not available so I see someone else in the practice, a young doctor with long, perfectly curled tresses.

"You were just here," she states as she glances at my chart.

"I know, but I think the antibiotics I took for the UTI gave me a yeast infection, so I'm back," I say.

"OK, I'm going to prescribe a pill for you, you take it once and that's it. The only downside is that it may take a day or two for the itching to ease up."

I ask for something that works faster and she offers a cream that some women don't like because it's messy.

"That's fine, I'll use the cream," I say.

"OK, and also, no sex for a week," she says as she starts writing out a prescription.

"Oh, um, is that true with the pill too or just with the cream?" I ask.

Her pen stops in mid-air and she looks up at me with a withering look.

"Just don't have sex for a week. Your body needs to recover. You have to let your pH adjust back to normal. Can you do that?" she asks.

"Yes, yes, of course I can, I just wanted to clarify if the no-sex rule applied to both treatment options, it's not like I have to have sex every five minutes," I say, reddening. Truthfully, I did want to know if one of them didn't have the no-sex for a week rule as suddenly a week seems like a daunting amount of time. In the past, a week of mandated abstinence from sex would have been a most welcome gift, but now, it looms.

CHAPTER 25

Hot Potato

I give #5 another chance, but I'm leery of him. I have never been in a relationship in which I haven't been trusted implicitly and it makes me feel like I'm lying even when I'm not. I've not only been trustworthy but also apparently *too* trusting of other people. I mean, obviously, if your husband carries on an affair for months and your teenage daughter is suspicious but you're not, you have to accept that you're lacking a self-protective sheath of wariness. Also, thinking about whether or not to keep dating #5 right now is the least of my problems. One day, as he flips through the newspaper on my kitchen counter and I cobble together lunch for us out of leftovers in my fridge, my phone rings. I see, with concern, that it's Hudson's school. I motion to him that I am going to take the call in my bedroom. The principal tells me that Hudson was caught smoking pot near school that morning, which means that he likely has drugs in his backpack on school premises, which warrants expulsion, and further, that he does not believe it to be an isolated incident.

I urgently need help with Hudson. This threat of expulsion from school, the place that feels like our one lifeline, sends me into full-blown panic. I vomit out words to the principal, filling him in on our current home life, telling him of Michael's sudden departure eight months earlier and that Hudson has cut him out of his life; that Hudson was kicked out of his camp in Israel over the summer and that he's been angry and unreachable. If we lose this school too, we will be completely lost. By the time I finish choking the story out, my voice is barely more than a squeak in a river of tears. I am mortified by my sobs and loss of self-control, ashamed that I have failed as a mother and have been reduced to begging for help from a man who is, for all intents and purposes, a stranger. When he tells me that he and the counselors at school will help Hudson, he says it with such conviction that I believe him and cry even harder at the relief of having a compassionate adult in my corner.

I am splashing water on my face to clean myself up when the guidance counselor calls. I share my tale of woe all over again, this time ending by pleading with him to find a way to get Hudson to open up to him. He says it will take time for Hudson to trust him but that he will stay the course until he does, and I am flooded with gratitude. I do not like to ask for help – I like to be the one who gives it. This latest episode has forced my hand, causing me not just to ask but to beg, and I am shocked once again to find my world populated by sympathetic adults who are not put off by my deep need. It seems amazing to me that these men want to help my son with no expectation of anything in return, and the recognition of their generosity fills me with hope that perhaps this latest hurdle is actually a blessing in disguise.

I am so lost in thought that I am surprised when I turn the corner to the living room to find #5, who I had assumed had already left, reclining on the sofa. He inquires as to how I will handle the situation when Hudson comes home later. I shrug, saying I want to help him, that punishing him is beside the point.

"Hey, you know, I can use help teaching swimming classes after school, that would keep him busy. You think he would be interested?" he asks.

"That's such a nice offer. I don't know, let me think about it," I say.

"Just don't be a pushover, Laura," he says briskly. "Don't let this kid run your house. You have to maintain authority. I don't agree with you about not punishing him."

"Well, luckily you don't have to agree with me," I say. "Not only do I not need your parenting advice, I don't want it. And feeling judged by you is extremely unhelpful. I have to leave soon to get Georgia so you need to go."

*

The next morning, I bring Georgia down to the lobby to meet Michael for her walk to school. I suggest that we all walk together so that we can drop her and then have a chance to talk. Georgia is delighted, walking between us and chattering away as she swings our hands. That it is now a novelty for her to be with both of her parents at the same time pains me. Daisy and Hudson had their entire childhoods with us together, but I doubt she will even remember a time we all lived in the same home.

After we drop her, we walk to the park, which is quiet at this early hour and will give us more privacy than a coffee bar. I tell him about Hudson and the phone calls from school; he is upset but helpless.

"If you would let me into the apartment, Hudson would be forced to acknowledge me. It's demeaning that I'm not allowed in to pick up or drop off Georgia," he says.

"Michael, you and I are on the same side. I too feel it's critical that he let you back into his life. There's no part of me that is prepared to continue being a single mother to a teenage boy. You had the whole summer coming and going from the same house and he never once acknowledged you, so proximity is not the issue. If I were you, I would write him a note every single day, let him know you're thinking about him and miss him. He's blocked you from his phone, so you'll have to drop off handwritten notes. It's a start. And maybe his guidance counselor will be able to reach him," I say.

"OK," he says. "I'll try."

We are both quiet then, watching the park come to life as strollers pass by with babies headed for the swings and dogs bound toward the dog park.

"Michael," I finally start. He looks up at me expectantly. "What are we doing?"

"Right now?" he asks.

"No, in general. We've been back in the city for weeks and neither of us has so much as mentioned couples' therapy. We aren't moving forward at all. What do you want?" I say.

"I don't really know, I've been waiting for a cue from you. You're so angry all the time, it's hard for me to understand what you want," he says.

This is the response I feared, confirming that the decision about our future has become a hot potato that we are going to hurl back and forth at each other, neither of us willing to be the one to hold it and let it burn. I wait for more, but he just looks at me. I will myself to say the words that have been trapped inside me for months; they're so close to the surface, but getting them out feels like I will have to shatter a glass wall to do it.

"OK, well," I say, sucking in a deep gulp of air. "I guess what I want then is to agree that we're done. I want a divorce. I don't think there's anything left to salvage between us."

The word "divorce" explodes between us, littering the space with shards of glass so that the path between us is no longer passable.

"I think we could be together if we both wanted to. But if you don't want to, then we can't," he says, his previously neutral tone now edged with anger and sadness.

"Michael, I thought we would always be together. I can't imagine what life without you is going to look like. I'm terrified. But I can't find a way back to you," I say, understanding that this is really it, that he won't be fighting for me unless I give him a signal that it's what I want, and I don't want it.

"I'll always love you, Laura. You gave me the most beautiful family. I don't want you to be scared, I'll always take care of you. It will make me proud to know that I can do that for you," he says, choking on his words.

Tears openly stream down our faces.

So this, I think, is what the end of our marriage looks like, almost like the beginning of it: a declaration of everlasting love, loyalty and support, sitting on a park bench just as when we got engaged 23 years earlier. We are, for a moment at least, two people who remember how purely they once loved each other, how much they have given each other, how permanent it was always meant to be. In the background are laughing children and exhausted young mothers, scurrying dogs and birds and squirrels, college students sleepily drinking coffee, joggers rhythmically making loops around the park. All the chapters of the life we shared unfold around us in the images of these passers-by, just another blessedly ordinary day except that for us, on this day, there are no more pages to turn together.

"I'll tell the older kids. I'll let them know this was a mutual decision. Maybe having this new information will give them some feeling of closure that we all need to start healing. We'll plan a time later in the week to tell Georgia together. OK?" I ask. He nods his head and I continue, "I guess that's it then."

He walks alongside me the five blocks back home, back to what is now my home. Under the awning outside the building, he pauses, asking if he can run upstairs with me for a few minutes so that he can write and leave behind a note for Hudson. I picture him sitting on a stool at the kitchen counter, carefully choosing his words as he scrawls them in his customary oversize, lopsided letters. I cannot bear the image of it, the physical presence of this man who is no longer going to be my husband. I shake my head, asking him instead to borrow a pen from the doorman and write the note in the lobby.

"Oh, OK. I guess I'll write it when I get home and drop it off later. You know how forgetful I am, I just don't want to forget to do it," he says.

"I would imagine this is the most important thing you have to do today, I doubt you'll forget. I'll see you," I say, stepping inside.

Upstairs, I lie flat on the living room sofa, close my eyes, hold my hands over my heart and breathe, as deeply as I can, in and out, deeper with each breath, through the catching in my throat and the whinnying sounds of my exhales. I press down on my heart as if I can contain its pounding, and finally, when my breathing sounds more like gasping and my heart threatens to erupt from my body, I weep. Heaves and wails burst out in a hideous, tortuous cacophony and I give over to it, allowing anguish to utterly consume me. I knew this day was coming, for months I could feel that this decision was inevitable, but the grief still comes at me like a sucker punch of agonizing pain. I howl for the past, present and future of what I am losing, my fervent desire for a steadfast family, my unwavering life partner, my best friend who I sometimes cherished and other times loathed but who I intimately and painstakingly knew – who it turns out I only thought I knew.

After some time passes – minutes maybe, though it feels like years – I rise from the couch. I could stay here immobile until it's time to pick up Georgia in a few hours, or I could rummage through my closet for a pretty sundress, press a cold washcloth over my eyes to ease the swelling, swipe on some pink lip gloss and go to my book group, which is meeting at Mara's house today. Copious amounts of Prosecco will be served and if I can't manage to keep it together, I will have the soft cushion these friends provide. Together, we have experienced the illness and death of a spouse, of parents, heartaches and heartbreaks of our kids. My pain won't scare them. The phone rings and I see that it is Michael.

"Hey," he starts, his voice coming at me like a sharp bark. "It's best for both of us that we help each other. I don't appreciate that you didn't let me up to the apartment today. I just committed to busting my ass to support you forever and in return you can't even give me five minutes in our home that I'm only staying away from out of respect to you."

"I'm sorry, I really needed to be alone, it doesn't mean I'm not supporting your efforts with the kids," I say.

"Well, that's how it feels. I'm still paying for this apartment you won't let me into, you should try to remember that."

"Right, the apartment you don't live in anymore because you chose to have a relationship with another woman, maybe you should try to remember that fun little detail," I say with a snarky laugh.

"You know why I had the affair, Laura?" he snarls at me. "To get out of our marriage."

The words land with a crash, startling me, making me audibly draw in the stale air of my apartment.

"That's a cruel thing to say," I finally sputter out.

"It may be cruel," he says, "but it's true."

I hold onto the smooth marble of the kitchen counter, feeling its cool weight under my hands. I imagine prison bars, Michael trapped behind them, leering at me.

"You're very angry, but I know you don't mean that," I say calmly, willing him to take the words back.

"I do mean it though. I couldn't figure out how else to get out of it. I knew an affair would end it," he says, still seething.

"I'm going to hang up now before one of us says something else awful," I say quietly, and then end the call before he has a chance to respond.

Michael so rarely gets angry, and in this state of fury he is no longer recognizable. The Michael I knew and loved is gone – in fact, may as well be dead minus the financial support he has vowed to give me. I am as perplexed as I am grief-stricken. It's as if the word "divorce" I used this morning released toxic fumes into our orbit, like a skunk spraying its fetid stench and penetrating every atom of the air around us. The foulness of the word charged the molecules between us and irrevocably changed our trajectory. Before that word, there was hope between us, paltry and fading, but present nonetheless. Now that it's gone, hope replaced by divorce, there is no need for either of us to continue our attempt at civility, to protect each other from the blows we could have landed months ago. We are out for blood now.

The word "divorce" has effectively changed everything.

CHAPTER 26

Outlook

My friend Leslie, who had been one of my college roommates, calls to chat and offhandedly asks me if I have heard the news that a couple we know, Alan and Liz, have broken up. Alan is one of Leslie's brother's best friends and I met him when Michael and I bought our first apartment eighteen years earlier when I was pregnant with Daisy. He was the co-op board president and Michael and I had to be interviewed by him to be allowed to buy in the building. We were in our late 20s and had scraped together every dollar we could find to purchase a lofty studio. The building had an elevator and a doorman, and the dishwasher, washer/dryer, and bathroom faucet in which hot and cold water mixed together in one glorious tap so that we would no longer have to choose between icy cold or scalding hot water made me feel that adulthood was finally within our reach. This man was all that was standing between our faking being adults and our actually becoming them. He turned out to be kind and welcoming and we were surprised by how readily he had ushered us into the building and our new state of maturity. Over the ensuing years, we often ran into him and his wife; perhaps because he had unwittingly played such a large role in this milestone moment, I had always felt indebted and even deferential to him.

Leslie tells me that he just moved out of his family's apartment into his own place, and I suggest she drop it into conversation with him that I happen to be single now too.

"You sure?" she says. "Seems like he has his hands full right now."

I snort and say, "Oh please, who doesn't? If I use that as criteria, everyone will be off limits and I'll definitely be untouchable. Ask your brother to mention it to him, see if it piques his interest."

A few days later, she calls me back, her voice breathless with excitement, to tell me that Alan jumped enthusiastically on the news of my being single and said he will not only call me, he wants to take me out for dinner.

"OK, so pass along my number. I mean, he's cute and nice, right?"

"Yes, very cute, fit, nice, and an amazing cook. You can give him any random ingredients and he could make something delicious out of it," she says.

That's all I need to know: nothing is as tantalizing as the idea of dating a man who cooks for me.

He wastes no time, texting me that night so we can set up a time to talk after I get Georgia to sleep. We talk about how odd it is to find ourselves single and living alone, about our kids and what the impact of our marriage dissolutions has been on them. His voice is deep and sonorous and, now that I'm allowed to think of him this way, sexy. We make a date for dinner on Saturday, on the late side as I will be volunteering all day at Georgia's school Halloween fair. I have known this man in such a specific context and I am trying now to think of him in a new way, but also to define how he sees me – not just as the friend of a friend or Michael's wife or part of the striving young couple he first met decades earlier. I want him to see me as a strong, sexy woman, not the broken half of a unit he used to socialize with on occasion.

I am still talking daily to #5, and lie to him about my plans for Saturday night when he asks if I can go out after the school fair. For years it has been a tradition for a bunch of my friends and our kids to pile into the Chinese restaurant across the street for a raucous dinner after the fair. #5 doesn't know that these friends have long since left the school, and I tell him much as I would love to see him, I can't disrupt tradition. I am adamantly opposed to lying, blame it as the corruptor of my marriage, but I justify it by blaming it on his possessiveness and jealousy. After all, my date with Alan might be totally innocent. Why I feel the need to come up with such a detailed and elaborate lie gives me pause, makes me dislike the person I am becoming in order to keep things smooth with #5.

The next day Alan texts me, "I made a reservation for 8:30 on Saturday. I'm happy to pick you up, after all chivalry is not dead, or we can meet at the restaurant. Just wanted you to load it into your Outlook."

"Thank you, that sounds lovely," I write back. "I don't think I've ever been picked up for a date so I will take you up on that as long as you don't mind waiting in the lobby if Hudson is home. By the way, what's my Outlook?"

"It's an online calendar. We use it at work," he writes.

"Ah, I see. Maybe I need a job first and then Outlook," I write.

I text Lauren, laughing about my confusion over Outlook, admitting that I thought he meant my general outlook for life, like look out ahead, dinner approaching. With that, his name permanently becomes "Outlook" between us.

The next night he texts me late at night to see if I'm still awake, and within seconds of my responding that I am indeed awake, my phone rings. We chat about the events of our day and he expresses anxiety about the sale of the apartment in which he raised his children. I'm confused as to why he's calling me, waiting for him to get to the point, but it seems he just wants to talk. It's sweet, but also worrisome – is this a red flag that he is needy? The next night he doesn't call, and the night after that he calls again. I like talking to him – he asks me a lot of questions and is empathetic and interested – but I'm concerned that maybe he doesn't have anyone else to call.

*

On Saturday, Georgia and I bake six small cakes and decorate them with orange frosting, candy corn, and as many Halloween-themed sprinkles as I've been able to find. She dons her panda costume and I put on my annual costume of a pink tutu with a garland of flowers in my hair to be a quasi-fairy princess. Michael will meet us at school to take Georgia to the haunted house and the craft rooms while I man the special cake room. As the fair begins and a sea of pint-sized princesses and Harry Potters fill the classroom, a man dressed in a '70s-style kelly green leisure suit and platinum blonde wig hands me a hefty cake box to add to my collection. I thank him and turn away, but he puts a hand on my shoulder and says, "Laura, it's me." I turn back and realize it's Michael. I raise my eyebrows. Every year that we've attended this event, I have put the kibosh on his wearing an elaborate costume, reminding him it's for the kids and just a small touch of a costume will suffice for adults. He is finally free to do what he wants now and he has gone all out, kicked my token costume squarely in the ass. Behind him I see Karen laying cakes out along the long table and I shrug my shoulders while she rolls her eyes and shakes her head.

"Let's take a picture," he says, and calls Karen over to snap it, handing her his phone.

I stand stiffly, pulling my lips into a tight close-mouthed smile, while his arm snakes around me and presses firmly against my waist. I am pleading with Karen with my eyes to take this photo quickly and let it be over. When he finally releases me and leaves the room with Georgia, she lets out a long sigh.

"Well, that was awkward," she says.

"He doesn't get it," I say. "I do not want to be touched by him. I do not want to be in photos with him. I wouldn't talk to him if I didn't have to."

An hour later, he posts the photo of us on his Instagram account with the caption "Can't make this up" and I ponder for longer than I care to admit what he means by this: can't make up that at the moment we loathe each other but are dressed up at a Halloween fair together? That he's finally allowed to be the full extent of his masqueraded self because I don't get to be the boss of him anymore? The photo mystifies my friends, from whom I receive a litany of texts ranging from, "I hope you're OK, you look miserable" to "Has he kidnapped you and is he holding you hostage?" to "It looks like that hold he's got on you is very tight." Daisy texts me and asks, "I'm confused by this photo, are things good now between you and Dad?" I'm furious that he feels he has a right to me and that for the sake of my kids, I really have no choice but to play along.

When the fair ends, Georgia and her friends run around the classroom while the other moms and I sweep up cake crumbs. Georgia suddenly runs headfirst into me, pressing her face against my stomach, tears dampening my shirt.

"I heard the other kids talking about me. They called me bossy," she sobs.

"Well sometimes you are a little bossy. It's OK, love," I say.

Her small body heaves as she wraps her arms tightly around me. She is a proud child who doesn't like to show feelings of sadness so I know she must be really upset to have unraveled like this. She presses her face even deeper into my stomach until Tina gently pulls her onto her lap so that I can finish cleaning up. She weeps and Tina strokes her hair. I know that she would never get this upset about her friends, that her grief at seeing me and Michael together, at having us in the same room but about to go our separate ways again, is more than she can bear. She looks small and piteous as the black and white eye make-up we painted on earlier streaks down her face.

When we all leave the building together en masse, I give her a hug and wave goodbye as she stands forlornly, holding Michael's hand. It is Saturday night, her night to stay with him. I have to let her go, even though my maternal instinct urges me to take her home, help her get cleaned up and curl into bed with her while we accept that this is how it is now, even though sometimes it's hard and often it physically hurts. I have to let Michael adopt this role too, learn how to be a nurturer. I know his love for Georgia is deep and abiding, but that he's usually played the role of fun uncle. If I take over every time the going gets tough for her, he will never learn how to be there for her in all circumstances. Ultimately it is best for her and best for him if they wade through these murky waters together without me. The only person it's not best for is me, who has never viewed motherhood as a walk-on role. I have to let Michael be Georgia's father. It does not devastate me to let him in, but it does devastate me to walk away.

Tina and I huddle under an umbrella as we turn in the opposite direction from Michael and Georgia, and she puts her arm around me.

"Oh boy," she says with a sigh. "I'm sorry. It's heartbreaking to see Georgia like that."

I nod my head, tears too close to the surface for me to get words out. She asks if I want to get a drink before we part, but I remind her that I have a date picking me up in twenty minutes and I gesture helplessly to myself, wondering aloud how I can pull myself together that quickly.

"Oh, right! Yay, a date! That'll be fun!" she says enthusiastically. I look at her askance so she keeps up her sales pitch, "Go home and get in the tub."

"I don't like baths," I say.

"Really? In that huge tub of yours? Go. Light a candle. Throw in some of those bath salts I bought you in Paris that I know you've been letting Georgia use. Please? Just try? Remember you're the one who always says, Saturday night, legs up?" she says.

"OK, fine, you're hard to refuse. Saturday night, legs up," I say, hugging her goodbye.

By the time Alan rings my bell exactly one minute before he is due, I am bathed, rose-scented and dressed in a black silk jumpsuit, which he will later tell me he found profoundly unflattering. We greet each other with a quick hug and kiss on the cheek and he looks much as I remember him – tall, slender, kind green eyes, gleaming bald head. He is interested in the renovations we did in the apartment, so I give him a tour and then he says we should get going. There are no good shoe options to be worn in a downpour like this and practical as I am, I'm not wearing rain boots on a date, so I put on a pair of impractical suede open-toed wedge heels and we set off. He has brought an umbrella large enough for the two of us and though I'm hoping we can jump in a taxi, we start walking instead. We walk quickly, heads down, as I delicately jump over puddles at the curbs.

"You can come closer, I don't bite," he says, holding his arm out for me to grab onto so that I don't continue to stray from the umbrella's cover. At the restaurant, he encourages me to order a glass of wine even though he doesn't drink. I drink it more quickly than I mean to and he orders me another one. I confess that it's been a long day, that switching modes from mom to single woman often feels like a herculean effort, but that I know if I give myself an out I will forevermore be on the sofa on Saturday nights, eating ice cream out of a tub and watching Netflix series about other people living their lives.

Our conversation meanders for hours, about his complicated upbringing and my own, about podcasts, religion, dating and his passion for cooking and surfing and fishing. He is easy to talk to, funny, and he listens, really listens. He picks up the check when it arrives and comes around the table to help me put on my jacket, saying once again, "Chivalry is not dead."

We walk back toward my apartment, passing his apartment on the way, and he asks if I want to come up. His apartment is sparsely furnished and he is apologetic, saying he just moved in three months ago. I sit on one end of the sofa, curling my feet beneath me, and he sits on the other. I am waiting for him to make a move, but he doesn't. I try every trick in my short book, tilting my head to the side, widening my eyes, gently shrugging my shoulder, which Lauren insists is my signature move, but nothing. We just talk. After an hour, he asks, "What time do you turn into a pumpkin?"

"I am pumpkin-proof tonight, Hudson is out with friends," I say.

We talk for a few more minutes until he repeats his concern that my curfew is looming. I take the hint that I'm being seen more as Cinderella approaching the strike of midnight than the sexy vixen for which I was aiming. He walks me outside; a taxi is approaching as we exit the building and Alan raises his hand for it to stop. Our goodbye is quick and clumsy, with my thanking him for dinner while he gives me a chaste kiss on the cheek and quickly closes the door once I'm in the taxi. I wish I could crawl under the seat as I give the driver my address, a mere ten blocks away, as I am so embarrassed. A less than subtle suggestion that I head home and then not even a kiss goodbye? I can't figure out at which point the date took a wrong turn. My experience so far has been that everyone wants at least a kiss goodnight.

CHAPTER 27

Instincts

In the taxi, I check my phone and see several missed calls from #5 and a series of texts from him starting with "How's your night?" and ending with "Not cool that you're not answering me." I call him and he answers on the first ring. He sounds drunk, is talking loudly and angrily, accusing me of lying to him and demanding to know where I've been. I did indeed lie to him, which makes me feel bad, but I also question what I'm doing spending time with someone about whom I don't care enough to be honest. Being spoken to like this is not worth the great sex – I mean, a little bit it is, but rationally, I know that it's not really enough. I tell him that I won't talk to him until he calms down and I hang up.

Upstairs in my apartment, I text Lauren to let her know I'm home safe and sound, and she asks for details.

"I don't have any, I'm sorry to disappoint. We had such a nice time but then he stuck me in a taxi and barely kissed me on the cheek."

"Oh, Outlook, come on!" she writes. "That's not how my girl works."

"I know. It's a bummer. And he ruined my streak. Meanwhile I'm supposed to see #5 tomorrow but I have to cancel, he's too much."

"OK then, don't go and move on. You know my feelings. You don't owe anything to any of these men. Bye-bye #5."

I toss and turn all night and at dawn text #5 to let him know I'm not coming as planned, and furthermore, I don't think we should see each other anymore. I am hopeful that with that off my chest, I can get some sleep but he texts me back within seconds, apologizing for speaking so harshly to me the night before and insisting that I come as planned, that he's been looking forward to it all week. I decline again, reminding him that I had told him I would give exclusivity a try, but that it's not working for me, I have too much going on with Michael and my kids to also manage his expectations.

The phone rings but I don't pick up, so he texts again, "Please come. I want to see you. If you want to date other men, we can work it out. Give me a chance. Please. I had a special day planned for you."

I am confused by him, his alternating belligerence and warmth. I think back to some of the conversations he's had with me about his ex-wife, how roughly and unkindly he spoke about her, but how loving he is when I hear him on the phone with his daughter. I wonder if when Michael talks about me he does so with respect for the fact that I'm the mother of his children, or if his frustrations with me are so great that the anger comes first, and then the acknowledgement of the love we once shared. I decline #5's invitation once again, but he persists.

"Please. I like you so much, Laura. You're the first woman I've opened up to in a long time. Just come spend the day, we'll work this out," he writes.

I cave. I don't know if it's compassion or my ego, but this line of reasoning works on me, makes me feel I'm special to him and I dare not disappoint.

When I arrive at his apartment, he looks at me forlornly and opens his arms to embrace me. I allow him to wrap me in a hug and he murmurs apologies in my ear, then guides me to the couch when I say that I am exhausted. He lies next to me and wraps himself around me. I am out of sorts, knowing I shouldn't be here and feeling upset with myself that I let myself be so easily convinced, once again. After a few minutes, he rises and gently tucks a blanket around me. I hear him moving around in his small kitchen, making himself breakfast, and I drift off to sleep. When I wake up and look at my watch, I see that I have been asleep for two hours. He is working on his laptop at the table and smiles at me when he sees me rise, saying we should go to the health club soon before it gets too late.

"OK," I say, groggily. "Let me eat an apple or a banana or something first."

I check my phone while he rummages in his kitchen for a piece of fruit. There is a long text from Alan, "Good morning Laura, as we both know from literature and movies, NYC taxis either never show up fast enough or come too soon. Last night I felt the latter, a quick goodbye rather than a longer hello. I'd love to see you again if you're interested, if not c'est la vie, no explanations or excuses required."

#5 comes back from the kitchen, proudly holding up a Red Delicious apple he seems surprised to have discovered in his fridge. He motions to my phone, asking if everything is OK. I feel uncomfortable being here; he is closely watching my every move and I'm well aware this is the last time I will see him. I shouldn't have come and it feels like play-acting with him now.

"Yes, all fine," I say. "I just need a cutting board."

When he goes back to the kitchen, I text Alan, "Yes that's quite true about the quick arrival of the taxi. I would love to see you again."

"I don't have a cutting board," #5 says, back again.

"You must," I say. "What do you cut on?"

"I don't know, I guess I don't cook anything that requires cutting," he says.

The one or two times I had opened his refrigerator, I had seen stacks of styrofoam containers, leftovers he had taken from Monday night dinners at the firehouse. This strikes me as unbearably sad and lonely, his inability to stock his fridge, to make his kitchen feel like a home. Or maybe I spend too much time with my many cutting boards and need to tone it down a bit.

He takes the apple and slices it for me on a plate. I obediently sit at the table and eat the thick slices, and he sits next to me and helps himself to a few. We don't speak, just gaze at each other and chew, and when we are finished, we rise to leave.

The health club is in a massive building on a commercial tract, and we sign in at the front desk. #5 has a free guest pass which requires me to fill out forms, sign waivers and release my email address so that I will receive emails in perpetuity from which I cannot successfully unsubscribe and so am forever left with this memento of my day here. We decide we will work out first and I head to an elliptical machine while he heads for the weight corner. Every ten minutes he comes to check on me as if I might escape when he's not looking, and finally I suggest that I go to the weight corner with him. When we finish there, we head to the locker rooms to change for the jacuzzis. We lean back against the jets, our faces flushed from the heat and my hair curling around my face from the humidity.

"I'm sorry about the way I've spoken to you recently," he says. "I would like to explain."

"OK, I'm listening," I say, and he explains the origin of his lack of trust in other people, which he knows is not fair to me yet is deeply rooted all the same. I try to be compassionate and kind, but I'm no longer invested in whatever this was going to be with him, so I don't push the topic or probe as I might with someone else. By the time we are dressed and ordering salads for lunch in the café, where he lets me know he didn't bring his wallet so I will need to pay, I am counting down the minutes until I can say goodbye.

*

By Monday morning, #5's good behavior has worn off. His phone call to me as I amble home from a Pilates class is tinged with rage, as if we hadn't achieved some level of peace less than 24 hours earlier.

"When were you going to tell me that you've already started dating other men?" he asks. "I know you went on a date this weekend. Just tell me his name."

"OK, I'm done. I give up. I don't want to see you again and I don't have to explain myself," I say.

He is adamant that I tell him my date's name.

"No," I repeat, "and I want to make sure you understand what I'm saying, that I do not want to date you anymore, that we are done."

"Tell me his name and I'll leave you alone," he says.

"OK then, his name is Alan."

"Alan. Aha, I knew it. That's all I needed to know. I thought you were different, Laura, but you're just like every other woman I've ever known," he says.

"OK, then it shouldn't be too hard to let me go," I say, but I can't figure out why he needed to know Alan's name, what that solidifies in his mind.

"You're a liar and a tease and you led me on. I really cared about you, I was falling in love with you. I'm disgusted," he says, with such fury that I stand still on the sidewalk and look around in paranoia, worrying he might be nearby.

I hang up, but the phone immediately rings again. Over and over he calls as I walk the few blocks back to my apartment, contemplating what the name Alan means to him, and then I realize: while I was sleeping on his couch, he had gone into my bag and checked my phone. It was locked, but he would have seen the new texts that had popped up on the screen, including the one from Alan about the night before and the taxi coming too soon. He's right to be upset with me – I did lie, and I was caught in my lie – but still, the violation of my privacy and the intensity of his reaction gives me the creeps.

At home, I lock the door behind me, shower and change for my lunch date with Lanie, an old friend. The phone rings over and over again, so I mute it. Then the texts start pouring in: "I'm sorry", "Please pick up the phone", "I just want to talk to you for a minute", "I understand what you're saying", "I want to suggest something to you", "You've been so good to me, you didn't deserve the way I spoke to you", "Just give me five minutes, I talked to a friend and have calmed down".

I call him back as I walk to the café where I am to meet Lanie.

"Thank you for calling me," he says in a tight voice. "Please give me another chance."

"No," I say. "Anything else?"

"I have a proposition. I understand that you don't want to be in a relationship with me, but you have to admit we have amazing sexual chemistry. We don't have to date to have sex, we can continue to meet up during the day as we've been doing, no strings attached," he says.

I can't help myself: I laugh, loudly.

"You're serious?" I ask.

"Why not? The sex is great for both of us. Why give that up?"

"Oh wow, I'm not even going to respond aside from an emphatic no. I don't want to see you again and I'm asking you to stop calling and texting. I have to go now," I say as I open the door to the café and spot Lanie seated at a table.

I bend over to give her a quick hug and then slide into the booth.

"Tell me everything," she says, her eyes lighting up. "I cannot imagine what it would be like to start dating again at this point in my life. It seems like yesterday you were visiting me in Brooklyn with sweet Daisy strapped into a BabyBjörn. And now you're single and dating, like your life is going in reverse."

"It feels that way to me too, like I'm sowing the wild oats I should have sown in my 20s," I say, and then tell her about my one-night stand with #1, my debacle with #2, my summer flings with #3 and #4, the disaster that #5 has turned out to be, the promising potential of #6.

"Oh wow, you've been busy!" she says. 'I'm impressed with how bold you've been and that you keep forging ahead even when you have experiences that aren't positive."

"I'm surprised too that I haven't been deterred by the more unpleasant experiences. The pros outweigh the cons I guess, and every date with a new man is an adventure. It's exciting to walk in with no idea what to expect and see where it goes. And it turns out that I really love having sex. I feel like I'm insatiable. I imagine at some point the novelty will wear off, but right now I'm trying to make the most of it."

"Have you had anal sex?" she leans forward to quietly ask.

"No, and it's funny you should ask because a few of the men have asked me about it. I'm pretty open-minded, but that terrifies me. I'm squeamish even thinking about it."

"I swear to you it's the best thing ever. It makes every other orgasm you've ever had feel like a warm-up. You just have to get over it mentally. When I have sex now that's not anal, it's totally humdrum," she says.

"Huh. I would not have expected you to say that. I will try to work up the courage," I say.

"Laura, please start writing all of this down. It might be cathartic for you and you have a lot of good stories," she says.

I give her a half-hearted reply, saying I will think about it but don't think I have enough of an attention span to write coherently.

*

The barrage of phone calls and texts from #5 continue well into the night. Sometimes they're sweet, "I will miss our morning hellos and the sound of your voice and the way your hair smells", and sometimes full of fury, "I can't believe I opened up to you, you're such a liar, I never should have trusted you. And here I thought you were different from other women."

I text him back one time to let him know that I will not be responding anymore. The onslaught goes on for days. Lauren suggests that I block him but I am convinced he's going to make an appearance at my building or wait for me after I drop Georgia at school, so I would rather get his texts and ignore them to know if he's still at it or trailing off. She offers to send her husband over to keep an eye on things for me, but I insist that I will be fine without a bodyguard, that #5 is unstable but probably harmless.

The calls and texts taper off, although months later, he will still on occasion text me to wish me a happy holiday or say he's thinking of me. Even a full year later, he will try to "friend" me on Facebook. Another lesson learned: I have to start trusting my instincts.

CHAPTER 28

An Older Man

I treasure most aspects of motherhood, with one notable exception: the constant planning. From the very beginning, while our babies are still gestating, we earnestly and optimistically create our ideal birth plans. Despite the fact that few of us end up with a birth that works out as we had methodically outlined, we continue to make plans for our unpredictable and fickle babies that require surgical precision and an ability to juggle ten competing needs into a one-hour time slot. As the kids grow older, planning takes on a new level of finesse and magnitude – after-school activities, play dates, tutors, school interviews and orthodonture appointments and meals. My God, do kids really need three meals a day AND snacks? And no two children ever seem to have the same palate, which means with three kids eating three meals, you could conceivably be planning meals a whopping nine times a day or 63 times a week.

So when Alan texts me during the week to let me know that he's planned our Saturday evening – having made a reservation at

a Japanese restaurant in Harlem to be followed by a jazz club down
the block – I am awestruck that he has taken this responsibility
out of my hands and relieved me of the pressure of having to
figure out what he might like and what the right atmosphere is
– quiet and romantic, noisy and fun, upscale, a dive? He picks me
up at my apartment again, but this time Hudson is home so I
meet him in the lobby. I suggest we take the subway and we disa-
gree about which one to take so I follow his lead. When we get
off the train, he has no idea where we are, and after hopping in a
cab, he agrees that maybe my route had been the right one after
all. He is getting a tiny glimpse of how much I love to be right
when I raise my eyebrows and give a small smile.

The restaurant is fairly empty, which seems odd as he had told
me this was a hard reservation to get. We opt for seats at the sushi
bar and he runs through the menu to see what I like, then orders
a plethora of dishes for us to share. Even more than I love how
he plans our evenings, I love how he orders. What joy it brings
me to cede decision-making to another person, even if it is something as inconsequential as where and on what we'll dine! There
are so many decisions to be made every day, for myself and my
marriage and my kids, so the way he takes over with a menu brings
me a momentary reprieve. I am pleasantly surprised when he
remembers all the particulars of my culinary preferences – to be
listened to like this, to actually be heard and for someone to care
about what I like and don't like, feels like a true wonder. There's
something old school about him that I find utterly appealing:
picking me up for our dates, holding doors for me, helping me
with my jacket, ordering for me, insisting on paying the bill as if

my even reaching for my wallet offends him. Being treated well, being doted on, having someone make me feel exceptional – a quiet, hopeful part of me dares to believe that maybe I deserve this.

Once again, our conversation comes easily and ranges from the mundane to the difficulties of our marriages to the challenges of our childhoods. As dinner continues, we start leaning closer to each other, touching each other's arms to emphasize a point, and when he returns from the restroom, he approaches from behind so that I don't see him coming and kisses me on the nape of my neck. I take in a quick, audible breath, my heart quickening.

He sits down next to me and continues the conversation without skipping a beat. After he pays the bill, he looks up at me, asking intently, "Shall we go to the jazz club as planned or do you want to go home?"

"I think we should go home now," I say, meeting his gaze.

It turns out that the correct subway is about ten steps from the restaurant, and also that this restaurant is not the one he intended to take me to – thus the confusion. We chat as the train barrels downtown, but the tension between us is palpable. I am curious to see how this well-mannered, courteous man will devour me, which is all that I am hoping will happen when we get back to his apartment. He lets his fingers brush against mine as we ride the elevator upstairs, but otherwise maintains a gentlemanly distance.

I slip out of my shoes at the door and take my jacket off so that I am down to my skinny jeans and a ruffly silk blouse with spaghetti straps that are easy to slip off. We settle on the couch for a moment, in the same spots as last Saturday night, but it only takes a moment for him to breach the space between us. He kisses me with passion and a lot of tongue so that I pull back a little to get my bearings. It's already clear to me that I had been silly to worry about his being too genteel to be an ardent lover. Soon I am lying on the couch and he lifts the blouse over my head, then runs his finger along my clavicle, down my breastbone to my navel, slowly but finally landing at the button to my jeans, which he easily opens with one hand. He slides my jeans down my legs, taking his time to kiss the soft spot of skin where my thong touches my bikini line, along the inside of my upper thighs and then down my legs, delicately lifting my feet to free me of my jeans. I watch wordlessly as he puts my toe into his mouth, gently sucking on it as I arch my back and let out a long, slow breath. He rises from the couch, then takes my hand and leads me to his bedroom.

His bedroom is small but his bed is hotel-quality, with a crisp white duvet covering a fluffy down quilt and copious pillows with matching white pillowcases and navy blue piping. It is elegant and enticing, but also masculine without signs of the bachelor beds I've seen haphazardly thrown together and usually covered in dog hair up until now; decidedly metrosexual, which hits my sweet spot. I lie back against the pillows and he kneels between my legs, saying, "I'm dying to taste you."

He pulls my thong down, his thumbs hooked around the lace waistband, and slowly runs his fingers down my legs. When he puts his head between my legs, he inhales deeply and says, "Your smell is intoxicating."

With these words, I'm at a loss. Am I supposed to respond? And what exactly would an appropriate response be – a delighted, why thank you? A sidebar that the smell is deeply indebted to expensive Parisian rose oil that never goes on sale so he's lucky I used some of it for his benefit? A sultry and absurd, "You know it baby"? Flummoxed, I remain silent and hope my silence will be a hint that I'm all action and no conversation once I'm in bed. I am not quite so lucky though, as it appears that #6 is going to take the time and effort to observe every detail of our sexual encounter and verbalize these observations.

"You are so wet and so sweet," he says, and my mouth twists so that I am biting the corner of my lip. He's kind of far away so if I do speak I'm going to have to do it in a loud voice, which means I'm going to have to really assert myself, say whatever I can muster up with some degree of gumption. I am running through all the possible responses, trying to come up with one that registers I hear him but offers only the most banal words so that I'm not forced to follow up with even more words.

"Yes," I finally say, and to be perfectly honest, I am pretty proud of that yes, as it took everything in me to choke it out. I have never talked during sex beyond a few basic and brief assessments and acknowledgements. I have never watched pornography or even read pornographic material, so I don't know how this is supposed to be done. I, who pride myself on my literary and verbal skills, am utterly speechless.

Other than the talking, he is doing a good job down there. He seems not to tire of it and uses his tongue delicately and then more urgently until finally I use my words to ask him to please make his way inside of me. He pulls himself up and reaches over to his dresser drawer, saying that he needs to get a raincoat, which gives me pause. It seems like such an old-fashioned, odd way to say condom – for all his verbal straightforwardness, this is where he's going to use a euphemism?

He pulls it on and enters me with a quick thrust. It is only a matter of seconds before I come, digging my nails into his back and letting out a cry of pleasure. My whole body loosens and he stops moving, lying against me as I catch my breath. I apologize that I couldn't wait for him.

"Don't be sorry, you did exactly what I wanted you to do," he says.

"How generous of you," I say with a laugh.

"Seriously, do you have any idea how thrilling it is for a man to make a woman come so easily?" he asks. "Most women I've been with don't come like that, it takes a more nuanced effort."

But we are not done with each other yet. He slides back inside of me and I push him to the side so that I can be on top. I still have my strapless bra on and as I sit up, he wraps his arms around me and snaps it open, then flings it to the side.

"I couldn't bear to take this off earlier. If I saw you all at once I would have come on the spot, it would have been more than I could handle. You have amazing tits," he says and I blanch; I loathe that word, finding it crass and demeaning.

He runs his hands along my nipples, gently touching them and pinching them, then runs his hands down to hold my hips as he guides the rhythm of my movements on top of him. I watch as his breathing becomes shallow and his eyes close. When I feel him pulsing inside of me, I stop moving and lean forward to lie on top of him.

He runs his fingers down my back and I press my ear against his heart as I listen to it slow down. We drift off to sleep for a few minutes until he whispers that he should get me home. I roll off him and head to the bathroom to clean up. When I emerge, I note that he has assembled the clothes that had been thrown with abandon in various parts of the apartment and neatly arranged them on his bed. He pulls on sweatpants while I put my jeans and flouncy top back on.

"You don't have to get dressed. I'm going to walk home, it'll take me ten minutes," I say.

"No, chivalry is not dead, I'll put you in a taxi," he says.

I shake my head and insist that I am fine to walk home on my own. He kisses me goodbye, asking me to text when I arrive home, which I do exactly ten minutes later. I also text Lauren to let her know I'm home.

"How was it? Please tell me you're back in action," she writes.

"Indeed I am. Sex was great. He's very oral and very verbal and I'm not sure how I feel about either, but I do like him so we'll see."

*

Like clockwork, he starts to text me every night around 10 asking, "You awake?" and I write back, "Indeed I am" or "Why yes, how lovely to hear from you," and within seconds he calls and we talk about our days and kids, articles we've read and what we cooked for dinner. He listens with exceedingly fine attention, following up on previous comments I've made or issues that have concerned me. On Wednesday nights, he casually asks what my plans are for the weekend and we book Saturday night dates. I love that he takes the game-playing and guessing out of dating. He makes it clear that he wants to talk to me and see me, so that I look forward to getting that daily "You awake?" text without having to worry whether or not it will come. If he hasn't made a reservation for dinner in advance, he has come up with ideas and we ride the subway from borough to borough on Saturday nights, eating Greek food in Astoria, Russian food in Brighton Beach, and Malaysian food in Chinatown. We are both adventurous eaters who prefer an authentic ethnic meal at a casual dive to a formal, upscale restaurant – though sometimes he takes me to those too.

One night he asks if he can cook for me and I arrive at his apartment to find the small table for two set with linen napkins, candles, even a crystal pitcher of water. I try to help in the kitchen but he says no, I should pour myself a glass of wine and keep him company while he cooks. He is apologetic about his cramped kitchen with its peeling counters and '70s stove, but I tell him he could be cooking in a cave and I would be equally enchanted. When dinner is on the table, glistening scallops from the fish-monger at the farmers' market, a bright green salad, long stems of roasted baby broccoli, fresh focaccia from the Italian market, I stand by the table with my hands pressed together over my heart. He urges me to sit down before the food gets cold.

"I will in a minute, I'm just taking it in. It's always been my dream for a man to cook for me. Sorry to tell you one man beat you to the punch by preparing a lovely picnic for me this summer, but this is next level. I really appreciate it," I say and am quiet; if I say more, I will cry.

Our nights always end the same way, with my going back to his kid-free apartment after dinner if we have eaten out, or straight to the couch and then bed after cleaning the kitchen if he's cooked for me. He is intrigued and enthralled by how easily I can orgasm and peppers me with questions about my previous liaisons.

"Your confidence is a huge turn-on," he says one night after we have depleted ourselves and are lying naked in his bed. "You have so much power."

I appreciate the compliment and love that this is how he views me, but I clarify that I'm more curious than confident. I've slept with twice as many people in the past four months as I did the rest of my life until now, so having sex has become something of a fact-finding mission for me at this point.

"Yes, but you have to have enough confidence to get to that point. I don't have the same insatiable curiosity as you do, maybe because I had so many years as a bachelor before I got married. And honestly, it's enough for me just to keep up with your sexual appetite," he says. I laugh and he continues, "No, really. I was forty when I got married. That's a lot of years of bachelorhood. I'm older than you and you have a ton of energy."

"You're not that much older than me," I say. He raises his eyebrows, so I ask, "Wait, how old are you?"

"62," he says.

"Oh come on! How old really?" I ask, propping myself up on my elbow, my hair spilling over his bare chest.

"62," he repeats.

"No way!" I shriek, my eyes widening. "I'm shocked. You have a six-pack for God's sake! Are people as old as 62 even capable of having six-packs? You're my first older man. I've slept with men a little older but this is a big age difference. You're fourteen years older than me!"

"I thought you knew my age. Is this an issue for you?" he asks.

"No, no, it's fine, I guess, I'm just surprised. This could be fun, now I get to be the younger woman, like a trophy for you. You should be proud of yourself for ensnaring me," I say, laughing, but really I'm not so sure. I know the adage that age is just a number and he certainly looks younger than I would imagine a 62-year-old could look, but still, he's only three years shy of getting senior citizen benefits. I have envisioned myself with a man my age or younger, so I file this new information away to deal with at a later point when I can figure out why it might concern me.

CHAPTER 29

Saturday Night, Legs Up

My kids' pediatrician and I have always been chatty and friendly, but the last time I saw her in the spring, I struggled to keep up my side of our usual banter, tripping over my words and looking morosely out the window. When she was done writing out a prescription for Georgia's ear infection, she sent her out of the room to give us a minute alone.

"What's going on? Something is off," she said, watching me closely.

I didn't mince words, quickly spitting out that Michael had had an affair and we had separated, that the older kids wouldn't talk to him. She sucked in her breath, rolling back in her stool until she could lean against the wall.

"I don't know what to do. I'm so overwhelmed. I don't think I can take him back even if he wants to come back, which is not certain to me," I wept.

"Laura, I want to tell you something. After my first son was born, my husband and I got divorced. The man I'm married to now is my second husband. I know what you're going through and I promise you, no matter what happens, you're going to be OK. Here's my advice to you: don't stay for the money, don't stay for the kids, don't stay because you're scared to be alone."

"Those are the only three reasons I can imagine staying. I'm scared of financial instability, I feel horrible about the kids and I'm terrified to be alone," I said.

She raised her eyebrows.

"No one can tell you what to do, only you know what is best for you. But staying because you're afraid not to is not a good reason to stay," she said.

Now, seven months later, sitting in the Mickey Mouse-themed patient room for Georgia's annual check-up, she again sends her out of the room to give us a chance to catch up. Georgia reaches for the phone I'm holding outstretched to her and rolls her eyes, asking me not to take too long. As soon as Dr B closes the door behind Georgia, she tells me that she is relieved to see that I look much healthier than the last time she saw me, that my color is back and I don't look painfully thin anymore. I thank her for her words to me months earlier, telling her they gave me clarity, that Michael and I are going to get divorced and I'm dating again.

"Good girl!" she says in her most encouraging pediatrician voice. "You're a hot catch. I'm sure you're very popular on the dating scene. Can I please set you up with someone?"

"Not yet, but eventually. I just started dating this man I like. I'll let you know when it runs its course and you can do your match-making then," I say.

"No way, it's too soon for you to be invested in one person. Just have fun for now. Keep dating the guy, but date other people too. Please, I have someone great for you. My best friend's friend. He's a lawyer, very successful, recently separated. I'm giving him your number," she says with the authority I so love in doctors.

"Give me a few weeks. I'm not good at juggling men," I say.

"Fine. I'm checking back in with you very soon," she says, and ushers me out the door.

*

A couple of weeks later, on a Friday night, I go to a cocktail party at Tina's apartment. She is a woman who was born to throw a soirée and does so as often as possible, with free-flowing wine and tequila and oysters and her famous clam dip. The kids play downstairs so that we can almost forget that they're there except when they run up the long elegant staircase of her duplex for snacks. Hudson texts to ask if he can stay over at his friend's house and I realize that I am down to just Georgia for the night so could sneak a visit over to see #6 if I leave her with Tina. When I ask Tina if that's OK, I can barely finish my sentence before she says, "Mama, absolutely leave her here with us for the night, go, enjoy."

I call #6 and ask, "Hey, what are you up to?"

"Oh you know, it's Friday night and my harem is here, wearing me out."

"Want an addition to your harem?" I ask.

"If it's you, then yes. How have you come to be free?" he asks.

I tell him I am not just free for the evening but have been given a one-night reprieve.

"So where will you sleep?" he asks.

"What are my options?" I say.

When he asks if I want to sleep over, it feels like a significant invitation, our first sleepover. As nonchalantly as possible, I say that I will stop home to get a few things and then come over.

I run downstairs to give Georgia a kiss goodbye and sing out a tipsy farewell to a group of my girlfriends. Johanna asks why I'm making such a hasty retreat.

"Just got a booty call," I say.

"Ohhhhh," she says. "Fun!"

"Well you know me, Saturday night, legs up!"

"But it's only Friday," she says, laughing. "Chasing the weekend down, I love it. Go, Mama, go!"

At home, I jump in the shower and speed through some last-minute grooming. I start to get dressed but realize it's all about to come off anyway, so instead wrap myself in a short silk bathrobe and a pair of leggings, zip a long puffy parka over it and walk the ten blocks to #6's apartment. He texts to ask what's taking me so long.

"Sorry, I was saving time on the back end," I write.

"What does that mean?" he asks.

"You'll find out soon enough."

When he opens the door, I unzip my coat, throw it on the floor and then unwrap my robe and let it fall open.

"See how much time I saved? I've already cleaned myself up and done all the necessary preamble. Now I'm ready for you," I say.

He drops to his knees and pulls down my leggings, pressing his face against my stomach and then working his way down.

"I love how efficient you are with your time," he says laughing, and after a few minutes of his inhaling me in the foyer I confess that I'm freezing and would love to get under the covers with him. I am a little bit drunk and more than a little excited to be kid-free for the whole night, so I do not hold back. I come over and over again and each time accompany the physical release with satisfied cries and then screams of joy. When we quiet down and start to fall asleep, he lies curled on his side of the bed facing away from me. I am unsure what to do. I have always been a solitary sleeper and barely move in my sleep, but this is our first sleepover and I want him to curl around me, not to be able to get enough of me. I settle for placing my hand on his back so that we have a particle of physical connection.

I awaken early in the morning when he rises from the bed. I assume he will come right back, but I hear water running in the bathroom and a few minutes later he sits next to me on the side of the bed where I am lying. He is fully dressed.

"Hey," he says softly, and I gaze at him with sleepy morning eyes. "I'm going to the farmers' market and then to yoga. Stay as long as you want, the door will lock behind you when you leave," he says.

My eyes widen and I grimace.

"In other words, don't let the door hit me on the way out," I say.

"'No, not at all. I like to get an early start on Saturdays but that doesn't mean you have to. We'll talk later, OK?" he says.

"Sure, OK, bye," I say, closing my eyes.

A moment later I hear the front door close behind him. I am

flabbergasted, not understanding what I did wrong to make him run out like this. I feel silly for having expected something more – a luxurious morning in bed, a cup of coffee, a shower together – and instead I am naked and alone while he shops for kale and organic eggs. I rise from the bed, smoothing the crisp white sheets and pillows so it looks like a hotel room after housekeeping has come. That's how cheap I feel; I want him to look at the made-up bed and see my humiliation and loneliness in the perfectly fluffed pillows.

My phone rings as I walk into my apartment, juggling keys and a cup of coffee I picked up on the walk home.

"Yes?" I say brusquely, after letting it ring a few times.

"Where are you?" #6 asks.

I tell him that I'm home and he sounds surprised, saying he thought I would sleep in.

"I felt weird staying there once you were gone and you weren't going to be back for hours anyway," I say.

"But I came back," he says, and I can hear his voice echo in the empty, still under-furnished apartment. "I'm so sad. I came home and expected to find you in bed but all your stuff is gone and the bed is made, like you were never here."

"That seemed how you wanted it to be. It's not every day you have your first sleepover with a man and he leaves you alone to go to the farmers' market and a yoga class. That seemed like a good cue for me to leave," I say.

"Please come back," he says. "I canceled my yoga class, I messed up."

I hesitate, having already settled on my couch with my coffee and the newspaper, and still feeling stung by his rejection a mere half hour ago.

He continues, "Please. I'm sorry. Just come. I made a mistake."

I walk the ten blocks back to his apartment. When I get there we climb into the freshly made bed. For a long time to come I will tease him about leaving a warm naked body in his bed to proceed with his usual Saturday morning routine and he will confess that once at the market, he phoned his friend Jeff, who called him a moron and demanded that he go right back home. We laugh at the absurdity of it, but I understand that he has a rigid structure he finds uncomfortable to stray from and I'm not certain I fit into it, or even want to.

CHAPTER 30

Plurals

With this ambivalence fresh in my mind, when Dr. B texts to ask me if she can pass my number along to her Brooklyn lawyer friend, that she's told him about me and he's dying to meet me, I agree. #6 is a lovely and decent man, but I'm still smarting from that Saturday morning of feeling unwanted, and I don't know if I have the patience to wade through the murky waters of his newly single life. Dr. B asks for a few photos of me and in return she sends back one of Mark – he's nice looking, sporty, has a sweet and genuine smile. He texts me right away and we make a date for the following week.

We meet at a small, crowded coffee bar in midtown that is close to his office, and sit on high stools at a narrow bar overlooking the street. He is of medium height and stature, with glasses and thick salt and pepper hair. There is nowhere to hang my coat or bag, so I sit on my soft, fake fur jacket and hold my tote bag in my lap. My jacket is slippery, so every few minutes I have to brace my foot against the base of the stool and push myself back up so as not to slide off. I think I've got it down to a subtle routine when he asks me kindly, "Do you always have a hard time sitting still?" I laugh and admit that I am logistically challenged at the moment, and he generously helps me arrange my pile of winter garments onto the tiny counter in front of us.

He is fun to talk to, deeply into sports and his kids, well-read and quick to smile. When he invites me to brunch at the apartment that he's just moved into with his teenage daughter from his first marriage, I readily accept, though I do make a mental note that he's a few years younger than me and already exiting his second marriage.

*

With two men now in my life, I come to the inevitable conclusion that my underwear drawer, overstuffed with stretched-out pastel cotton panties and practical bras that once fit, with a few black lace thongs thrown in that have recently seen more than their fair share of action, is no longer adequate. I have long aspired to be the kind of elegant, sophisticated woman who wears matching sets of underwear, and while realistically I know that I have neither the patience nor the finances to make this a reality, I can definitely kick things up a notch.

I head to the local outpost of a British lingerie shop, ready to have my breasts manhandled and squeezed into sexy, lacy, over-priced contraptions. I am led to a fitting room by an older woman named Marisol, who eyes and measures me and agrees that my left breast is slightly bigger than my right but is undaunted by it.

I confess that I have not bought new bras in longer than I can comfortably say aloud and want some pretty ones that are sexy without being flashy. She nods knowingly and leaves me while she picks some out. When she returns, she has bra straps up and down her arms and instructs me to stand still, then to bend forward a bit so she can maneuver my breasts into the cups. She shakes her head at the first few – too flimsy, too pointy, too tight – and then finally stands back to admire a black bra with delicate scalloped lace along the edges.

"I like how this fits you," she says approvingly.

I turn so that I can see how it looks from the back.

"Oh no," I say, dismayed. "Very pretty in the front, but the back is too wide and bulky."

"Who cares?" she asks. "Who's looking back there?"

"Umm, a lot of people," I say quietly. "I'm newly single, and a lot of men are looking back there. This would have been sexy enough for my husband, but I've got a whole Saturday night stratosphere to please now."

"Ohhhhhh," she says, nodding. "OK, Mami, I get it. You've got plurals."

"Plurals!" Delighted with this phrase, I burst out with a peal of laughter. 'I've never thought of it that way before."

"I'm taking all of these and coming back with date night options. Give me a few minutes," she says, pulling the curtain closed behind her.

When she returns, she is swimming in a colorful sea of lacy, skimpy bras and thongs. She stands back to assess each option, looking at me from the front and the back, and together we choose an eggplant purple lace bra with metallic stitching, a sheer black bra with skinny spaghetti straps, and a deep red lace bra with tiny flowers stitched on. She insists on bringing me matching thongs, but I confide in her that I know I can fill in the bottoms with cheap substitutes and am already spending more than I should.

As I watch her gather the dozen bras strewn around the room, I feel overwhelmed with gratitude for this woman's attention and care and I turn to thank her, telling her I am continually moved by the kindness of strangers. She tells me it's her job, but I say no, her job was simply to fit me in a bra that suited me, not to make me laugh or understand my plight and then cheer me on.

"Oh, honey," she says, embracing me. "I haven't had this much fun with a customer in a long time. You go out there and get your plurals. Come back and tell me how they liked your new bras."

CHAPTER 31

Dollar Store Candles

On Saturday morning, Mark texts to find out what time I will arrive, and when I ask what I can bring, he suggests a Spanish red wine to go with the cheese and charcuterie he's preparing. I take the subway to an area in Brooklyn I haven't been to before. It is mostly residential, the streets lined with stately Victorian houses featuring sweeping front porches. His apartment is on a small commercial strip and I pass it a few times before finding unevenly placed numbers at the top of a dirty, banged-up metal door. The ground floor contains a futon store that looks like it's been here since the beginning of time – I wonder, do people still actually buy futons?

Mark had asked that I call him upon arrival since his buzzer is broken, so I call now to let him know I'll be downstairs perusing the futons until he comes to fetch me. A couple of minutes later, the door swings open to a teenage girl wielding a granny cart piled with dirty laundry. She smiles shyly at me and I see Mark right behind her.

"This is my daughter," he says, and we exchange hellos. "She's on her way to the laundromat."

He nudges her along with his eyes and a nod of his head. She walks away, the overloaded metal cart clanging behind her on the uneven sidewalk. He holds the door open and I follow him up two long flights of stairs to a narrow landing covered with sneakers and boots. Stepping out of my heeled clog boots and lowering myself by about two inches, I leave my shoes in the pile in the hallway and enter his railroad apartment. It is small and dark, with windows placed at either end, one of which is his bedroom and the other his kitchen and his daughter's bedroom, so the narrow living space between is windowless and dim. It's comfortably furnished and carpeted but feels like a starter apartment, striking me as odd for a successful lawyer at this stage in his life. This makes me feel like an unbearable snob, but it's less about my thinking it's not good enough for me than about wondering why it's good enough for him.

He ushers me into the kitchen, where he starts slicing a baguette and laying chorizo and wedges of cheese on a platter. Again, I brace myself against my inner snob, watching in dismay as he unwraps plastic wrap from hunks of cheese on which I can see price tags from the supermarket. Lately, my brother has been teasing me about how bougie I've become, as I appear to be simple but with a country house and an SUV and an apartment on lower Fifth Avenue. I am frugal about certain things — happy to buy clothes and dishes at thrift shops, throwing cheap bottles of conditioner in my grocery cart and upgrading only when Tina insists I try one of her rarefied Parisian products — but when it comes to certain categories like food, reading material and hotels, I am highbrow: sheepish about it, but highbrow nonetheless.

When he's assembled the platter to his satisfaction, he asks me to grab the wine and follow him to the living room. We sit on the loveseat and as we talk, he scooches closer to me and sets down his wine glass.

"You really are so beautiful," he says. "I'm so happy Jill gave me your number. She said you were dying to meet me, but I feel now like it should've been the reverse."

I can't help but laugh to myself, remembering how Dr. B had been so persistent, telling me he was so excited to meet me and could I please allow the precious passing along of my phone number? She diligently worked both ends to make this set-up happen.

Within minutes, the platter still largely untouched, he leans toward me and kisses me, continuing to murmur about how beautiful I am and how happy he is to be with me. A noise at the door startles us and we pull away from each other. A moment later, his daughter is tiptoeing through the room apologetically, saying she forgot something, and then she is back out the door again and he returns to his spot next to me. I pull back, expressing concern that she will come in again, so he takes me to his bedroom and closes the door behind us. His bed is king-size on a large mahogany frame, covered in a worn patchwork quilt. Framed photos of his kids line the dresser, along with a few candles that he lights, saying, "This is the best thing about living right next to a Dollar Store, they have absolutely everything." I think longingly of #6 with his fastidiously chosen bedding and expensive, delicately scented candles culled from artisanal markets.

We undress, facing each other, and he lays me back against the bed and asks if I am OK with his going down on me. I nod my assent and after a few minutes he grabs a condom from his night-stand and we both quickly come. When we are still and lying next to each other, I say, "I want to ask you a question, something I've been pondering lately."

"Sure," he says, "go ahead."

"Why do men love oral sex so much? I don't mean receiving it, I mean giving it. Every man I've been with finds it a huge turn-on, and many love it or seem to need it more than intercourse. Why is that? What is it about it that you find so alluring?" I ask.

"Isn't it obvious?" he says.

"No. Don't get me wrong, I really love having sex. I like being the recipient of oral sex and like giving it, but it's not the main attraction for me. I always wonder why men love to be that up close and personal with a woman's pussy," I say.

"Well, first of all, it's not every pussy. They're not all the same. Some aren't appealing at all. You just happen to have a really nice one," he says and a short, loud laugh escapes my lips.

"Why? What about it?" I ask.

"The way it smells. The smell is very important. The way it feels. Yours is wet and soft and inviting. The way it tastes, like nothing else in the world," he tells me.

"Fascinating," I say.

I am amazed. I could not say these things back to him if he asked me what I find enticing about giving blow jobs. Mostly what I like about them is that men like them and it seems so easy to please them.

Maybe, I think with growing concern, *I don't love giving them because I'm not good at it.*

When I am dressed and ready to leave, he asks when he can see me again. I suggest a weekday if that's ever an option for him, realizing that I want to reserve my limited weekend time for #6, and he asks about the coming week. Is it a bad sign that I don't want to be wanted this badly by him, that I put him off by telling him that scheduling is a challenge for me and I will have to get back to him? He dons a scruffy parka and old sneakers to walk me to the subway. On the walk, he holds my hand and grins at me. I like him – he's kind, educated, isn't into playing games – but holding hands feels like too much familiarity too soon.

CHAPTER 32

Hair Removal 101

I am not yet accustomed to having open pockets of weekend time, having filled my Saturdays and Sundays for the past eighteen years with swimming lessons, birthday parties, and trips to the zoo. Now that I can do whatever I want without having to entice Michael or the kids, it seems as if I am magnetically drawn to activities that make me pine for my family. I make a mental list of neighborhoods I've wanted to explore and restaurants I've wanted to try so that the free time feels like a gift instead of a reminder of all that is being stolen from me.

"You know what I've never done before and have always wanted to do?" I say to #6 as we meander through a Thai cultural festival in Union Square on Saturday afternoon. It's a beautiful late fall day, so the square is teeming with people. "I know it's not terribly exciting, but I've always wanted to ride the tram over the East River to Roosevelt Island and have never made the time to do it. Any interest?" I ask.

"Sure, let's go check that off your bucket list," he says, smiling.

Time is ours to fill, a notion that is both liberating and intimidating.

We take the subway to midtown and then walk a few blocks east to the tram. I am delighted when it rises high over the river. We press ourselves against the glass to look down as he points out sites and orients me. It takes only a few minutes to get there, and when we disembark, I ask if we can explore, having never been on this small island so close to our own. He's usually game for whatever I suggest as long as we are outside. We walk to a monument on the island and he explains the history of it as we sit on a stone ledge in the sun, Manhattan on one side and Long Island City on the other. He lies down and rests his head in my lap, and I am pleasantly surprised by this rare display of affection from him. When the sun starts to dim, we agree that we are starving and realize we are only a few stops away from a Thai restaurant in Queens that we've wanted to try. While we wait for a table, he heads to the restroom. The hostess approaches me to say that she has a table ready, but can't seat us unless we're both here.

"No, it's OK, we're both here. My, um, my . . . he just went to the restroom, he'll be right back," I stammer.

I squeeze my eyes shut in embarrassment, realizing I could have just called him my friend, that she wasn't seeking an explanation of who we are to each other. Who are we to each other anyway? On the outside we look like a middle-aged couple who've been married beyond the point of anyone caring, but the novelty of being out and about with a man who is not my husband is still very real to me. When he returns a minute later, I tell the hostess,

"OK, he's back, we can sit now," as if we have some secret under-standing of who "he" is.

Later that night, talking in his bed before I have to head home, I sigh and tell him, "I need to up my blow job game. I want you to know that I know, lest you think I'm unaware."

He lets out a long, soft chuckle, asking why I just said that out of the blue.

"I was just thinking about it. I'm not good at giving blow jobs, I need to improve. I'm a single woman and men love blow jobs. I'm on the case," I say earnestly. "And don't respond. If you tell me I'm good, I'll know you're lying and if you tell me I'm not I'll be insulted. So whatever you're about to say, bite your tongue."

"Well, I was just going to say you could use your teeth a little less," he says.

"What did I just say? I don't want feedback, I just want you to know I'm actively engaged in improving my skills. And I'm really sorry I'm not as old as you are and still have all my teeth," I say.

"Hey, while we're talking about things we want to get better at, you know what I would find such a huge turn-on?" he asks, and I brace myself. "If you shaved all the hair from your pussy."

"All of it? 100 per cent?" I ask.

"Yes, that would be so sexy," he says.

"First of all, no one shaves all their hair off. I would cut my vagina and the idea of how itchy it would be growing back in makes me feel like I have poison ivy. Second, it would have to be waxed, which seems unbearably painful as well as humiliating. I don't wax, the pain of it is barbaric," I say.

"I'd come hold your hand," he offers.

"How generous of you! Yes, that's exactly what I want, for you to see me naked and splayed open on a table while I writhe in pain and cry like a baby. For *hair removal*," I say.

"So many women do it, how bad can it be?" he asks.

"Bad," I say.

"Just think about it," he says.

"OK, I will contemplate putting myself through extreme pain to present you with a smooth pussy that will make me look like a child," I say.

*

The next day, despite my best efforts to remain stalwart in my position on the removal of pubic hair, I google the difference between waxing and sugaring. I am torn, wanting to remain true to my own ideals of beauty and sex appeal but not confident my ideals work for the men for whom I want to appeal. Two out of seven men I've slept with have asked me to go hair-free; the first, #5, I was often wary of and didn't want to alter either my thinking or my body on his behalf. But #6 asks for little from me and gives me so much – feeding me, wanting me to come before he does, buying me gifts big and small that he knows will make me smile or solve a problem. I could do it not because he's asked me to but because I want to give him a gift, temporarily change a part of my body for the sole purpose of pleasing him. If I think of it that way, as a gift that I have the autonomy to give, I don't have to feel that I am sacrificing my standards of sex appeal for his.

Ever since the first time I had my bikini line waxed when I was fifteen, I have waxed only under duress. The hot, sticky slathering on of wax, the slapping on and pressing of the paper, the bracing for the ripping off, over and over again, on top of the abject humiliation of lying with my legs spread while a beautician frowns at the seemingly endless amount of dark, coarse hair she has to rip off: no, thank you. But it's been decades since I've done it and surely there have been improvements to make the process more efficient and less painful. Plus, I've given birth three times, so obviously my pain threshold is not what it was when I was an innocent teenager who had no idea what true physical agony felt like.

I fall down a deep rabbit hole, reading endless reviews of sugaring salons versus waxing salons and decide to book a sugaring appointment for complete bikini hair removal at a salon around the corner. I take a screen grab of the appointment and text it to #6, adding, "I hope you're happy." He sends back a happy face emoji in which if I look hard enough I'm certain I can see a drooling, oversexed teenage boy.

"Ugh, the things we do for love," I write back, and then immediately realize my mistake. "Well, not love, just for sex," I quickly clarify.

"You're going to be a convert, you'll see. You'll love how smooth it is," he texts.

I tell him he will be the first to know if that turns out to be true.

The next evening, I show up at the salon already in a cold sweat. I anxiously ramble to the young, bored technician that I'm newly single and I understand this is what men want now but back in the day when I was last single women wore their bushes with pride. By the time I am using one hand to hold the skin in my pubic area taut for her so she can get every last hair and the other hand to bite down on to distract myself from the pain, I am so miserable and embarrassed that I can't imagine sinking any lower. Then, she tells me to roll over and hold open my butt cheeks and I realize this is actually a bottomless well of mortification and physical torture. She keeps promising that there's just a little more to go, all while repeatedly pressing and ripping and asking robotically if I am doing OK.

"Define OK," I say.

"Just tell me to stop if you can't take it anymore," she says impatiently. Finally, she adds the words I have been waiting for: "OK, all done. It won't be as bad next time. There was just *so much* to remove today." She emphasizes the words "so much" to fully drive my humiliation home, holding aloft the hairy, sticky ball of sugaring paste in her hand like it might bite her.

I roll over and sit up, catching my reflection in the mirror across the room, horrified that my face is flushed and damp, my hair a messy halo around my face. I am trying to salvage what little self-respect I have and also make her see that I am not as unmanageable from the neck up as I am from the waist down, though it seems hopeless at this point.

"I'm curious," I say. "Am I the worst client you've ever had?"

She shakes her head.

"Not the worst," she says. "Some people ask me to stop and then walk out, so you did OK."

"You know, I've given birth three times. Vaginally. So I'm no

stranger to pain," I say, because now I can't stop trying to prove
to her that I am not only not weak but also that I'm self-aware.
She hands me an ice pack and suggests I lie down for a few minutes
with it wedged between my legs and then, blissfully, I am alone.
If I could throw my clothes on and skulk out of this place I would,
but of course I have to face her again at the front desk as I pay
for the torture I just endured and throw in some exfoliating products she says will help maintain my new smoothness.

I text #6 as soon as I leave, "Worse than expected. I kind of hate
you right now."

"Come over, I'll make you feel better," he texts.

"As if I would give you the reward of seeing it now," I write,
and walk home alone to tend to my sore vagina and bruised ego.

CHAPTER 33

Definitely Not a Good Morning

When I trek back to Brooklyn for a weekday tryst, #7 doesn't notice my newly bald hairstyle. #6 was delighted and appreciative when he saw it days ago, admitting that he had been very surprised, disappointed even, when he discovered during our first sexual interlude that I had any pubic hair at all. Now I don't know which is worse, his initially distasteful opinion of my pubic hair or #7's total unawareness of it.

#7 tells me that he's made a reservation with a group of his friends for New Year's Eve at a local restaurant and he's added a seat for me. New Year's Eve is weeks away and it feels too soon for me to spend such a momentous occasion with him and his friends, and alarming that he would want me there. If I had plans with my friends, which I sadly do not, the last thing I would want is a date to accompany me.

"Can I see a picture of your ex?" he asks suddenly. "I want to see what I'm up against."

"You're not up against him," I say. "That's why he's the ex. You sure you wouldn't prefer photos of other people I'm dating? Your actual competition?"

"Sure, show me them too," he says.

"No, I'm kidding. Here, I'll show you one photo of Michael and then we're moving on," I say, finding an old family photo on my phone and handing it over for him to see.

After a few moments of studying the photo, he lies back with a satisfied smile and says, "OK, I'm happy. I'm better-looking than he is."

I know he is waiting for me to agree with him, but I'm speechless. I don't think he's better looking, and anyway, does he really think he has a right to assert an opinion of the man I've been with for decades, the father of my kids? I feel instinctively protective of Michael and embarrassed for #7 that he is comparing himself.

After a few moments of awkward silence, I start looking under his quilt for my clothes, both to make a statement and because I have to get home. He asks if I can stay for a late lunch but I look at my watch and shake my head. He laments that he never properly feeds me, asking if I can come over for dinner and spend the night, that he's dying to cook for me and have a whole night with me. I am noncommittal, saying I don't have many chances to be out for the whole night, but it'll happen eventually.

Fortuitously (or, as it turns out, unfortunately), the next week Hudson asks if he can go with a friend to his country house for the weekend and I ask Michael if he can take Georgia for an extra night. I have become maximally efficient with my windows of free time, so I offer #7 Friday night for the dinner and sleepover he has requested and save my Saturday night for #6. All week, #7 texts me with updates to his menu, verifying what I like to eat and what wine I would like with it and telling me how excited he is. On Friday afternoon, he texts me as he counts down the hours until my arrival, telling me he's at the butcher asking for a special cut of meat for a special date and at the wine store asking for a special bottle of wine. I am both touched by his extravagant preparations and put off by his enthusiasm. I want to be wanted, but this feels too easy, like there's no chase at all. Also, I'm perplexed, wondering if he really likes me or just likes the idea of me, needing someone special in his life at all times.

I ask him where his daughter will be for the night and he tells me she's going to hang out with a friend and will be home very late. I worry that she will feel uncomfortable with my staying over, as I wouldn't dare do the reverse and have a man stay in my home with my kids around, but he insists she's fine with it, that she hated his ex-wife and thinks I'm really sweet. I admire his openness with his daughter but also wish he would protect her from having to know so much about his private life. Also, there's a level of invest-ment he's putting into my sticking around that is starting to make me feel like a cornered animal.

When I arrive at his apartment that evening, he opens the door with a broad smile and instructs me to sit at the small kitchen table and pour myself a glass of wine while he finishes cooking. He bustles from the stove to the refrigerator, explaining he's not quite used to this kitchen yet. Finally, he presents me with a plate of sliced steak with grilled mushrooms, roasted potatoes and steamed asparagus. I tell him that I am impressed and appreciative and he beams. Having a man cook me a meal with such care, being taken care of by being served dinner – that will never grow old for me.

As we eat, he tells me that he's made plans for us for the night. A salsa band will be playing at a bar he frequents with his friends and he's excited for me to meet his gang. I murmur that it sounds like fun, but truthfully, it doesn't. I don't know him well enough to meet his friends and being with them at a noisy neighborhood bar sounds like the nights in college that were my least favorite. He is brimming with enthusiasm though and tells me that his friends are excited to meet me, so I smile and go along with it.

We walk a block to the bar and he greets his friend Jay, who is standing outside smoking a cigarette. Jay wraps me in a hug, telling me that #7 has told him so much about me. The bar is fairly empty and the band doesn't start for an hour, so #7 tells Jay we will return in a bit and we walk a few doors down to another, smaller bar, where he orders himself a tequila on the rocks. At his place we drank the entire bottle of red wine and started a second bottle with dinner and I'm not sure how many glasses I drank, so I order a club soda. We chat with a few people he introduces me to at the bar until he suggests we head back to the first bar, where the band will play. Bar hopping is another activity I haven't done since my college days and I still don't get what about it is supposed to be fun.

When we return to the first bar, it is packed. We have to squeeze through a throng of people to reach his friend Abby, an attractive brunette around my age, who is waiting for us. #7 orders another tequila and I order another club soda. He leaves me with Abby while he talks to a small group of people nearby, saying he really wants me to get to know her. Abby is friendly but seems wary of me. He's mentioned her to me frequently and told me she's his absolute closest friend, but now she's telling me that she moved here from the West Coast a few years ago and I am surprised to learn they haven't known each other very long. I ask Abby as many questions as I can come up with to keep the conversation going while she remains fairly uninterested in me, and I am relieved when #7 returns to us. I see him catch her eye but can't interpret the meaning of the look that passes between them. *Have I just been approved or rejected?* Before I can decide, a sudden dousing of cold liquid down my shirt and into my lap makes me jump up. #7's friend Dylan, who can't be more than 25 years old, has spilled his entire mug of beer on me and is slurring out an apology as he tries to grab napkins and pat my chest dry.

#7 looks at me in dismay and then sternly tells Dylan he's had enough to drink and should go home. Dylan is too close to me, apologizing over and over with his yeasty breath, and #7 gets angry, pulling him away from me and demanding that he leave. I say that I'm fine and not to worry about it, but #7 is upset, shaking his head and repeating that this is totally unacceptable. I can't help but feel that Abby isn't at all sorry. When Dylan finally makes his exit, #7 turns sympathetically to me, asking if I want to leave since I'm wet and probably uncomfortable. This time I don't sugarcoat it, I tell him I am eager to leave. We say goodbye to Abby and again hug Jay near the door and walk the block home.

"Isn't Abby great?" he asks. "She's my best friend."

"Yes, I know, you did mention that," I say in a tight voice, wondering as with myself which version of her he likes more, the actual Abby or the idea of her.

When we get upstairs, I peel off my wet, sticky clothes and throw them in a corner. I am soaked through my bra and underwear, so I strip down completely and he gets me a washcloth.

"I hope you like the scent of beer as much as you like my usual rose oil," I say.

"I like your smell no matter what it is," he says, kissing me a little more sloppily than I would like. I run through the evening in my mind, calculating how many drinks he consumed.

"You are so beautiful," he murmurs as he pulls a condom on. When he gets on top of me and buries his face in my hair, he whispers, "You know, our mutual friend thinks we should get married." It takes me a minute to understand that he means Dr. B, and I am appalled and horrified.

Rising from the bed to use the bathroom, which is down the hall, I ask when his daughter will be home and he says not until very late. I suggest that he check in with her before we go to sleep, but he insists that she's fine so I decide that I have time for a quick naked run to and from the bathroom, not having any clothes here that are easy to throw on. I grab my toiletry bag and head down the dark hall. In the narrow bathroom, I take out my contact lenses and wash the makeup from my eyes, wiping dry on the small, well-worn hand towel next to the sink. I hear #7 pass by the bathroom on his way to the kitchen and I quietly open the bathroom door to step into the shadows of the hallway, standing naked as I brush my teeth, silhouetted by the light from the bathroom behind me. I see him in the kitchen leaning into the open fridge, appearing to pick at leftovers from dinner and eat with his fingers straight from the plastic containers. I'm about to comment about his late-night snack, but when I squint my eyes to get a better look and he slowly turns his head toward me, I realize with horror that it's not him, it's his daughter – the daughter who was not supposed to be home for hours.

I take a flying leap backwards into the bathroom, grabbing the door to pull it shut behind me. Not thinking about how narrow the bathroom is and panicked in my mad dash to get out of the daughter's sight, the heel of my foot slams into the bathtub and I land with a smashing thud on top of the flimsy wicker wastebasket – no doubt from the Dollar Store downstairs – wedged between the tub and the toilet. I had grabbed the shower curtain in a futile attempt to steady myself on the way down and succeeded only in bringing the entire rod and curtain down on top of myself. I lay now, jammed between the porcelain tub and the toilet with the garbage can pressing painfully into my back, a damp plastic shower curtain draped over me and toothpaste dripping down my chin onto my chest. I'm stuck, lodged between two large objects that have no give, and realize after taking a few deep breaths that the pain is not coming from the location of the trash can, it's coming from my ribs, which I'm immediately certain I've broken.

I catch my breath, hoping my shockingly loud crash followed by the fall of the shower rod will bring #7 running to help me, but the apartment remains eerily silent. I slowly wiggle myself forward an inch at a time until I am out of the narrow sliver of space and can sit up, disentangling the shower curtain from my arms. I wince in pain as I try to rise to my feet.

"Shit, shit, shit, shit," I whisper to myself over and over again. A moment later there is a light tap on the door, which I assume is the daughter who has been waiting patiently to use the one bathroom in the apartment. I freeze.

"Sorry," I say finally, in the most cheerful, sing-song voice I can muster. "I'll be out in a minute."

She doesn't say anything and I don't hear footsteps, so I am unsure if she's waiting at the door for me to exit.

I push the rod, which had been secured by suction to the walls before I disturbed it, back into place, recoiling in pain as I lift my arms and cause another flash of pain to sear across my ribcage and down my legs. I right the trash can and pick up the used Q-tips, dental floss and dirty tissues that spilled out when I landed on top of it and are both on the floor and pressed into my lower back. Finally, satisfied with my cleaning job, I survey the room, desperately seeking something to use as a cover when I bolt back to the bedroom – but the only towel I see is the small hand towel I used a moment ago. I give it 50:50 odds that #7's daughter is standing mere inches away from me on the other side of the door, curious to see me emerge. I step back to the shower, deciding the only solution is to take the flimsy shower curtain off the hooks and wrap myself in it, and almost cry with relief at seeing a bath-size towel that must have fallen into the tub during my ordeal. I pluck it out of the tub, wrap it around myself, open the door and attempt to walk out in a ladylike fashion, all but ready to curtsy to the daughter waiting for me. Thankfully, she's not there, so I dash to #7's room and slam the door shut behind me so she will know the bathroom is now available and I can get #7's attention.

No such luck. He is lying naked on his back on the bed, exactly where I had left him minutes earlier, and he is snoring. Loudly.

"Mark," I say sharply.

He continues to snore.

"Mark," I say again, this time more urgently, pressing on his shoulder. "Wake up!"

"Oh hey," he says sleepily, blinking his eyes open and smiling up at me. "Sorry, I must have fallen asleep."

"Yes, I see that. Your daughter is home," I hiss at him. He continues to grin moonily at me, thanking me for letting him know. I remind him that he assured me she wouldn't be home for hours.

"I guess I was wrong," he says simply, fueling my rage.

"Yes, well do you remember that I suggested you check with her? She's home and I was marching around the apartment completely naked," I say indignantly.

He laughs, reaching for his phone, and then says, "I don't think she saw you. She would have texted me by now to yell at me if she did."

"OK, well, forget her for a minute, I jumped to get out of her line of sight and fell and broke my rib. Maybe multiple ribs."

He laughs again, which enrages me, so I continue, "I'm serious. It hurts to breathe and I'm in pain."

"So sorry," he says. "I'm sure you'll be fine."

Within seconds his eyes have fluttered closed and he is snoring again.

I contemplate my options, desperately wanting to leave this apartment and be in my own bed, but it's too late at night for me to attempt to get home. I lie flat on my back under the covers and pray that my ribs are just bruised and will feel better in the morning.

#7's breathing is a raggedy cacophony and his blissful dream state is an affront to me. I lie absolutely still, gently nudging him away whenever he attempts to throw an arm around me, focusing on shallowly breathing in and out to avoid disturbing my ribs. My heart is racing and I know sleep will not come to me; I'm angry at #7 and wounded and mad at myself for being here in the first place when my better instincts told me #7 was not for me. By the time daylight starts to gently streak its way across the room, his breathing has quieted and I finally drift off. I hear him move in his sleep and then feel the bed shift as he rises from it, but I am not ready to greet him or the day, so I stay still and feign sleep. I hear him move around the kitchen, banging cabinets open and closed as he makes coffee, and then the familiar and welcome sound of the coffee machine burbling. A few minutes later he climbs back into bed. I open my eyes to peek and see he's got a mug of coffee and his iPad, so I try to fall asleep again. I dream that I am in a park with Georgia and she falls from the top of the slide, and I jerk awake, which makes me gasp with the pain the sudden movement has caused.

"Good morning, beautiful," he says, oblivious to my despair, looking lovingly at me.

"No, definitely not a good morning. I'm exhausted," I say, lobbing my words at him. "I was awake all night. My rib is broken and I'm sorry to report that you were snoring very loudly."

I glare at him. I know that I'm being ill-tempered and mean, but the innocent look in his eyes infuriates me. He responds nonchalantly that he doesn't snore. I snort, informing him that he's sadly mistaken, that he snores and not gently either, and that if he thinks I'm exaggerating about my rib, I am not, that I'm certain it is broken. It occurs to me that he might be someone who snores when he's drunk but not otherwise and that he truly is unaware of it. He offers to bring me coffee and says he's sorry about my rib, stroking my hair and then heading off to the kitchen.

I gratefully accept the lukewarm coffee and tell him I need to go home, but he asks if we can eat at a brunch spot he loves across the street before I leave. Thinking about a strong, hot cup of coffee, I nod my head. The café is crowded so we take two seats at the bar. I tell him I am really embarrassed by the scene with his daughter the night before, that no teenage girl wants to see a naked woman her dad is dating meandering around the apartment at night, but he insists she didn't see me or he would have gotten an earful from her by now. She texts him then to say she's hungry and he tells her to come across the street to the café so he can give her money to buy food. Before I can escape to the bathroom to avoid her, she is next to us, holding out her hand for the $20 bill he's reaching out towards her. I smile at her and say good morning.

"Are you OK?" she asks, looking intently at me.

"Yes, I'm fine thanks," I say quickly, averting my eyes.

"That's good," she says. "I wasn't trying to rush you out of the bathroom last night. It's just that I heard a huge crash and then absolute silence. I thought someone had died in there. I was so relieved when I knocked and you answered."

"I'm sorry I scared you. I slipped. It sounded more dramatic than it was," I say quietly, meeting #7's bemused gaze with narrow, angry eyes. I am too overtired and cranky to soften my anger and I dare him to find me a hot catch after this sleepover. When I leave him with a perfunctory kiss a few minutes later, I know that I will not be seeing him again.

CHAPTER 34

Onward

I rally, despite my broken rib situation, lest I lose a precious Saturday night. #6 and I decide to see the Freddy Mercury biopic and I invite him to stay over at my place after, as long as he feels confident he can give my ribcage a wide berth. He enthusiastically agrees.

At the theatre, he produces a clementine from each pocket for a snack, which makes me laugh. He is always eating clementines, throwing peels in small garden plots we pass on the street, claiming it's permissible because they're biodegradable. I fuss every time, appalled that he appears to be throwing trash in the bushes. He's over-the-top eco-conscious, recycling even the small pieces of foil that are wrapped around Hershey's Kisses. During the movie, he keeps his hands in his lap but occasionally reaches over to place a hand on my knee, withdrawing it after a brief moment, or placing his hand over mine and then putting it back in his own lap. His touches are fleeting but so gentle and intentional that I feel a small thrill with each one.

Onward

Back at my apartment, which he likes to call The Four Seasons compared to his "Shiteau", he asks for a clean towel and sets up a makeshift massage station on my bed. He produces a tube of coconut lotion from his bag and instructs me to lie down, saying it is his sole mission to take care of me. I remind him about my rib and he promises to be gentle. He is methodical, making sure not to miss a spot on my body and to give equal treatment to both sides. Every couple of minutes, he asks me how he is doing. I suggest that the only improvement would be if he could stop talking, that we should keep this professional. Ever since I got a massage when I was at a spa with Jessica and the masseuse made me open my eyes to look at a photo she kept in her pocket of a sighting she insisted she had of the Virgin Mary, I have believed silence during a massage is key.

"I don't want to get a bad Yelp rating. If I give you a happy ending, will you give me more or less stars?"

"Depends how happy it is. Now shhhhh," I say, closing my eyes again.

When he has worked all the way down to my toes, his hands make their way back up my legs, slowly, teasingly, as he massages my inner thighs and finally puts his finger inside of me. He lingers there until I roll onto my back, sucking in my breath in pain as I do, having forgotten about my rib.

He strokes his erect penis against me, starting to enter but then pulling out and telling me to hold on so he can get a condom, but his penis, warm and hard, is still pressing against me.

"Please, no condom, I just want to feel you inside of me," I say.

He pauses and looks hard at me.

"Promise that you'll be safe with any other partner you may have?" he asks.

"Yes, I promise, everyone else will use a condom," I say. "Please."

This man is so methodical, inflexible with his routine and self-made rules, that I know what I am asking requires him to take a leap of faith, to trust me and to go outside his comfort zone. He asks again if I absolutely promise. I solemnly vow that I will and he pushes hard inside of me, both of us inhaling sharply at the same moment. The condoms are essential, but there is no denying that they dull the sensation for both of us. This skin-to-skin contact feels totally different, and I can tell that he feels it too. Whatever relationship is developing between us has just been kicked up a notch, as this particular degree of intimacy will be reserved for just the two of us, even if we date and sleep with other people.

*

On Monday morning, I call Lauren for advice on how to get rid of #7.

"Is this a real question? You broke a rib in his bathroom while he lay passed out drunk on his bed. You just move on," she says.

I demur, saying I don't want to hurt his feelings.

"Do you owe this man something that I don't know about?" she asks, knowing I do not.

I confess that I'm feeling too wimpy to call him so she tells me not to, that a text will suffice and that ghosting under these circumstances would even be fine. I call her a bully, but thank her for the pep talk and write him a brief text: "It's been great getting to know you, but I feel like you're looking for a relationship while I want something more casual, and our different intentions make me feel like this isn't going to work. I wish you all the best in finding the special someone you're looking for, she will certainly be lucky to have found you."

I feel a load off my shoulders after I hit the send button and walk out into the cold, bright day to see if my favorite baker is at the farmers' market so I can treat myself to the sourdough bread that I will likely eat in its entirety, slathered with salted butter, by tomorrow to celebrate my extrication from #7.

By the time I hit the market, there is a text from him.

"This is the first time I've been dumped by text," he writes.

I blanch at having been called out for something I have to agree wasn't the best choice to begin with.

"Sorry," I write back, pulling up short next to a pile of carrots at a tented stall so that I'm not in the flow of foot traffic. "I find it easier to be clear in writing. I trip over my words when I'm nervous and I really wanted to explain."

He asks me to clarify, asking bluntly if what I'm saying is that I don't want to see him again because I think he's more into me than I am into him.

"Well, more into the idea of me perhaps than the actual me. I just don't think our feelings align," I write, but he wants further clarification, asking why I would think that.

"Maybe when you whispered in my ear on Saturday night that Jill thinks you and I should get married," I respond.

"What? I never would have said anything like that!" he writes back.

"I promise, you said it. You'd had a lot to drink so maybe you don't remember. But I was pretty shocked, so I am certain of what I heard. You also think you don't snore. Just something to think about."

He seems angry in a passive-aggressive way and won't let the subject go, so I wish him well again and abruptly end the conversation.

I text Dr. B, aka Jill, right away: "Thanks so much for setting me up with Brooklyn Lawyer. He's a good guy, but not for me. Also, just out of curiosity, did you tell him that you hoped we would get married?"

"What? No! Why would I have said that? Onward," she writes.

CHAPTER 35

Thanksgiving

Amidst the sadness and tension between Michael and I over how to navigate our first holiday season as a fractured family, there is one significant bright spot. Hudson has responded to one of Michael's notes and they have arranged to meet at a nearby coffee bar before we all walk to our synagogue to watch Georgia sing Thanksgiving songs with the children's choir.

After Hudson leaves, Georgia says that her stomach hurts and she can't go. She looks heartbreakingly small and sorrowful, so I gently tell her that we will stay home. She has been adept at going with the flow, but I can see when the mixed-up world of her family drags her to a place in which she yearns to retreat. It is painful enough that her father no longer lives with us, but the mystery of why her brother and sister have cut off contact with him is beyond her capacity to understand. Usually I can propel her forward through the routines and events in her life, but right now, I don't have it in me. Anxious about Hudson's meeting with Michael and knowing that tomorrow, Thanksgiving, will be loudly populated by my family and notably absent Michael – the first time in 26 years we won't be together on this favorite holiday of his – has left me feeling weary and craving a retreat too.

I await Hudson's arrival back home as I fold around Georgia on the sofa, watching *Frozen* for the umpteenth time. The more time that passes, the higher my hopes rise that Hudson and Michael are having a productive conversation that connects them to each other again. The last time they talked was nine months earlier, at a diner the week after we learned of Michael's affair. Hudson had told Michael that he didn't want further contact with him and that if we divorced, he would live with me. His stubborn streak combined with his intense loyalty has made him stick to his word beyond the point of reason. I had retained little hope of their reuniting anytime soon, so the sudden willingness to talk was a wholly unexpected and welcome surprise.

When Hudson walks in hours later, I play it cool. I know that he feels he is betraying me by extending an olive branch to Michael, even though I have told him over and over again that I want him to have his father in his life, that he could never betray me by having a relationship with him. I call to him from the family room to say hello.

He sticks his head in the room, looks at Georgia with concern and asks, "You OK, little G?"

"My stomach hurts," she says pitifully, and he nods his head sympathetically.

"How'd it go?" I ask, attempting casualness, and he mutters that it was fine, averting his eyes. I turn my attention back to Georgia to let him know he is dismissed from further inquiry. A few minutes later, Michael calls, breathless with excitement, telling me that Hudson had talked for hours about school and theatre and friends, like he had been saving it all up and it came pouring out.

"I'm so glad. I hope this is a new start. Did he indicate that he would see you again?" I ask.

"I walked him home and he was still talking, so he kept walking with me. It was so good to see him and hear his voice. When I first saw him, I cried. I couldn't believe how different he looked since I last saw him. He's changed a lot, he's grown and his face has morphed into a more adult face. It was amazing to see him but heartbreaking to know that I've missed so much," he says.

"Yup," I say, because what else is there to say? Missing almost a year of your son's life is indeed heartbreaking. He asks if he can stop by tomorrow before my family arrives to say a quick hello to the kids and drop off some treats for them.

"Yes, sure. I'm sorry that I can't invite you for dinner. I hope we can get to that point someday, but the older kids aren't there yet and then there's my family, most of whom you haven't seen since before all of this," I taper off. I had pleaded with him in the immediate aftermath of our separation to reach out to my parents, but his avoidance of them for five months until his visit to them in the summer, caused damage that I doubt will ever be undone.

The next night, after my family says their tenth goodbye and finally exits into the dark, cold night, and every roasting pan and serving platter has been dried and put away, I crawl exhausted into my bed and call #6 to say hi. We chat quietly in the dark, comparing menus and the chaos of the day, and then my bedroom door bursts open with Daisy rushing in, "Mom!" she says urgently, "I found this new curly hair product and brought some home for you to try. You're going to love it."

"Hang on," I whisper to #6, and then to Daisy, "Thank you so much, darling. Will you leave it next to my sink?"

"Yes, but you have to smell it," she says excitedly, walking around the bed to my side. When she gets closer and sees that I am holding the phone, she pauses, asking who I'm talking to.

"A friend," I answer, flustered. She frowns, so I continue, "A friend you don't know."

She looks at me with alarm so I hang up without even saying goodbye to #6.

"I was talking to a friend – well, a friend I've gone on some dates with, we used to live in the same building, that's how I know him," I say, rambling.

"I don't care how you know him, Mom, I can't believe you didn't tell me you were dating. What else are you keeping from me?" she asks, her voice rising.

"It's not that I've been keeping this from you, I didn't feel the need to tell you. I'm entitled to privacy, and this is private," I say, attempting to delineate boundaries for us where they had not existed before.

"I hate being here so much," she says angrily. "Home doesn't feel like home anymore. You tell me so much about you and Dad, it feels unfair for you to pick and choose what parts of your life you're going to share with me."

"Are you angry that I'm dating or angry that I didn't tell you?" I ask.

She pauses, the fury and hurt in her luminous eyes apparent even in the dark.

"Both. It's too soon. You've been single for like five minutes," she says, rolling her eyes.

"It may be too soon for you, but it's not for me. For the record, it's been nine months. The alternative is that I wallow in misery and stay home. You don't have to be part of my finding my way, but you might consider what the alternative would look like," I say.

"Mom, I want you to be happy, I really do," she says, miserably.

"So what should I do? What works for me or what works for you? You're off at school living your life as you should be. Do you want me to sit home alone on Saturday nights, waiting up for you on the few occasions you're here, so I can hear about the life you're living while mine has stopped?"

"Yes! That's exactly what I want," she shouts.

I understand that beneath her irrational words are rational feelings of anger, hurt and betrayal.

"I'm sorry, Daisy, I know this is really hard," I say, watching her back as she walks away and slams my door behind her, but my voice is more condescending than I intend for it to be, as if there are things she just can't understand and I'm tired of feeling I have to explain them to her. I know it would likely defuse her anger if I were to follow her and wrap her in a hug, but I'm too angry myself and who is here to defuse my anger? If I am to be the repository of Daisy's rage, then Michael has to be the repository of mine. It all has to stop somewhere and it seems fair to me that he should be the end of the line.

I text him, tapping away at my phone furiously, "Daisy is broken-hearted, so upset that I'm dating. In her mind, I may as well be having an affair. This is not what I imagined my daughter's first time home from college would look like. I want you to understand all the ways in which we suffer because of you. Actions have consequences, Michael, and unfortunately we are all impaired by your actions even on what should be happy occasions. Did you ever once stop to think about how your affair would affect the rest of us?"

"I'm sorry, Laura," he writes back. "I know how excited you've been to have Daisy home and now she's taking her anger out on you because you're a safe person. It's not fair and it's my fault. I wish I could help. You're a great mom and are single-handedly getting our kids through this terrible time. They're so lucky that you're their mom."

Tears spring to my eyes. Finally, a real apology. I have waited months for this, wondering how our trajectory might have been different had he shown regret and compassion from the beginning instead of anger and resentment.

"That doesn't ease the blow of Daisy's anger, but it means something to me that you've acknowledged how hard this has been on me," I write.

"As much as you're dealing with now, just know that I will forever have to live with the devastating knowledge that I traumatized the people I should have protected. You didn't deserve this Laura," he writes.

I put the phone down and weep. It's been so long since Michael has been recognizable to me, and here is a shred of him that matches up with the Michael I had fallen in love with, the Michael who had been gracious and loving and kind. I have been so incensed at him for upending my life, smoke pouring out of my ears when

I think of him, overwhelmed by fury and loss, that I have not allowed myself to admit that I miss him desperately. He had been my partner for 27 years and then he was gone, overnight. In this brief exchange of texts, I see him again, and the grief that it elicits feels unbearable. I miss him, I long for his friendship and his calming words, his optimism and support, but I understand too that our marriage is over, truly and irreversibly over. I don't want to be with him going forward, I want to go back in time and hold tight to all that was good between us for my entire adult life thus far. It's like seeing a ghost who has come to reassure me that I hadn't misunderstood who he had been all those years of our life together, that the essence of him is still in there.

I move through the next days in a new state of grief, trying to piece Daisy together before she leaves again, feeling a heavy sadness envelop me. I'm still angry but I can feel the anger being replaced by sadness, and I suspect that sadness and I can comfortably cohabitate in a way that anger and I have not been able to.

CHAPTER 36

Restoration of Faith

By the time Daisy arrives back home a few weeks later for her month-long winter break, Michael and Hudson are cautiously, tentatively, back in each other's lives. Michael and I agree that we will each separately spend a few days with the kids in the house upstate, but we will overlap for Christmas so that neither of us has to miss being with them. Georgia is delighted, Hudson is wary and Daisy is indignant that it appears everyone but her has forgiven Michael, and we're going to pretend we're one big happy family for the holidays. I assure her that we all have different timelines and definitions of forgiveness, but neither he nor I are willing to forgo this time with our kids. I know I will have to accept that she may choose not to be with us and it pains me to imagine her spot empty under the Christmas tree. I do my best to assure her that Michael and I have made leaps and bounds of progress since she was last with us together and to please give us a chance.

So here the five of us are on Christmas morning, the lopsided pine tree laden with twinkling lights and an overflow of brightly colored gifts stuffed beneath it, me in my fleecy pink bathrobe putting ancient Christmas albums on the record player and Michael snapping photos and refilling our mugs of coffee – for all intents and purposes, a family. Michael and I are on our best behavior with each other, nicer and more helpful than we ever were when we were married, working overtime to prove to the kids that this reorganized family does not have to be a tragedy. He stuffs piles of torn wrapping paper and bright red ribbons into garbage bags while I assemble the ingredients to make our traditional Christmas dumplings with my parents, who will arrive any minute. When we all sit down for dinner late that afternoon amidst steaming platters of pork dumplings, Michael is effusive in his praise, saying our dumplings get better every year, and I see my parents stiffen and then glance at the kids, trying to accept his presence for their sake.

When Michael leaves the next morning, I silently congratulate myself, thinking how far we've come, how much we put aside successfully for the benefit of our kids. Daisy takes only a few hours to break my reverie.

"Mom, I gave it a chance and I'm so glad you and Dad aren't fighting anymore, but I'm *never* doing this again. It felt so normal to be with you guys together, to be the family we were, and now I feel bereft all over again. It was a reminder of what we used to have that we will never have again. I feel worse than before," she calmly states, and now I see it clearly too. I'm not going to be able to pick and choose when we are a family the way we used to be, the kids need it to be one way or the other. Either it's over and they grieve and move on, or they get it back. Flashes of normalcy merely feel like a cruel taunt. I tell her I understand and thank her for trying.

A few days later, I take a train back to the city to spend New Year's Eve with #6, while Michael stays upstate to usher in 2019 with Georgia and Hudson, and Daisy heads off to visit friends. We had started an annual New Year's Eve celebration with Erika and her family nineteen years earlier when I was pregnant with Daisy, over the years adding five children to the mix who tumbled around in penguin-like snowsuits while we grilled shish kebab on the deck. This beloved tradition is yet another casualty of the collapse of our marriage and tugs at a worry I've had recently as I've considered the long-term effects of our split. We had a circle of friends with whom we spent time as a couple and as a family, but the perfect balance of spouses and children has been altered irrevocably.

I'm not worried about dividing up friends as I know some are steadfastly loyal to me, others to Michael, and yet others are struggling with how to embrace us both, which is what I want. I have never needed my friends more than I do now and I know the same is true for Michael – I may wish he spends the rest of his life bemoaning that he missed out on my sexual heyday, but I don't want him to cry about it alone. I do, however, miss being part of a posse as a couple and family. My friends always make me feel welcome and wanted on my own, but I've had to reluctantly accept that it's not the same as it was and I can't get it back – one more loss to swallow.

A few friends have invited me to come to their New Year's celebrations, but they will have younger kids in tow and I fear I will find it painful to be around them without Georgia in the mix.

Other friends have invited me to stop by with #6; but we haven't met each other's friends yet and doing so feels like a level of commitment for which we are not yet ready. We are on our own, which is how we like it at this point and what we can comfortably handle, safely nestled inside our little bubble for two.

*

#6 leaves his office in the late afternoon so we can meet at a theater for an early movie. It's pouring with rain as I walk through a deserted Washington Square Park to meet him. I am the only person standing by the fountain in the center as the park's street lamps flicker on. As I pause to take in the moment I feel a sense of peace descend on me; in the past I would not have slowed down long enough to experience this lovely stillness, the darkening sky, the rhythmic sound of the rain beating on the pavement. I am aware that I am present in a way I have not been in the past, but now I relish these moments of beauty and serenity.

Let the world stand still for a few breaths, I think.

A few minutes later, I see #6 waiting for me in the lobby, tickets in hand. He is so unlike Michael that sometimes I fret I'm attracted to him solely for the ways in which he meets those of my needs that Michael couldn't: he's always on time, is organized and prepared for every potential scenario – like a Boy Scout, he likes to say. Next to him, I'm a slacker, an odd and new experience for me but not entirely unpleasant, giving me the feeling that I'm laid-back and easy-going, two qualities no one has ever assigned to me. If I were to add up all the hours I had spent waiting for

Michael, I would probably get back entire months of my life. Time was a fluid concept to him, whereas for #6 it is fixed and one has to be accountable for it.

After the movie, we debate what to do next. We aren't intimate enough yet that we understand intuitively what the other wants, so it's a bit of a dance. We set off into the rainy night, pressing against each other under the big umbrella he's thoughtfully brought for us to share. We walk west to Hudson Street and peer into restaurants that beguile with their warmth and festive decor. The city feels like the park did a few hours ago, eerily quiet, and we are amongst the few who ventured out for a stroll. We pause outside of Red Farm, where there is usually an hours-long wait for a table, but tonight we see empty seats and agree this is just what we want – shrimp dumplings, crisp-skinned chicken, a cocktail for me.

Tucked into a cozy booth for two, I let #6 do the ordering, appreciating the way he orders food – expansively and generously, making sure there is enough of an assortment for us to share. Michael and I used to share food too, but he was notorious for absentmindedly eating both my share and his, so I always eyed him suspiciously as he ate to make sure there would be enough left for me. #6 is the opposite, serving me first and always saving the last bites for me too.

After dinner he consents to a taxi home because I'm convinced I will wash away in what has become a monsoon. At home, we light tall white candles I have set on the ledge of the bathtub and I sprinkle lavender bath salts into the water, turning off the lights and putting on quiet music Pandora has helpfully made into a "Romantic" playlist. #6 undresses and slides into the tub.

"I should have brought my snorkeling gear, this tub is so big," he says, lying back and watching me slip out of my clothes and attempt to climb gracefully into the deep tub, which is fairly impossible as I have to swing my leg high to get in and then teeter with one leg in and one leg out while I regain my balance. I have avoided bathtubs assiduously for as long as I can remember, afraid of wiping out on the slippery bottom and cracking my head on the marble edge, but ever since I took a bath to get ready for my first date with #6 at Tina's insistence, I have begun to appreciate its many merits.

No sooner have I gotten both legs safely inside than I hear my phone ring and see that it's a FaceTime call from Georgia, who probably wants to wish me a happy New Year. I catapult myself out of the tub, grabbing my phone and singing out, "Hello sweetheart!" As soon as I do, I realize my mistake: I'm naked and there's a naked man in the tub behind me and the room is aglow with candles. I quickly hang up, hoping she caught only a blur of me; she calls right back. I decline the call and call her back without using video. She asks me suspiciously where I am.

"I'm home. What are you up to?" I ask.

She tells me that Hudson went out with his friends and she and Michael went out to dinner and are now waiting for the ball to drop. Then she says the words that land with a thud on my heart, that she misses me.

"I miss you too, but I'll see you tomorrow and we'll do something special," I say.

"OK, but what did you do tonight? Are you OK? Are you lonely by yourself?"

Both moved and dismayed by her concern, I am proud of her for her compassion but sad that she feels she has to worry about me. I reassure her that I spent time with friends and am thrilled to be home now, dry and warm and snug, and she seems satisfied. I blow her kisses as I hurry to hang up the phone and turn it over so I don't have to see the screen again. I want to turn it off completely, but I don't like the kids not being able to reach me whenever they need to and dread the recriminations when I am accused of not being available because God forbid, I didn't come right to the phone. Fresh in my mind is my most recent debacle when Daisy's shower backed up with her alone at home, leaving inches of water that seeped into the carpet in her bedroom in the 45 minutes it took for me and #6 to have quick afternoon shake-off-Thanksgiving sex at his apartment. By the time I turned my phone over to find ten missed calls from her, a few from Michael and a couple more from the building's super, the shake-off sex was rendered null and void and my parenting acumen was on the line.

"OK, sexy bath scene take two," I say, jumping in without attempting grace this time. I lie back, closing my eyes and pressing my feet into his thighs to keep myself from sliding down.

"I love the look on your face when I enter you," he says, shifting toward me and watching me. He moves his hips as the water rises above us like ocean waves until I push him away so that he is lying against the tub and I am leaning forward to straddle him.

"Ah yes, so Laura is in control now," he says, raising his eyebrows.

I am still not used to talking during sex. I know that #6 finds it incredibly sexy, needs it even, my voice as tantalizing as the rest of my body, but I'm at a loss as to what to say. Giving words to my physical desire is like learning an entirely new language. When I try to talk dirty and use words like "cock" or "pussy", I pause before saying the words, uncomfortable and certain that my reluctance is more of a game-stopper than a turn-on. I visibly cringe when he uses the word "tits", finding it crass and demeaning, so that now he apologizes and corrects himself when he says it. He's asked what word I like in place of it and that perplexes me too: "boobs" sound childlike and "breasts" sound clinical. Is there another choice? The words "cock" and "pussy" are, surprisingly, growing on me when he says them, but when I use them they catch in my throat. Then again, using the words "penis" and "vagina" makes me feel like I'm giving an anatomy lesson, which is a turn-off even to me. Hasn't anyone come up with anything better yet? A world full of wordsmiths and the best we've got is a male rooster and a cat to describe our most intimate and mysterious body parts?

When I had sex in my married life, I wanted to come quickly so I could call it a night and go to sleep, but now I want sex to last as long as it can. Finally, when even my head feels like it's detached from my body and is gently floating in space, I let out an ecstatic sigh, arch back and then collapse forward onto him. I am still, again.

Now my other favorite part: I take his hand, place it over my pounding heart, and then I put my hand over his. We stay like this, hand over hand over heart, until my breath calms and I become aware again of where I am. I allow myself these few moments to revel in what feels like an epiphany in my body before turning my attention back to him.

He likes to wait to come until I have and the more times I can orgasm before he does, the happier he is, but I have become much more interested in the quality of my orgasms than the quantity. The ones that move up my body and consume it in its entirety – those are the ones I want, not just the ones in which I can feel the release but I'm otherwise largely unmoved. These bodily orgasms are life-affirming and transporting to the degree that when I open my eyes, I am often shocked to find myself in #6's room or in my own bed with my head hanging off the side across from where I thought I was. I appreciate that he wants to please me all the time, but I also want to please him.

I stand up and reach down for his hand, ready to leave the now-chilly water. We quickly pat ourselves dry and land dripping on my bed. I straddle him again and kiss his inner thighs, then move my tongue up the shaft of his penis and flick my tongue against the head, which is a recent trick I've picked up from *Cosmopolitan* magazine.

"You're teasing me again," he says and I laugh, but – and here's where a blow job really comes in handy – I don't have to say anything because my mouth is full and I can't talk! One of the surprises of sex with #6 is that it's not linear, it's not just a means to an end. He loves the process and sometimes wears himself out before he can come; whereas I worry that makes the sex a failure, he doesn't judge it by this one set of criteria. I am such a goal-oriented person, so have to adjust my thinking: if an orgasm is not the goal, then what is? Touch, words, sensuality, exploration, intimacy, vulnerability. I am learning that there is no bottom line in sex as I thought there was.

"You make me crazy, Laura," he says, as I climb on top of him, his rhythm becoming more persistent until he takes in a deep breath and pulses inside of me.

"Thank you," he says, when we have quieted down. I look at him with my eyebrows raised and he continues, "For restoring my faith in intercourse."

"What do you mean?" I ask.

"It's been a long time since I've had sex with a woman who loves it and gets as much pleasure as you do from it. Now I see it's possible for a woman to be empowered by her sexuality and her ability to orgasm. I'm in awe of it, all I want to do is please you," he says.

"Well then, you're welcome. And Happy New Year," I say, laughing, and then curl into a ball to sleep.

CHAPTER 37

Slimegate

With a sense of alarm, I admit to myself that I'm developing real feelings for #6, feelings that make it matter whether or not he becomes a more integral and consistent part of my life. I like how he reaches for my hand when we cross the street and a car turns too fast toward us. I like how he bought me a cashmere hat because I didn't have a warm hat even though I complain relentlessly about being cold. I like how he cooks dinner for me on Monday nights when Georgia is with Michael and sends me home with labeled containers of soup to eat for lunch during the week. And I like how he keeps a toothbrush for me in his medicine cabinet and conditioner under his sink that he calls "cream rinse" in the most old-fashioned way. I might be falling in love with him, but it's hard to say as I have no context for what falling in love at this point in my life should look like, and anyway, love is an intimidating word I am wholly unprepared to use. I am at a crossroads, not wanting to flee from him but also knowing that I don't have the wherewithal for a serious relationship.

As I ponder my plans for the upcoming weekend, I decide to test the waters. Georgia will be with me all weekend and Hudson is going skiing with a friend. I've invited Georgia's friend to sleep over on Friday night and I'm looking forward to making a fire and having a cozy night with the girls, but I've become accustomed to spending at least part of every weekend with #6 and I would like to see him too. I call Lauren for advice, asking if she thinks it's OK for me to invite #6 over for dinner on Friday night and introduce him to Georgia, just as a friend? I worry that it is too soon and too forward, the equivalent of a marriage proposal. She tells me not to overthink it and to proceed, that it's just dinner.

It takes about ten phone calls for me to work up the courage. Dinner itself isn't a big deal, but dinner with my kid? It feels like I'm kicking things up a notch, but this seems like a natural progression if we consider ourselves to be in a relationship. Finally, I bite the bullet. I'm standing in my bathroom and I squeeze my eyes shut and sit on the side of the tub.

"I was just thinking," I say, on the phone with him midday. "Georgia is going to be here Friday night with a friend, do you want to come over and we can maybe cook dinner together?"

"No thank you," he says without hesitation. "The last thing I want to do on a Friday night is stay in and make slime with your daughter and her friend."

I reel back as if I've just been slapped. I am silent and so is he.

"Well," I finally muster, "no one said anything about making slime, I had only mentioned making dinner, but OK, it was just an idea."

He says he has to get back to work and I hang up the phone.

My eyes fill with tears. I am not even sure what I want with him, but this had seemed like an organic extension of our path. I get it if he's not ready, but to speak of the possibility of spending time with Georgia with disdain is not something I can live with. I call Lauren again to let her know the conversation did not go well, that he most definitely does not want to meet Georgia or come over when she's here. I am hurt, but I am also confused, as maybe I don't want him further enmeshed in my life either. I don't want a boyfriend, I don't want to be married again, I don't want to live with a man, so do I just want a man who wants to meet my kids and be a bigger part of my life without actually meeting my kids or being a bigger part of my life?

Why am I so terrified to want more than that?

*

I go back on Tinder and Hinge. I've let the dating apps sit dormant on my phone these past months while I've been spending time with #6, but now I'm hankering again to see what kind of single men are out there, and I want to get back to the simple, fun part of dating that involved a lot of sex without a lot of complicated feelings.

A couple of weeks after the unfortunate slime conversation, as #6 and I are lounging in my bed early on a Sunday morning, I know that I have to address my recent wounds, unburden myself and clear the air. I would rather scare him away than keep him around while I harbor resentment and insecurity. I tell him how stung I was by his response to me.

"Oh boy," he says, sighing and staring up at the ceiling. "I'm sorry, I didn't mean to hurt your feelings, it's just the last thing I want to do after an exhausting week of work is hang out with a couple of eight-year-old girls."

"You're not making it better," I say quietly. "You've basically repeated the exact thing that offended me to begin with, just taking out the bit about making slime."

"You're right, I'm sorry. You caught me off guard when you asked me and I had a million things distracting me at work. That's a classic example of a moment when I should have hit the pause button and asked you if I could think about it and get back to you," he says.

"Fair enough, but the part that's bothering me is not that you didn't think about it but that you seemed so genuinely horrified by the suggestion of it. It was hard for me to work up the courage to ask you and being shot down like that really hurt and frankly confused me."

"Laura, at this point in my life I don't want to play daddy to other people's kids. I don't see myself standing on the sidelines of Georgia's soccer games, cheering her on."

"She doesn't play soccer and I didn't suggest that you play daddy. Georgia already has a father. I was just asking you to join us for dinner, not play a role in my family. But OK, you've made your feelings clear and now I understand that," I say.

"It's not about you, Laura, or your kids. I'm at a difficult place with my own kids right now, so it's impossible for me to imagine having relationships with someone else's kids. You're so in love with your children, you can't possibly understand," he says, still staring at the ceiling. "I suspect this will be the last time I look up at that crack on the ceiling."

He points to a spidery crack over the bed with a sad smile.

"Quite possibly," I say with an equally sad smile.

Yet, we manage to forge ahead, spending our weekends together when I don't have the kids, and talking on the phone every day when he calls me from work and again before he goes to sleep. There is a rhythm and an easiness to being with him, and we have sex that is thrilling and nourishing and continues to keep me intrigued. At the same time, I question myself: what does this mean, what are we to each other, shouldn't I still be having sex with lots of different men? Isn't it too soon for me to feel I'm settling down with only one man, especially when that man doesn't really want to be part of my life beyond my private relationship with him?

CHAPTER 38

Laura's Liberation Tour

I've maintained traditional views of monogamy and relationships throughout my life, firmly believing one relationship at a time takes tremendous effort and concentration and that part of loving someone is loving only that someone. All of my relationships had been goal-oriented though, existing to culminate in a potential future together. I understand the motivation I had at the time – I had been young and looking for a husband, craving a family. If I'm no longer seeking a settled life with a man, don't want a husband and already have a family, what's the point of continuing to be steadfast about my views on monogamy? When I casually dated #3 and #4 simultaneously over the summer, it had felt different, less substantial. Now that my relationship with #6 is something, ill-defined and shapeshifting but something weighty nonetheless, I need to rethink how I feel about being with one man at a time.

One evening at #6's apartment after he's cooked me a dinner of roasted sea bass he has professionally deboned and filleted himself, complete with cloth napkins and wine, I tell him I have a confession to make, that I have a coffee date later in the week with a man I met on Hinge.

"Ahhhh, she's back on her apps," he says with a wry smile and a sigh.

"I just wanted you to know. We've discussed that we're not exclusive with each other and I've promised you that I won't sleep with another man without using a condom. But we see each other enough that you should know."

He thanks me for my honesty, but wonders why I am going on this date, why I am active again on my dating apps after months in which I haven't been.

"Because I'm still curious about being with other people. We have great chemistry and I love being with you, but I don't want to be tied down by any one relationship. And," I pause here, closing my eyes to brace myself for the vulnerability I'm about to lay out for him, "I have strong feelings for you that only seem to be growing with time and I don't know what to do with them and I don't know if they're reciprocated. And they don't have to be, I'm not asking for a declaration of your feelings. I don't even know what I want, but I do know that I'm getting attached to you and it unnerves me, so I have to keep moving."

"Laura, here's how I think about it: you were on this journey before you and I started dating and you've just picked me up along the way. I see it as a caravan in motion. Let's call it Laura's Liberation Tour. You're driving along and you're seeking something. I'm just one stop on the tour. Keep going. If I try to stop you, you'll resent me and always wonder what's out there. So onward your LLT goes," he says.

"But what about you? Can you stick around while my tour continues or is this too much for you?"

He hesitates, then says he can stick around. His pause is long enough that I ask if it makes him uncomfortable or if he's perfectly fine with it. It seems impossible that he is so willing to share me, and if he is indeed so willing to, does he really care about me at all?

"I'm definitely jealous, but also intrigued by your power. I understand there's a risk here, that I might lose you to someone else you meet on your tour. But it's not right for me to try to stop you."

I find his lack of possessiveness remarkable and very attractive. I recognize that it's not that he's so confident I will keep coming back to him but that he respects the space and freedom I need to get my bearings right now. He sees me as a fully separate entity from himself, but he wants to know too if the same is true in reverse, how will I feel if he dates other women?

"Terrible," I say, and he laughs. I explain why I have a double standard, that our situations are completely different, that he didn't get married until he was forty years old and by that age in my own life, I had been married fifteen years and had three kids. He had years to sleep with different women and explore what he wanted in a sexual relationship, whereas I had none of that, so have to make up for lost time now. I admit that it's unfair and hypocritical, but emphasize that even owning up to that won't make me feel any less insecure or jealous.

"Would you want to know about it?" he asks.

"Yes, definitely. Wait no, definitely not. I don't know, don't do it and then I don't have to choose," I say, pouting, and he responds that it's unlikely he would anyway, that he's already having more sex with me than he's had in years and doesn't think he could handle more.

"OK, let's make a deal," I say. "Have sex with anyone you want, but not in Manhattan. Go out of town, go to another borough, just no one local."

"Would that make you feel better?" he asks.

"Yes, because then it won't be so easy for you to make it a regular thing. Enjoy your ferry ride to Staten Island," I say snarkily, and we both laugh.

CHAPTER 39

Confessions

I do not follow my own outer-borough rule and later that week, take the subway to the Upper West Side to meet potential #8 for coffee. He lives in Harlem, so this is equidistant for us and I'm thrilled to get out of my neighborhood lest I run into someone I know downtown. We had spoken on the phone after connecting on Hinge and our conversation was easy and he had laughed a lot. He doesn't have kids of his own but he enjoyed my stories of what it's like to be a parent who is surreptitiously dating, and since I always laugh uproariously at my own jokes and stories, I appreciate anyone who goes along with me.

I arrive at the café early so have time to shed my multiple winter layers and catch my breath before he arrives. When I'm sitting and trying to perfect my open-for-business-but-not-too eager face, I hear a loud and animated voice belt out, "Laura!" I look up and there is my friend Johanna with her warm smile beaming down at me.

"What are you doing here?" she asks.

"Ummmm," is all I can get out and my face immediately reddens, so she starts laughing, knowing that I am awaiting a suitor's arrival. I pick up my collection of outerwear so I can relocate my seat away from her, warning that despite my love for her, if she so much as even glances in my direction, she will be dead to me.

"Go to the back, I promise not to peek. You look beautiful by the way," she says and returns to her friend at the next table.

I settle at a table in the back of the restaurant where we will be safely tucked away. I recognize #8 right away when he comes in – he's got a huge smile, sparkling white teeth and is substantial, tall and broad. He spots me and heads my way, his sizable frame filling the space between tables. When he reaches me, I stand and he gives me a hug. This seems to be the standard greeting with men I've met online and it always reminds of the '80s TV show *The Dating Game*, when a couple would finally meet face to face after talking behind a screen and instantly embrace as if to claim their prizes. I glance in Johanna's direction and see that she is very determinedly averting her eyes, but still, I feel self-conscious. Johanna and her husband are amongst our closest friends and after all the time our families have spent together, I know it must be bizarre for her to see me with another man.

"You look just like your photos, but even prettier," he says.

"Why thank you," I respond, blushing. "Has it ever happened that you meet a woman who looks nothing like her pictures?"

"Oh yeah, all the time. First of all, the majority of women lie about their age," he says. "And I'm not talking about a couple of years, I'm talking more than a decade."

"I'd be too nervous to lie," I say.

"Actually," he says laughing, "I have a confession to make. I'm really 53 not 48 which it says on my profile." I purse my lips together and give him a quizzical look, so he continues, "So many women won't like your profile if you're over 50. The playing field gets way too small."

I ask if lowering his age has worked as he had hoped and he concedes that it indeed has and gestures to me as proof.

We've successfully broken the ice and can now get to the basics. He's never been married and he tells me a story about a woman he was engaged to who turned out to be pretty wacky, so I get the sense that he's not serious relationship material, which is just fine with me. When I see Johanna walk by our table on her way to the restroom with a hand shielding the side of her face so she can make it clear she isn't looking at us, I laugh. As the waiter clears our mugs, #8 tells me that he's had a great time talking to me and asks if we can see each other again.

"Yes, that would be lovely, thank you. Just one thing I have to be upfront about. I'm dating a lot right now, I like to be open about that from the beginning so there are no misunderstandings later," I say, blushing again. He laughs, so I ask earnestly, "Is that too much to share? I'm not suggesting you're looking for anything exclusive, I just have to say it or I'll worry I've been misleading."

"No, don't worry, I appreciate your being so open. And I'm dating lots of women too, so we're even. But while we're confessing, I may as well tell you something too," he says.

"What, you're not really 53, you're actually 83 and preternaturally youthful-looking?"

"Ha, no! I'm a recovering alcoholic. I've been sober for five years.

Some women find that unappealing, they want to be able to go out and let loose and drinking is a big part of that. I mean, I don't mind if you drink, I just want you to know why I won't."

I thank him for sharing with me, but let him know it's not an issue.

We head back outside into the cold. Walking next to him, I feel tiny. I don't think I come up past his shoulders. I have long since recognized that I like being smaller than men I'm dating, but I don't particularly like feeling like a child. We head down into the subway station together and he walks me to the downtown platform to say goodbye. We feel a rush of wind as the train zooms into the station and suddenly he is bending toward me, his lips pressing against mine. The doors of the train are already open and I smile at him as I hastily jump on before the doors close. There is something decidedly unromantic about being kissed in the middle of the day on a dirty subway platform under dingy fluorescent lights, but I guess the kiss goodbye is as mandatory as the hug hello?

That Sunday, as we clean up after a lunch of tuna niçoise salad at #6's apartment, he asks if I want to walk to the international grocery store where I love to peruse the aisles and get dinner ideas for the kids. I tell him that I can't, that I actually have to leave soon to meet a friend. He rattles off a list of my friends, asking who I am going to see: Lauren? Mara? Jessica?

I shake my head.

"Ah, I see. A friend," he says slowly. "A date?"

"Well, yes," I say sheepishly.

"And she's off!" he says with a bemused smile.

I give him a quick kiss goodbye before we have a chance to

launch into further conversation. I feel equal parts guilty and empowered, but my honesty has prevented me from being in the uncomfortable position of having to lie.

The sun is starting to go down, if it ever really came up at all – it's one of those winter days that feels like snow is about to blanket the city. I sit at a darkly lit tapas bar, order a glass of mulled wine, and contemplate how it is that I came to be sitting at a bar in the middle of a Sunday afternoon with a glass of wine, having just left one man's apartment to go and meet another. Where are my children? I should be home drinking hot apple cider, eating popcorn and playing an epic game of Risk with them. A year ago my life was perfectly ordinary, deceptively steady, centered around my family life that in actuality was only weeks away from combusting.

Thankfully #8 dashes in before I can get totally lost in my thoughts, which will swallow me whole if I give them room to grow. I am struck again by how large his physical presence is, how much of the small room both his solid build and dazzling smile take up. He rushes over, apologizing for being late, giving me a chaste kiss on the cheek and explaining that he has to go to a party after this and couldn't decide what to wear. I note his deep blue cashmere sweater and pressed jeans.

"So this is pretty weird, but the party I'm going to is actually a sex party and I've never been to one so I had no idea what would be appropriate to wear," he says.

"It seems to me that if you're going to a sex party, what you wear is totally beside the point, but OK, do tell," I say, my eyes popping open. He admits that he is nervous about the party and not sure what to expect, but that he has been dating a woman who is in an open marriage and that she has been trying to get him to come to one of these parties she and her husband host every month. He hasn't met the husband yet and all he knows is that there's a regular group of people who attend and they pair off depending on what they're looking for.

"Well, this is definitely out of my comfort zone, so I have no advice for you," I say.

"Yeah, mine too," he says laughing.

Having just loosened the reins on my policy about monogamy, I am now facing the opposite extreme, but who am I to judge? Maybe if Michael and I had had an open marriage, we would still be married, or maybe a sex party is the greatest thing ever. I can't imagine myself being so comfortable in a group that I could just let go, but who knows? If I've learned nothing else from this past year, it's that there's a lot less I know for sure than I thought I knew.

#8 promises to report back to me, and I advise that he work hard to try and get the details down as I will have a lot of questions. I stand to use the restroom and his eyes shoot down my body, linger, and then slowly work their way back up to my face.

"You look good in tight jeans," he says.

"You have sex party on the brain," I say and saunter off, knowing he is watching me.

When we part on the corner a few minutes later, bundled back into layers of winter clothes, he leans down to kiss me goodbye and I stand on my tiptoes so that I can put my hand behind his neck. The kiss, outside a row of brownstones whose

Christmas lights are still twinkling, is a vast improvement over the subway kiss.

As he heads down to the subway and I walk toward home, my phone rings. It's #6, who has likely waited what seemed to him like an appropriate amount of time before checking up on me. For all his encouragement that I go off and live my life freely, I suspect it's not a comfortable position for him to be in, just as he fairly pointed out it wouldn't be for me if the tables were turned. When I pick up the phone, he barely says hello before asking me about my date.

"It was nice, thank you for asking. Are you checking up on me?" I say.

"Yes and no. You left your stuff here – the soup I had packed up for you. Do you have time to come get it before your kids get home?" he asks.

I know he wants to give me the soup but I know too that he needs reassurance and I am touched by it. It continually surprises me that not so much changes from the time we are teens first dipping our toes into the world of intimate relationships, terrified of being left behind by someone we like. We may mature and evolve, have kids and learn how to handle emergencies with aplomb, but feelings of vulnerability stay remarkably the same.

CHAPTER 40

Bald Monkeys

"It turns out sex parties are not for me," #8 writes to me the next day, inviting me over for a lunch of his self-proclaimed famous crab cakes so that he can tell me about it in person.

Wednesday morning, I go through my pre-tryst routine: touching up my bikini area – which I have succeeded in keeping bare with an electric hair trimmer after I vowed never to undergo the pain and humiliation of bikini waxing or sugaring or any other inhumane torture again, rubbing rose body oil all over, donning a black lacy thong and bra that match closely enough. I text Lauren to tell her I'm heading uptown, keeping my promise that I will always let her know before I go to a man's home so that someone is keeping track of me.

It's a beautiful winter day, a bright blue sky melting off heaps of snow and icicles that drip rhythmically onto the sidewalk. I find his building, a charming brownstone that has been divided into apartments, and buzz his apartment. A moment later, I see his considerable frame filling the narrow staircase as he jogs down the steps in Puma sneakers to let me in. Up in his apartment, I am struck by the simplicity of the decor. It is clean and tidy, but feels makeshift, like a glorified dorm room. The furniture is comfortable but shoddy and there is a huge TV screen filling the wall across from the sofa.

I have been getting the feeling that #8 is commitment averse in every aspect of his life and maybe even a bit of a Peter Pan, refusing to grow up. The fact that this apartment could have been put together by a 20-something man right out of college verifies this for me. His saving grace is that he seems to know his way around his kitchen and tells me to make myself comfortable while he heats a pan already filled with oil and takes a platter out of the refrigerator with softball-sized balls of crabmeat. I take my glass of wine and nestle into the faux suede chocolate brown sofa, noting that the huge TV is on in the background.

He calls from the kitchen that he will be just one more minute, and soon after appears with two plates bearing pencil-thin spears of asparagus and what I want to call crab-balls for their profoundly large and round shape. I am impressed – a man who can simply get food on a plate still blows me away, and I mentally give him bonus points for the vegetable.

He smiles and sets each plate down on small foldout tables he had already set with checkered cloth napkins and silverware. He pulls one table in front of where I am sitting on the sofa and the other beside it. I thank him and wait for him to sit next to me before eating, but he is standing in front of the TV, flipping through channels until he settles on *The Graduate*, which has just started.

"I love this movie," I say just to say something, but I'm taken aback that he seems to be watching it attentively as if I'm not here. I don't know if I'm supposed to talk or if I will be interrupting the movie if I attempt conversation, so I concentrate on nibbling the unwieldy crab cake. I am poking the food around my plate and anxiously contemplating how to deal with this television-versus-talking situation when suddenly he is pressed against me from behind, kissing my neck. I glance over and note his empty plate.

"Oh, OK, I guess lunch is over?" I say with an awkward laugh, attempting to be cheeky but mostly sounding child-like and confused. It is now clear that he invited me here to have sex and that the crab cakes were a polite ruse. How I have gotten all the way to #8 without instinctively understanding the dynamics of these situations astounds me, and I realize assigns a certain naïveté to me that I am no longer entitled to. I have inexplicably managed to retain an innocence, even a demurity, that should have been tossed aside many numbers ago.

"Yes, Laura, lunch is over," he says, reaching his arm around me so that his hand can inch its way along my neckline and then down to the edge of my bra. I can feel his hardness against the small of my back as he leans into me. I feel enveloped by him, his kisses against the back of my neck becoming breathier, his hands working their way deeper down before finding my nipple. He is not physically threatening but he is moving quickly and persistently, and for a fleeting moment I wonder, if I wanted to stop now, would he let me? There is something about the urgency of his movements, coupled with my tepid response, that unnerves me. The power here is most decidedly not in my court. As for the paucity of my physical feedback, I am more than a little distracted – by Dustin Hoffman's bumbling machinations across the room, by the sun beaming through the windows which affords no darkness in which to hide, by the crab cake congealing on my plate in front of me. My mind is wandering so much that I start to panic – am I losing my interest in sex, have I used up my post-divorce allotment? I am attracted to him, so why do I feel like I can take this or leave it right now?

He pushes back from me, swings his legs around to the floor, and takes my hand to lead me to the back of the apartment. Passing by the bathroom, I extricate my hand from his, indicating that I'm going to make a quick stop first. When I enter his bedroom a minute later, he is lying on his back on the bed, stripped down to a pair of boxer shorts. His bed is neatly made beneath him, a purple geometrically patterned comforter covering a low platform bed. I pause at the side of the bed, pulling off my sweater so that I am down to a sheer camisole. I lie next to him and he immediately rolls over so that he is on top of me, tugging off my jeans and then my thong. When he sees my bare pubic area, he pauses and raises his eyebrows.

"I did not expect you to have a wugget," he says, smiling.

"A what?" I ask, furrowing my eyebrows.

"A wugget," he repeats and I continue to look questioningly at him.

"A bald monkey," he adds, unhelpfully.

"Translation please," I say.

"A shaved pussy," he clarifies.

"Wow, you're a walking urban dictionary! Yes, well, surprise, here it is. I am told this is what men like now," I say. "Would you like to weigh in?"

"Yeah, I like it," he says.

"But do you prefer it this way? Is the presence of pubic hair a dealbreaker for you?" I ask.

"Ha, no! Not much is a dealbreaker for me in terms of hair. But it's a bold choice. I guess I would think with your daughters up in your business all the time, you might have wanted to keep some hair," he says.

"Just to be clear, my kids are definitely up in my business, but not the business of my vagina," I say and he laughs.

Within seconds his mouth is on my wugget, my bald monkey, my shaved pussy. I am definitely in some kind of weird clinical mindset because I am evaluating all that is happening to me without feeling any physical arousal. Am I just flat-out having too much sex so that I can't even be bothered to feel anything anymore? Why does this suddenly feel like work?

I always feel like I should reciprocate – and I use the word "should" here as frankly, even though my blow job skills are improving, I still don't totally get the appeal – but honestly, he is so well-endowed, I can't fathom putting him in my mouth. I am wholly intimidated by it, sheepish even, not confident that I have the skills yet to tackle this particular one.

For the moment, I am off the hook as he reaches across me into his night table drawer for a condom. With the condom on, he aggressively thrusts inside of me and I can barely catch my breath before he has single-handedly flipped me onto my stomach. I raise myself to my hands and knees so that he can enter me from behind. It feels like he is propelling himself into me and I am too focused on not clumsily toppling over to really feel much excitement myself.

It's not unpleasant exactly, but it is decidedly athletic and more physical than erotic. Soon he wraps his arm around my waist from behind and flips me onto my back again, taking one of my legs high in the air and placing it on his shoulder and continuing his energetic penetration. A physical sensation builds in me quite suddenly and when I come a moment later, the tightening of my muscles is so intense that when they release, it feels like every single muscle in my body goes slack and I jolt upright, squeezing my legs tightly together to stop myself from peeing on his bed. I am appalled and too scared to see if I really did pee or if I just felt like I was going to, but he doesn't seem to take notice. What just happened? I wonder with alarm. I felt absolutely nothing and then this? Did I not just pee in his bathroom ten minutes ago? On top of having to worry about sagging boobs and spider veins on my legs, am I now going to have to add incontinence to my list of middle-aged indignities?

After subtly verifying that there is in fact not a wet spot on the sheets beneath me, I lie back and within seconds, he is inside me again, vigorously pumping. I feel like a contortionist, with my legs high in the air while he presses my thighs back even further toward my head. Suddenly, I feel so tired, physically spent. I don't want to lie dormant like a rag doll, but I cannot match his vigor and size. I have, for better or for worse, been outmatched. When he closes his eyes, gasps and then collapses on top of me, I feel nothing so much as relief. He rolls off me, pulling off the used condom and disposing of it in the bathroom. When he returns, he lies next to me on the bed so that we are now both on our backs, staring up at the ceiling.

"You're quite flexible," he says, smiling and glancing at me. "Clearly doing yoga or a lot of stretching."

"Nah, just having a lot of sex," I say with a coy smile.

"Ha, OK then. Speaking of a lot of sex, I haven't told you about the sex party yet," he says.

"Oh yes, I've been waiting for a full report. Please start at the very beginning, when you walked in the door with your blue cashmere sweater. Was everyone else already naked?"

"Not at all, in fact it kind of felt like a support group. We sat in a circle and went around the room saying what we wanted to get out of the night," he says.

"And when they said what they wanted, was it like a sharing circle? Hi, my name is Laura, I live in NYC, have three kids, my favorite ice cream is Breyers vanilla, and I'm hoping to have three spectacular orgasms tonight?" I ask.

"Take out the part about ice cream and add to the orgasms that you're hoping to get fucked by two men simultaneously and you'll get a little closer to the circle," he says. He tells me that he confessed that this was his first time and he was looking forward to observing and participating, but that other people were very specific and graphic about fantasies and S&M, sex toys, blindfolds and whips, women on women, men on men, threesomes, foursomes and anal sex. I nod along, my eyes wide, as he continues that they split into groups depending on what they wanted, but that it was understood that he was going to be with the hostess since she invited him to be part of her fantasy of being with multiple men at the same time, while her husband went off with his girlfriend.

"That kind of defeats the point of the group sex party, doesn't it?" I say.

"True, well maybe his fantasy was having sex with his girlfriend while his wife was being gang-banged in the bedroom next door," he says and I blanch, but maintain my determination to understand the logistical set-up, asking if there were enough rooms for everyone. He explains that the apartment was pretty big and that all rooms were used, even the open living room and the kids' bedrooms.

"I wonder how the kids would feel if they knew that. My kids would drop dead on the spot, they would feel so violated," I say, mortified.

His answer, that her kids know that she and her husband have an open marriage so maybe wouldn't be as scandalized as mine, is a reminder to me that he doesn't have kids of his own. I prod him to keep going with the story, now that they've moved into a bedroom with other men.

"So she wanted to have a dick in her mouth while she was being fucked from the front and back," he says.

"I didn't know that could be done. Did someone call shotgun for the front position?" I ask.

"No, she told us where to go. She had been with the other two men before, so they knew what to do. I was on the bottom and she was on top of me and then another man was on top of her. And the third guy was right behind my head so she could put him in her mouth."

"Whoa!' I say, finally and genuinely speechless.

"Yeah," he agrees.

We are quiet for a moment.

"Did you like it?" I ask. "Because that's several comfort zones away from one's average sexual encounter."

"I felt really uncomfortable being with two other naked men. I've never been with men sexually before. And the guy above my head was very close to me and I was hyperaware of him, so that was awkward. And then the worst part, I can't even say it," he says.

I wait silently. There's no way I'm not getting the rest of this story out of him so I figure if the silence is uncomfortable enough, he will break it eventually.

"Well, the guy on top was really short, remarkably short, but he had a huge dick. *Huge*. The ratio of the size of it to the size of his body was jarring," he says. "I could feel him while I was inside of her. I mean, it's just a thin wall between her ass and her pussy, and I'm inside her pussy and I can feel him moving inside of her. It was too much for me. I'm glad I tried it, but I never need to do it again."

"Was there any part of it that you enjoyed?" I ask.

"Honestly, not really," he says laughing. "It reduced sex to something that felt purely animalistic. I like this woman, but this isn't for me. I haven't spoken to her since the party. I think she knows it spooked me. By the way, if you saw her you would be shocked. She looks quite prim and proper. She's petite, wears a headband and has a big job working for a bank."

"I don't think I could do that. I'm trying hard not to judge. I get that everyone needs different things to make them feel whole or turned on or alive or whatever, but the extremeness makes me wonder a hundred different things about her, why she needs so much at once. It seems violent," I say, and I can't help but wonder if he realizes that his own approach to sex, if not exactly violent, is definitely aggressive and feral. I sigh and changing topics, he asks me about the rest of my day.

"My parents are staying for dinner and we're going to try out the new air fryer I got for Christmas," I say. "My mom and I love testing out kitchen appliances."

He pulls up an instructional video on YouTube so that we can watch a demonstration. *How odd*, I think, *to be naked in a man's bed on a Wednesday afternoon discussing sex parties and watching a video about air fryers.* For at least the hundredth time over the past few months I am perplexed, puzzling over the path that led me to this spot at this moment. I was so certain of my life's trajectory and my vision definitely didn't include this bit of off-roading, it just involved more of the same: marveling as the kids grew, spending holidays with my parents, upgrading our iPhones, brining increasingly larger turkeys for Thanksgiving, clearing books we didn't love from the shelves to make room for new ones, arguing over who got more coffee every morning. I liked that life – it was predictable, safe, secure and cozy. It was enough, more than enough. In fact, I had so much that it would have been unseemly to have wanted more. It never crossed my mind to want something else, and yet – and *yet* – now that it's gone, I don't want it back, not if it means giving up this incredible freedom, this not knowing what comes next.

"So you probably need to go pick up your daughter," #8 says, interrupting my internal dialogue.

I glance at my watch and shake my head, saying that my mother is in fact picking Georgia up at this very moment. He is silent, and I realize he wasn't saying that out of concern for my schedule, he is simply ready for me to leave. I pick through the pile of tangled blankets and sheets for my clothes. *How quickly we can put ourselves back in order*, I think. In the living room, I see my plate on the small foldout table, a few thin spears of asparagus lying dejectedly next to half a ball of hardened crab cake. He offers to pack the food up for me to take home and I have to bite my lip to keep from laughing – I have never been shown the door with more urgency.

When he opens the front door to the brownstone, an older woman walking by pauses to look up at us. She shouts out a cheery hello and we wave back, for a fleeting moment the very picture of domestic bliss, then he bends down to give me a quick kiss and I am off. I feel my phone vibrate in my pocket and when I look, there are several missed calls and texts from Lauren. I call her back immediately.

"Oh thank God! I've been panicking. I thought I would have heard from you by now," she says.

"OK, nervous Nellie. I'm fine, heading home," I say.

"Can I just say how stupid we are? I thought I was on the ball keeping track of you but you didn't give me his address or phone number – not even his name – so I was trying to figure out how I was going to find you, call the police and say I'm looking for my girlfriend who is with #8 somewhere in Harlem? Next time I want an address," she says.

"Amateur hour," I say, laughing. "You'd think we would be a little better at this by now."

And with that, I hop on the subway, heading back downtown.

CHAPTER 41

G-spot

For all the ways in which I'm getting a crash course in sexuality at this unexpected juncture in my life, I remain in the dark about why the G-spot is so elusive. It appears to me from women's magazines that having your G-spot activated is like reaching the top of Mount Everest, a rare and inarguably lifelong achievement. Like the easily achieved orgasms I take for granted, I'm certain that my G-spot has gotten plenty of action, but I would be hard-pressed to describe it beyond the description I would give the intense pleasure of an orgasm.

Thus it is no small surprise to me the next morning, when I recount the details of my date with #8 to my friend Ana during our weekly coffee date after Pilates class, to hear her reaction. She loves to hear about my sexcapades and I describe the awkward scene, how he was watching a movie while we ate lunch and then how physical the sex was, how hard it was to keep up with him, then how when I came it was so strong, I actually felt like I had lost control of my bladder but that I had

379

checked the sheets and I had not, in fact, peed. I tell her that even the idea that I had peed in this strange man's bed was so embarrassing, that I am now re-thinking ever having sex with a stranger again.

"Could it have been that he hit your G-spot?" she asks, seriously pondering the situation I described.

"What? No, it wasn't like that at all," I say.

"Hmmm, because that once happened to me and it was so surprising, but it's never happened again," she says.

"What makes you think it was your G-spot?" I ask.

"I really don't know how I knew, I just did. I guess because it was so different from anything that had ever happened during sex before," she says.

I ask if she had been actively aiming for her G-spot, if she did something specific to get to it.

"No, it just happened, and I have never been able to make it happen again," she says.

"Like magic," I say, and she agrees.

"Who were you with? Was it someone very well endowed?" I ask.

"It was with my husband!" she says. "It's more about the positioning than size, I think. It felt exactly as you described, like my muscles had tightened so much that when they released, they overcorrected and everything just flooded open. I remember feeling like I had peed."

"I'm genuinely confused. I thought the G-spot was something totally different," I say. "I thought it was on the outside, like some mythical spot on the clitoris."

She smirks at me, suggesting that she's more of a sexpert than I am and I can't deny it. I pull out my phone and google "G-spot", study the images and then pout.

"I'm so upset. I squandered it! I stopped it in mid-air. Now it may never happen again and I'll never really experience the glory of it. I was scared of it, there was no joy or satisfaction, no earth-shattering thrill. I wasted my shot at the G-spot."

She suggests that the solution is to sleep with #8 again, but I admit that I don't want to. Instead, I will put #6 to work.

I leave the table to use the restroom and when I return, I am alarmed all over again.

"This might be TMI," I say, furrowing my brows, "but I think #8 broke me. I'm bleeding."

Ana bursts into peals of laughter, shrieking "TMI? TMI? Now it's TMI? You passed that so long ago! TMI went out the window the minute you told me you thought you peed in #8's bed."

We laugh long and hard, drawing a few looks from the waiter who normally witnesses us huddled in the corner, me wiping away tears while Ana reaches out to put her hand over mine. Now we are like hyenas, cackling and doubled over, crying with laughter. It's obvious to both of us that we have crossed the border into a land where bodies are just bodies and what they can do is a common experience, no reason to keep it to ourselves.

*

True to my prediction, #6 is wildly jealous that another man has located my G-spot and becomes obsessed with finding it himself.

I suggest that he go down one of the research rabbit holes I'm so famous for to figure it out.

"Now you're definitely going to see #8 again. Why wouldn't you?" he says mournfully.

"Actually, he texted me already to make another date and I declined," I say. "I told him that as much as I enjoyed my time with him, I have been dating someone for whom I am developing real feelings and thus it is starting to feel strange to sleep with other men."

"And what did he say?" he asks, though I was hoping he would respond to the part in which I declared vague but real feelings for him.

"He said he was happy for me," I say.

"So now the pressure is really on for me to find the mystery spot," he says.

"I'm parking my LLT for a while. I'm going to see what it feels like to date just you," I say.

He laughs; I know the way I said it made it sound like I was slumming it with him as my sole sex partner.

"Sorry, I didn't mean it like that. Obviously I have limited free time and I would like to spend the free time I do have with you. My sexual curiosity is calming down – I think I've got it now, and honestly, I'm exhausted. I like having sex with you, I like being with you, so my liberation train is going on hiatus," I say. "What do you think about that?"

"I don't know, I feel jealous when you're with other men but it's also a huge turn-on. I think you should do what feels right to you," he says.

"Better step up your game if you're going to be my only sexual partner," I say.

"I have to update my will," he says lightheartedly, but I can tell that he is relieved. "You may actually kill me."

CHAPTER 42

Lemonade

Michael proposes a family trip to a beach resort we've been to several times together. It had always been his rule that we never go to the same place twice no matter how much we loved it since the world is too big and there are too many places to see. This one resort in the Caribbean had broken the rule though, with its majestic beauty and absolute luxury – it was many dollar signs beyond what I could have stomached spending on a vacation, but because he had done marketing work for the resort, we were able to go once a year for free.

I am evasive in my response to him, saying the dates don't work and Daisy won't be able to come because of her college schedule, but he persists. It's not just the idea of taking a family trip with our newly revised family that is giving me pause, but a combination of the memory of what had once been a happy place for our family and the fact that Michael had been there with his lover in the midst of his affair. He doesn't seem to realize that his suggestion coincides with the one-year anniversary of our separation, but I am painfully aware of the timing.

The morning of the day that marks exactly one year, I am upstate with the kids for their mid-winter recess. I drop them off to ski and then drive to my favorite café for coffee and a flip through the newspapers on the communal table. I am overwhelmed with an unrecognizable feeling – the intersection of absolute joy and peace on one hand and grief and heartache on the other. I take a selfie as I sit with my mug of coffee and pile of newspapers, as I know that I need to remember this exact feeling. I am bundled in a cream-colored sweater with a thick indigo blue scarf knotted around my neck. I stare at the camera and tilt my head to the side, neither smiling nor frowning. The sun is streaming through the window behind me and light makes its way through my unruly curls. I am not wearing make-up and my eyes look sleepy and swollen. This is me, in my messiness and beauty, in a moment of solace that encapsulates the intense feeling of loss with the reassuring knowledge that the worst is safely behind me. I am sad, but I am whole. I post the picture on Instagram to commemorate the occasion, ensuring that I have a record of this moment. I caption it, "These last twelve months have brought particularly turbulent highs and lows to my life, but I am more than ever grateful that I can appreciate the small pleasures that make me feel peace and happiness: this view when I'm upstate, and a coffee at my favorite café. Sometimes that's enough".

Later, I ask Hudson if he can bear to be with me and Michael so that we can all go away to the Caribbean together, reassuring him that no matter what he prefers my feelings will not be hurt. He does not hesitate in saying he wants me there, that he doesn't want to go on vacation without me.

#6 is both amused by and wary of my upcoming family holiday, wryly suggesting that perhaps Michael and I will reunite. I tease him for being jealous, but he insists that the timing and location suggest an ulterior motive.

"Oh please, he wants me back as little as I want him back. He knows the kids will be disappointed if I'm not there and he's in love with the notion of our being an ultramodern family. He's too transparent to hide something like that and anyway, I've got bigger fish to fry. All the years we've been going to this place, I've been obsessed with the man on the beach who sells fruit and weed to tourists. He's gorgeous – Rasta hair down his back, mahogany brown skin, perfectly defined muscles and an accent that could bring you to your knees. If you want to be jealous about something, this is your target," I say.

"And this is your prey?" he asks.

"For years I've been innocently flirting with him but now I can do whatever I want. I mean, why not? Daisy and I used to walk down to the beach together to talk to him and then argue later if he was paying more attention to her or to me," I say.

"Back on the LLT," he says.

"Listen, who am I kidding? He's probably fifteen years younger than me and he sees gorgeous barely dressed women all day long, he's not going to look twice at me. It's certainly fun to fantasize though."

I tell my friends and they agree, why not try? It seems outlandish, but it's a good diversion – and anyway, haven't I proven that my formerly staid life has indeed become outlandish? Some of them suggest it would be karmic payback, but I'm not interested in revenge. I am hurt, but what I want from Michael is continued acknowledgement of how deeply he's wounded me, not vengeance. I don't want to get back at him, but I do want to experience aspects of life that have been unavailable to me up to this point, like Blaze, the current object of my fantasies. Frugal as I am, I am prepared to shell out big bucks for new bikinis that will help in my hunt.

I ask my friend Jen for help. We meet at a bathing suit boutique and carry dozens of options into the fitting room, treating this like a broad science experiment. What will it take to get a breath-taking 30-something man who sits on a beach and witnesses beautiful bodies all day long to notice a petite Jewish woman with a pancake ass who is nearing fifty? I have convinced myself that the secret lies in the suit I pick and attack it as such, finally landing on one bikini I think is adequate.

The next week, I fixate on needing another bikini. It's as if the slate of the past year is going to be washed clean if I can find the perfect bikini. Lauren and I head to Bloomingdale's, where I try on a string bikini with a tropical floral print. She walks into my fitting room as I am snapping a picture of myself to send to #6 to see if he thinks this will do the trick.

My phone rings and I assume it's #6 weighing in with an opinion, but it's Michael calling from a bag store I love in Soho to tell me they have a new line of backpacks that would be ideal for the new laptop he got for me and he wants to get me one as a gift. Meanwhile, #6 texts to say the bikini is a winner. Lauren looks at me agape, shaking her head and laughing.

"Girl," she says, "I never want to hear you complain again. Your ex-husband is sending over a fancy new bag for you, you're going on an all-expenses-paid trip to the Caribbean, you're sending photos to your boyfriend to advise if you can get a new lover with these bikinis. Talk about being handed lemons and making lemonade! If you ever complain to me about anything again, I will remind you of this moment."

"But—" I start.

"No, stop right there. I've lived through the past year with you. I've seen you at your lowest moments and I'm telling you, what you've pulled off is magic. Just take it in. You got yourself here, you crazy girl. Own it," she says, serious now and wrapping me in a hug that for once hasn't been prefaced by my weeping.

CHAPTER 43

Passionfruit

In the months since Lanie suggested that I write about my recent experiences with dating and sex, I have committed myself to shaping my random musings into something deeper and more structured. My pledge to write five minutes a day has evolved into longer sessions, hours at a time, which have become like therapy sessions for me. I ponder the images and words from my past that come back to me in vivid detail, firmly embedded in my memory, and those that seem fixedly out of grasp, no matter how I try to recall them. It fascinates me to bring back to life the conversations and situations that have been so critical to my growth, as of course in the moments when events are happening we rarely understand the lasting impact they may have on us.

When, in the pre-dawn hours of the day we are to leave for the Caribbean, Michael arrives in a taxi to pick me, Hudson and Georgia up from our building, I am holding my new shimmery backpack with my laptop tucked inside in case I find some quiet moments and feel inspired to write. Michael sits in the front with the driver and the kids and I bundle into the backseat, leaning against each other sleepily and talking about what we will do when we first arrive, swimming in the turquoise ocean, ordering virgin frozen daiquiris by the pool, walking down the beach to see if Blaze is there with his kayak of fruit.

We have only two assigned seats on the plane that are together, so Georgia and I take them while Michael and Hudson go further back to their individual seats. I remember how many torturous flights I went on with the kids when they were little, squirming in their tight seats, knocking over the cans of ginger ale they had begged for, propping open bags in case turbulence made vomiting a plausible threat, holding them as they screamed with ear pain, eyeing Michael to see if he might take over for a while and give me a break. Georgia is newly independent and I luxuriate in what it means to travel with her now – beyond minor iPad set-up issues and excited chatter, I am free to read my book and relax. I hear a cacophony of noise behind me and turn my head, just enough to catch a glimpse of a woman juggling toddler twins. I feel for her but am practically giddy that I'm not her.

The swelling of noise from the toddlers increases and falls and then becomes so intensely high-pitched that even Georgia raises an eyebrow and makes a tsk, tsk face. When we rise from our seats halfway through the flight so Georgia can use the bathroom, I see that one twin is in the window seat four rows behind us with her mother holding the other twin in the middle seat, and there, next to them in the aisle seat, is Michael. Oh, the justice of it all! I put my hand over my mouth to stifle a laugh.

"That's mean," she says.

"What's mean? I didn't put him there," I say, trying to position my phone surreptitiously to snap a photo of this uncomfortable trio.

"It's mean that you think it's funny and are taking a picture," she says.

"Well, come on, admit that it's pretty funny. Anyway, it doesn't look like he's struggling, does it?" I say, watching him sleep peacefully through the chaos, his neck encircled by a travel pillow. I know I could have been that mother, trying to contain a squalling baby – *his* squalling baby, not a random one – and he still would have been as peaceful. I snap the photo.

*

A few hours later, we are spread on chaise longues by the shimmering blue pool. I want to lie still for a few minutes, soaking in the smoldering heat of the midday sun, but the kids are antsy. Hudson wanders off to get the first frozen mocktail of probably ten that he will drink today, and Georgia begs Michael to walk her down the beach to find Blaze to get a coconut and if she's lucky, some passionfruit and soursop. Ten minutes later, Georgia comes bounding over, her hands sticky with juice and the skin around her mouth already orange from the mango she's been eating.

"Mommy, Blaze is here! He gave me extra soursop for you! He wants you to come say hi, can we go now?"

I pat the spot next to me and promise we will go as soon as she's done eating. I accept the wedge of dripping fruit she hands me and watch her tear into the array in front of her. Georgia has a voracious appetite and eats with such gusto that I watch with bemusement. She lacks self-consciousness, allowing juice to drip down her face and bits of fruit to stick to her cheeks, even her hair. When she is done, she smears the pulp from her hands and face all over the bright white, plush towel she is sitting on. I look askance at her but she shrugs her shoulders.

"Now can we go?" she says. "Blaze asked about you. He said 'where's the boss?'"

I stretch lazily and reach out my hand for her. We scurry through the hot sand until we reach the water and then follow the path, slowly and casually, to the end of the beach where a canopy of trees shade Blaze's spot. I see him turn his head to watch us as we approach, but I don't look at him, intently talking to Georgia and pointing out shells and crabs scuttling across the sand. He walks down to the water to greet us.

"You brought the boss lady," he says to Georgia, who giggles.

I smile broadly and his gaze at me lingers long enough to make me wonder if I could actually make my fantasy a reality. My heart is pounding as I watch him, his ropy muscles undulating with his every move. We make small talk in intimate, soft voices. His eyes flicker over to Georgia, who is standing nearby, looking into the clear water to find fish and shells.

"Come back alone so we can talk," he says, his eyes boring into me.

I nod, feeling his eyes on me as Georgia and I turn around and walk back toward the pool.

I make my getaway a couple of hours later, asking Michael to keep an eye on Georgia in the pool so I can take a walk on the beach alone. I head back in Blaze's direction, and when I get in his sightline, he stands and watches me approach. He gestures to the row of beach chairs he and his friends park themselves on for much of the day and we settle into seats next to each other. He asks how I'm doing and I quickly tell him that I'm single now and that fact pretty much sums up my year, and I ask what he had wanted to say to me earlier but didn't with Georgia underfoot.

"I've been waiting for you. Every day, I wait for you to come walking down the beach," he says.

I let out a loud laugh and say, "Oh please! I wish that was true. Tell me really."

"It is true. This is the time of year you usually come. I've been waiting," he says, staring at me. "I couldn't say that in front of your daughter."

"Were you going to tell me this whether or not I told you I'm newly single?" I ask.

He laughs and puts a finger on my hand, tracing my palm for a moment. My entire body feels like an electric current is running through it.

"I knew you would be single," he says.

I furrow my brows in confusion, but I'm too wrapped up in the potential of my fantasy taking this amazing turn to wonder at his statement.

"When can I see you?" he asks.

"Alone?" I ask, stupidly, and we make a plan to meet after dinner by the bar on the private beach. He says he will wait there for me as no one comes on that beach at night.

I calmly rise from my seat despite the thumping of my heart.

He catches my arm as I turn to go and pulls me down toward him so that my lips meet his for a kiss as passionate as it is quick. I have been rendered speechless, so I touch my lips with my index finger, give a small smile and walk away. It takes every iota of self-restraint I have not to leap down the beach, cackling with glory and laughter. Instead, I walk slowly, attempting to sashay, knowing he is watching my every step.

Back at the pool, the kids and Michael have disappeared so I dig my phone out of my bag and call Tina, who knows Blaze from her recent vacation here. I silently plead for her to pick up and when she finally does, I blurt out, "Tina, I have a date with Blaze tonight."

"Mama, what are you talking about? You just got there! Hang on, I'm at pick-up, school just let out. I have to tell Alexandra and Sarah, they're right here," she says, and I hear shouts of kids in the background as she excitedly tells Alexandra and Sarah that I'm calling from the Caribbean and I have a date with the object of my fantasy. There is joyous shrieking and laughter all around and then Tina comes back on the line, saying, "We are so excited for you. Tell us everything. And be safe!"

I call #6, feeling the need to confess, wanting to give him one last chance to say he can't have me sleeping with another man, but he doesn't answer.

CHAPTER 44

Lost Condoms

I still find it challenging to put my own needs up there with my kids' needs, but I know it's the only way forward. I have to take care of myself properly if I am to take care of them the way I want to, which means not just managing their basic care but showing by example how to live a life with joy, serenity, kindness and compassion. If I do not give myself opportunities to feel happy or at peace or filled up as a woman, how will I be a mother who can share these qualities with her children? I am consumed with feelings of guilt, terrified that if I let myself thrive in my life outside of motherhood I am sacrificing my children. Friends and books keep telling me I must grab the oxygen mask first for myself and second for the kids, but it sounds like validation for selfish behavior. On a rational level, I know that I am equating being a good mother with being a martyr, but on an emotional level, I am having a hard time letting go of this vestige of my previous life. I've been having sex with various men for months now, but the thought of having sex while on a family trip suggests that I am fully establishing myself as an independent human being outside of my relationship with my children. Sleeping with Blaze is a fantasy, yes, but it's also proof that I have given myself full permission to have a private life. I have proven in so many ways to myself over the past year that I am strong, resilient, adventurous, curious, passionate and open, but it turns out I have one last thing to prove to myself, that I can be a mother and a fulfilled woman and that the two are not mutually exclusive.

Sandy, sticky and freckled from the sun by early evening, I luxuriate in a long shower, scrubbing myself clean with the coconut-scented bath products the resort has provided. I shimmy into my favorite dress, the bright orange Indian-print halter I wore on one of my dates with #4, knowing this is the easiest access piece of clothing I own. I tuck a condom into my small straw clutch purse and then the four of us head out to dinner.

Michael snaps a picture of me, Georgia and Hudson sitting on the back of a tuk tuk, bouncing along the narrow road to the beach restaurant. Georgia is squished in the middle, one hand on my leg and the other on Hudson's, and his hand is wrapped over hers. In the photo, they are smiling widely, filled with joy to be in their happy place and, for Georgia, being with both of her parents at the same time. I have a small smile and am looking not at the camera but sideways at them, cherishing this moment and, as I've done a million times before, feeling gratitude for their extraordinary relationship. Georgia worships Hudson and he is attentive and kind to her, even now in the peak of his teenage years when no one could rightfully expect such tenderness. My kids are alright and I am on my way to being alright too. I think guiltily of the condom hidden inside my purse, trying to persuade myself that it's OK that it's there, that all of this – my thriving and my kids thriving – goes hand in hand.

Dinner takes a long time and when it finally ends, we drift over to the beach where a reggae band is playing. I cannot take my eyes off the singer, a petite woman with thick braids swaying as she moves to the beat. She sings with her eyes closed and is enraptured by the music. I envy both her smooth voice and the bliss she exudes, and I lean back on the wicker couch, tucked between the kids. Georgia is leaning heavily against me, her eyelids fluttering closed, and she pats me and asks if she can go back to the villa to sleep. I ask Michael to take her so that Hudson and I can stay and listen to the music.

I am keeping an eye on the time and know that soon I will have to make my getaway to meet Blaze on the beach if I'm really going through with it. Luckily, the band announces it is playing its last song, and when they are done, Hudson and I walk along the beach to get back to our villa. It's a beautiful starry night with a gentle breeze coming off the ocean and we walk in a contented silence. When we reach the end of the beach and the beginning of the path that leads to our villa, I tell Hudson I left my wrap on the couch and I will have to go back to get it. He offers to run back and retrieve it for me, but I send him ahead and tell him that I want to sit on the beach for a little while by myself anyway. I watch him walk up the path and wait a few more minutes. The wrap is inside my purse, where I stuffed it as we left the beach so that I would have an excuse to turn back. It's a few minutes after 10pm now and Blaze had said he would wait until 10:15.

When I am sure Hudson is far enough ahead, I walk along the path to the private beach, which is pitch-black and deserted. I take off my sandals and dangle them from my fingers as I try to gracefully make my way over shells and shallow pools of water to the bar, which is shut down for the night. As I approach, I hear a long whistle come from the direction of a stretch of empty chairs on the beach. I amble over, feigning casualness as best I can. The chairs are more like round beds, half covered by a canopy, and it's not until I get to the second one that I see Blaze tucked inside of it.

"Hey beautiful," he says quietly.

I say hello shyly, still clutching my sandals in one hand and holding up the hem of my maxi dress in the other. I didn't really expect him to be here and am surprised and nervous. He gestures to the enclosed seat. I drop my sandals and climb in, asking how he got to the beach since I can't picture him in a car, which seems too ordinary for him. He takes a long inhale of the joint he is holding and passes it to me, but I shake my head. Now that I'm trying to see him as a real person and not just the demi-god of my dreams, I'm curious too to know his real name. He makes me promise that I won't laugh at it.

"Ephraim," he says.

"A Biblical name. Does anyone still call you that?" I ask.

"My mother," he says.

"And how did you come to be known as Blaze?" I say.

"How do you think, Mama?" he says laughing and before I can answer his lips are on mine, so soft and pillowy that I want to bite them. His breath is a combination of cigarettes and weed, and I can smell cologne on his skin, which I find touching – an indication that he put himself together for me. He lies me back and looks meaningfully at me as he pulls my dress down and throws it to the side, so that I am lying naked except for a pale pink thong, which he also pulls down and throws to the side of the chair. I watch him closely but don't speak. He tells me that he's been watching me for a long time and then his lips are all over my body, working their way from my nipples down my torso, resting on my still-hairless pubic triangle.

"Mama, you have fat pussy lips!" he says, laughing.

"I don't know how to take that. Is that a compliment or an insult?" I ask.

"I have no insults for you," he says, burrowing his face between my legs. After a few minutes, he pulls himself up and unbuttons his shorts, reaches into his pocket and holds up a condom, saying, "No baby Blazes."

He thrusts into me and it takes me only a moment to come, but now he is energetically pumping, so much so that sweat is dripping from his long braids onto my face and along my neck. He pulls out to turn me around onto my hands and knees, but realizes the condom has fallen off. He pats the mattress and uses his phone as a flashlight, but we can't find it.

"It's inside of you," he says.

My eyes widen; in panic, I envision myself in a clinic as doctors do a scavenger hunt inside of me to find the missing condom. I try to exude calm, as if condoms regularly fall off inside of me, and say, "Just give me a sec." It doesn't take long for my finger to alight on the rubber, and I pull it, long and slippery, out of me.

Blaze sorts through the pile of clothing until he finds his shorts. He spills out the contents of his pockets and I hear coins and keys falling, but he soon holds up another condom, announcing that it is his last one.

He enters me from behind and I brace my hands on the back of the chair as his indefatigable thrusting continues. We both hear voices at the same time, a small group of people, and their voices get louder as they approach the area where we are. He pauses, saying "Shhhhh" to me. We are suspended in motion, silent, listening to the voices rise and fall and the ocean waves gently break on the sand a few feet away. I am squeezing my eyes shut, praying we can't be seen in the dark since we are mostly covered by a canopy anyway, and eventually the voices fade away. When Blaze gently turns me around again to get back on top of me, I hear him curse under his breath.

"What?" I ask.

He points sheepishly down at his penis, which is dark and erect and once again missing its rubber sheath. I wordlessly reach inside myself and pull it out again, this time handing it back to him so he can resume using it, and note that I should probably march myself back into my gynecologist's office and ask for yet another STD panel, even if I am chastened by the mere thought of it. Our bodies are slick with sweat and when he clamps his hips against mine and lets out a surprisingly high-pitched coyote-like yelp, I am relieved, as I am physically spent. He collapses on top of me, panting, and then rolls to the side. Suddenly curious about his age, I ask him how old he is, guessing that he's 35, but he's actually only 31.

"Oh wow. A baby," I say. "You like older women, huh?"

"I like beautiful women," he says.

"How often do you sleep with guests at this hotel?" I ask.

"Never. You're my first one," he says, unconvincingly.

I give him a skeptical look and he continues, "Sometimes three women in a month and then nothing for a few months."

I ask an improbably naïve question then, needing to know if these women have all been single.

He laughs.

"Married women proposition you?" I ask, unable to keep the shock out of my voice. "I guess they can't stay away – you exude sex."

"So do you," he says.

He starts putting his clothes back on, reaching in the dark for a collection of money, keys, matches and joints which had fallen from his pockets. I pull my dress on, shoving the thong he produces from under the mattress into my purse, which I remember just now is holding its own condom. He asks if he can see me again since I still have two more nights here, but I hesitate. This tryst has been validating, fun, a fantasy come true, but I am keenly aware of how tired I am and think longingly of the cool white sheets in my room. I'm even more surprised when I feel a sudden yearning for #6, for the comfort of being intimate with someone who is so careful with and sensitive to what works for my body, whose sole purpose often seems to be to please me. I offer a noncommittal maybe, explaining that I'm not sure I can pull off sneaking away from my family two nights in a row, lean down to kiss him, then walk back off into the warm, star-filled night.

CHAPTER 45

Another Confession

The villa is silent when I slip in, so I walk on tiptoes into my bedroom. I am surprised to see that it's only 11:30. The whole exchange took little more than an hour. Dropping my bag and sandals on the floor, I head to the bathroom to clean up. I laugh when I catch a glimpse of my reflection in the mirror: my hair a disorderly tangle, my skin a shiny, sandy mess. If anyone in my family had seen me come in, they would have wondered what experience I had just endured to come out looking like this, perhaps imagining a ceremonial purging process in which I shed the trauma of the last year.

I hear my phone ringing inside my purse in the bedroom and run to answer it before it wakes anyone up.

"Ah, Miss Laura, I'm surprised I got you on the phone. I figured you'd be too busy to answer," #6 says in his deep voice from what feels like a million miles away. I tell him that I just got home, hoping he will connect the dots on his own, but he doesn't so I explain that I was out with Blaze. He laughs, thinking I'm joking, but I remind him that I am efficient with my time. He is silent, so I tell him that I tried to call him before I went as if that will make this information more palatable.

"Was it all you hoped it would be?" he finally asks, his voice subdued.

"Are you upset?"

"Not upset exactly. Just surprised you did it so quickly. And intrigued," he says.

"That's why I called you. I tried twice. To give you a heads up," I say. "You sound angry."

He reassures me that he's not, but he wants to hear the story.

I tell him about our meeting in the dark on the beach, how intensely vigorous the sex was, how I had thought about him and even missed him when it was over, which he does not believe.

"You don't have to believe me. I'm not telling you to flatter you, I'm telling you because you want to know if the sex was all I had built it up to be in my imagination and I'm sharing that it both was and wasn't. I love the hunt, the flirting, the capturing, the moment when I know feelings are more than friendly, but I don't think I need to do it again. I'm fully satisfied now. And I did think about you," I say, putting the phone on the bed and climbing between the sheets.

"What did you think about when you thought of me?" he asks.

"I thought about how easy it is with you, how I'm comfortable with you even when I'm out of my comfort zone sexually. How new isn't always better. How you treat me like I'm more than just a receptacle for your pleasure," I say.

"All this while fucking the man of your dreams on a beach in the Caribbean," he says, laughing.

"Make all the jokes you want. I know it's hard for you to speak openly about your feelings. I'm telling you the truth, I have no incentive to conjure feelings to make you feel better about your manhood," I say.

"Do you think I'm a pervert because I want all the details?" he asks.

"Absolutely," I say. "But now I must sleep. My eyes are closing while I talk to you," I say, and immediately fall into a deep, blissful slumber.

CHAPTER 46

Writing

Parked on lounge chairs next to the pool under the blazing morning sun, Georgia asks me to take her down the beach to get a coconut from Blaze, a request I suggest she take to Michael instead. I watch them walk away, swinging their hands together as they run through the hot sand to get to the edge of the water. I feel anxious, knowing I have something weighing on me that I need to share with Michael. It's not about my dalliance the night before, as that's something I get to keep all to myself, it's about my writing. I've been working on it and I like doing it. It has been cathartic, allowing me to sort out my feelings as I put them into words on my computer screen or into the Wonder Woman Moleskine notebook #6 bought me, and my friends who work in publishing have told me they think it could be a book. I want nothing more than to take my heap of messy emotions and even messier dating stories and smooth them out, craft them together into a cohesive narrative, but the thought of revealing myself so publicly and outing Michael's indiscretion are roadblocks I can't get past.

When they come back a few minutes later, Georgia holds up her coconut for me victoriously and puts the straw into my mouth so I can take a sip.

"Look at Mama with her bunny hairdo and big sunglasses and tropical bikini," Michael says.

Georgia eyes me, then shrugs her shoulders. "She looks fine, I guess."

"What do you mean, she looks fine?" he continues. "You should feel proud that you have such a pretty mommy!"

Georgia eyes me skeptically and then hands me her coconut so she can jump in the pool. I am perplexed by Michael, unable to decide if he simply forgets that we aren't a couple anymore, or if he remembers but doesn't feel that should stop him from doling out compliments. I remember when I first met him, how I found his tendency to blurt out unsolicited opinions to be refreshing at times, disconcerting at others. It's not that I don't appreciate any and all compliments, but the way he says this now, so adoringly, is a painful reminder of how I once felt so cherished by him. It had seemed to me from our very beginning together that he was smitten with me; I cannot for the life of me figure out when that stopped being the case.

"I'm worried about Blaze," he says as he plops himself down on the double-wide chaise longue I am sprawled across. "He wasn't himself this morning, he was kind of subdued."

I am mid-swallow when he says this and I start coughing, the thin coconut milk coming back up my throat. He looks at me quizzically and when I catch my breath, I suggest that maybe Blaze was just tired.

"It was weird. You know how he always has so much energy and gets excited to do his whole coconut machete show for Georgia? He looked sad, kind of sedated," he says.

"I wouldn't worry. It may turn out he's simply human like the rest of us and is having an off day," I say, trying to play it cool as questions race through my mind. *Could I have worn him out? Could he be feeling guilty? Does he wish last night hadn't happened?*

Hudson jumps in the pool to join Georgia and they play their usual games, which involve a combination of shrieking, laughter and, eventually, tears. Michael and I are left alone on the chair, watching them and unsure what to talk about when we aren't talking about them. In moments like this, I have to remind myself that we are not who we used to be to each other, that a tranquil moment like this is hard-won.

"Michael," I start.

"Yes?" He swivels his head to look at me, seeming surprised and thrilled that I have initiated a conversation with him.

"You know how I asked you for a laptop so that I could do some writing?"

"Yes. I'm so glad you're writing. I really think you could get copywriting work, the stuff you did for me was great."

"That's not the kind of writing I want to do. I mean, if I can do that and make some money, I'd be thrilled, but I'm more interested in creative writing."

"OK, well do both. This could be a whole new direction for you," he says encouragingly.

"Actually, I want to tell you about a project I'm working on. Sort of a memoir about my life after marriage. It's not about you,

Available

but you obviously play a big role in it. It's my story, about finding myself again," I say cautiously. "I'm writing it with the hope that it'll be published. I'm writing carefully about you, I don't want to trash you. You're the father of our kids and I hope that we are moving into a new dynamic in which we can be friends, but the story of how we fell apart is included."

"Laura, I'm interested in the truth, in people speaking their truth. As long as you're honest, it's OK with me. I have nothing to hide," he says.

"You say that now because it's an abstract notion. It could feel different when it's spelled out on a page," I say.

"Let's cross that bridge when we come to it. For now, if it's making you feel good to write, do it," he says.

I nod my head and thank him.

"Hey, just to lighten the mood a bit, can I tell you something funny?" he asks, and continues without awaiting my response. "The doormen still sometimes call my cell phone instead of yours when you have visitors. I gather you're dating someone named Alan, because I get phone calls from the doorman like clockwork on Friday nights after I pick Georgia up for the weekend, asking if it's OK to send him upstairs."

"Oh my God, that's so embarrassing," I say, my face reddening.

"I'm telling you because I think it's funny. I want you to be happy. I'm glad you're dating," he says.

I realize it's especially awkward that he's getting these calls because it's always within minutes of Georgia leaving, like I haven't wasted a moment having a man up to my apartment, and I wonder aloud why he didn't simply tell the doorman at some point to call

408

my number instead. I make a note to have a chat with the doormen when I'm back home – I would like to feel I have some semblance of privacy, the same way Michael does.

In the afternoon, Michael and the kids convince me to walk down the beach to snorkel with them, so we borrow goggles and flippers from the resort and waddle to the water. The snorkeling area is all the way at the end of the beach, where Blaze sits. Mercifully, he is not in his regular spot at the moment, though I see his kayak at the water's edge, laden with ripe tropical fruit. We swim out until the ocean floor seems far beneath us and I float on my stomach, hearing nothing but my breath as I gaze into the turquoise water and watch schools of brightly colored fish dart around me. It is serene and imperturbable here, and I'm grateful my kids knew to drag me here despite my wanting to be left alone like a sloth with my book. When I finally lift my head, I see Blaze standing in the shallow end, watching me. I raise my hand to acknowledge him, and he is still standing there a few minutes later when we all swim back in. I linger for a moment as Michael and the kids run ahead to return the snorkeling gear and ready the next activity, a Sunfish.

"Did you have a good time last night?" he asks me quietly.

I smile and nod, so he asks if we can do it again. I demur, saying I'm not sure I can get away. The kids are gesturing to me so that they can take me for a sail, so I tell Blaze that I better go and that I will come back to talk to him after the sailing excursion.

Hudson is excited to show us his sailing skills, and we let him zoom through the water with the wind at our backs. By the time we arrive back at the beach after capsizing and bobbing in the water, waiting for the resort's motorboat to rescue us, Blaze is long gone for the day. I am both disappointed and relieved, as I still hadn't decided if I had the energy to have another go with him. I love the attention from him, but I had my adventure and think I'm done now.

CHAPTER 47

Authorship

Late afternoon is my favorite time of vacation days – a cooler breeze moving in, the crowds packed up and gone. Georgia and I stroll along the beach, holding hands and splashing the water with our feet.

"I don't want to leave here. I wish we could stay forever," she says wistfully.

"I know, me too. It's such a special place. Just think, someday you can come back here when you're all grown up with your own kids," I say.

"But I won't be able to afford it!"

"Marry well," I say, and am instantly horrified that these words have come from my empowered, feminist mouth. "Wait, pretend you didn't hear that, I take it back. Make your own money, then you can take your husband here someday."

She says that's not what I did, and she wants to follow in my footsteps.

"Daddy and I met when we were so young, and then once we

had Daisy and Hudson, I wanted to be with them all the time so I stopped working. I think I could have been as financially successful as Daddy is now, but we made a decision together and I gave up my career. You could do that too if you want to. I just want you to figure out who you are first," I say.

"Didn't you know who you were when you met Daddy?" she asks, and I raise my eyebrows at her and twist my lips, pondering how to answer. I am continually stunned by the way children can hone in on the heart of the matter, how they so earnestly ask questions that astonish with their simplicity.

"That's a really good question. I did know who I was and I knew I wanted a life with Daddy. But imagine, I wasn't much older than Daisy is right now, and over the years I changed and Daddy changed, and we grew up but not in a way that made it easy for us to be together anymore. I wouldn't change a thing, because if I did, I might not be a mom to my three amazing children, and truly all I ever wanted was a family. It's really hard for you to understand this right now, but I think someday you will," I say, and she solemnly nods her head.

"But we're not a family anymore."

"Oh, we're still a family, my love. We look different from how we used to look because we don't all live together anymore, but the love we have for each other will always be strong and that makes us a family," I say, and as I speak the words, I realize that I actually believe them, that they're not mere platitudes I am using to bandage her back together. All my childhood and into early adulthood, I mourned that I did not have a cohesive family, a nuclear unit that did not include stepparents and stepsiblings and half-siblings, a complex family tree that branched off in confusing directions. I wanted to create the family that I hadn't had and had felt deprived of, and when Michael and I separated, I felt he had stolen from me this chance to get it right. It wasn't just that he had irrevocably altered my present – he had forced me to reconsider my past and to reshape my future.

I think back to the fury and despondency I felt a year ago. I picture myself shifting shapes, molting skin, digging deeply inside myself to unearth the person who was in there all along, but so afraid of not getting things right that she was willing to bury herself until she was nearly impossible to find. As I groped my way through the dark months that followed my learning of Michael's affair, I fought with the child in me who wanted back the precious item that had been so unceremoniously ripped away, who questioned if I was willing to walk away from Michael, to give up on the notion of the ideal family I had so carefully cultivated over the course of my life. I could have stayed, and the realization of this astounds me.

I could have stayed.

At a crossroads, I had a choice: go back and salvage what I could, or forge ahead alone. I had been terrified, but I gave myself a chance anyway; I had run headfirst into a wall and decided not to retreat, but to claw my way over it to see what was on the other side. This did not happen to me, I made it happen, and now I know this about myself, that I am a person who can transform and endure.

I don't know if this part of my story is an ending or a beginning, but just as grief has no clear beginning, middle or end, I know that my story is a work in progress. Some days I feel like a warrior, fierce and reawakened; other days like a zen master, serene and grateful to have emerged with a new understanding of myself and determined to take one day at a time; and still other days, I still feel wounded, vulnerable, alone and scared. Yet every day I carry with me a newfound, life-affirming, woman-hear-me-roar knowledge. I gave so much of myself away over the years, gradually disappearing as I put all of my love and energy into my children and maintaining as perfect a home as I could. The fault lines were there all along, but I had been unwilling to acknowledge them until the earthquake erupted and gave me no choice. I embraced motherhood so completely that I neglected the woman beneath the mother, and the worst thing that had ever happened to me – Michael's betrayal – had set her free. I didn't lose my sense of self all at once and I won't find myself all at once either. It's been a year since I started along this path, clumsily and impatiently stumbling along, desperate to reach the end of it. Now I finally see: there is no end, just forks, detours, hills and valleys, an ever-shifting footpath that I have time, freedom, courage and insatiable curiosity to amble along. Most importantly, I am willing to let whoever is inside me emerge without rushing her along. All my life I've been a fixer, doer, plan maker, strategist – needing to know what's coming, and now, for the first time ever, I simply don't need to know. I would even go so far as to say that I embrace not knowing and will tenaciously cling to the right to evolve as I go along.

I think back to a recent conversation I had with #6 as I attempted to clarify our status, explaining that I love him and want him in my life, but not at the cost of my freedom. I had told him, you may not continue to be comfortable with my being with other men as we become more deeply invested in each other, and that's a choice you have to make. He had misunderstood my meaning, thinking I was seeking his permission, that I was requesting that he allow me to be with other men.

"No," I had said, shaking my head, "my freedom is not yours to give me or withhold from me, it's simply for you to decide if it works for your own needs."

I see now there can be commitment without monogamy and further that a lack of monogamy doesn't signify that a particular relationship is not enough. No matter how fulfilling a relationship is, it doesn't negate the part of me that still wants to be noticed and wanted, that enjoys the flirting and the hunt, as #6 likes to call it. I don't know what I want in a relationship and why should I? I am privileged to be able to live by my own rules and standards and am surprised to realize that what I avidly pursued ever since I first started dating as a teenager — security, stability, a sure thing — is less important to me than what I gave up to have those things and have since reclaimed, namely my self-awareness, independence and choice. It's no longer imperative that I understand what someone else can provide for me, but that I unflinchingly hold close what I can provide for myself. I am a woman and a mother, but no longer a wife, no longer looking for the sure thing that'll keep my life tidy, my future certain. I thought that going off script would crush me, but instead it has freed me to be fully present in my other roles as a mother, a lover, as a friend and as the author of my own story.

Afterword

There are only two groups of people I hope won't read this book: my parents and my kids. It's not that I have anything to hide, but I know how uncomfortable it is to imagine one's kids or one's parents having sex. You know abstractly that they're doing so, but you don't want to know what their sexuality looks like up close. One of the benefits for kids of their parents staying married is that their sexual identities are obliterated. It's easy for them to pretend it isn't happening or doesn't exist, but when your parents are single and dating, you don't have much of a choice but to accept that in all likelihood, sex is involved. I have never been bashful about intimate topics with my kids, openly discussing puberty, masturbation and birth control while they squirm and plead with me to stop talking. I don't shy away from their burgeoning sexuality – I want them to take the subject of sex in stride, knowing it can be different things at different times, a sign of love and intimacy, or playful and fun. Recently, I told Daisy's friends that I was their age when I started dating Michael and their jaws fell open – the concept of settling down anytime soon was unthinkable to them.

"Don't do what I did!" I admonished them. "Sleep with lots of people, find out what you like and always use a condom."

Some of the girls said they'd like to get married someday, and Daisy admitted she was interested in marriage mostly for the cake tasting during the wedding planning. I told her I would get her all the cake tastings she wanted and she could take her sweet time figuring herself out before she committed to another person.

My kids may choose to read this book despite my forewarning not to, and I can't stop them if curiosity gets the best of them. I hope they will take solace that I am whole, and maybe, just maybe, someday I can serve as a role model to them. My living life on my own terms and then publishing a book about it might be disquieting for them in this moment of time, but when they're older and less easily embarrassed by me, they might be able to see that, like a phoenix rising from the ashes, I turned the most devastating period of my life into the richest one. It wasn't an easy trick to pull off and involved a veritable SWAT team: girlfriends with the patience of saints and the enthusiasm of cheerleaders, my mother whose profound wisdom and unconditional love kept me safe, men who enticed me to come alive again sexually, therapists who helped me find my way to a path I had no faith even existed. I hope that witnessing my transformation from a front-row vantage point is a reminder to my kids that there will inevitably be major bumps and dark tunnels throughout their lives, but they have what they need inside themselves to pull through and know how to supplement whatever they can't locate inside with the love and guidance of other people, just like their mom did.

*

As I write this afterword, sitting on the porch of a Victorian inn at the Jersey shore on a stormy August day with #6 at my side, I feel content. To our mutual surprise and delight, we are still dating, almost two years after that first date in which he put me in a taxi and hurriedly shut the door behind me. An hour from now, I may feel sad and regretful, but I know that these feelings – the ones that make me sigh with deep inner peace, the ones that make me go mute with grief – come and go. When I walk down to the beach and watch children frolic in the waves and parents wrap them afterward in oversize beach towels, I miss my kids with unbearable intensity and I close my eyes, fighting with myself to be present.

I love my time without my kids, the freedom and ease with which I am able to move through my days, but I think about them and pine for them constantly. When I am with them, I call #6 at night, telling him he's been replaced by Georgia in my bed, venting about an argument I had with one of the kids, missing him. I have a full private life now, separate from my fulfilling and busy life as a mother. It's a delicate balancing act to keep myself aloft, but it's not terribly complicated. My kids are my priority; when they're doing their own thing, I am free to spend time with #6 or my beautiful gaggle of girlfriends or to write or occasionally, still, to wander.

#6 is gracious about relinquishing me to my children, saying he is attracted to me in part because I am such a committed mother. He has yet to meet them beyond a quick hello and that's my choice now. When I'm with them, I want to be wholly with them. I suggested to him recently that he would be better served by a girlfriend who has more time to spend with him, but he waved the suggestion away: quality over quantity. We know we have a good thing. We make each other laugh, we care about each other and we have great sex – this seems like enough.

As for my wanderlust, that's a part of me that I steadfastly refuse to let go. #6 gives me everything I want from a man except for one significant thing that is impossible for him to provide: newness. I still want to be noticed, desired, flirted with, seen in all my naked glory; I want to peel clothes off men and run my hands along their warm skin. I won't demean myself by not being forthright with #6, and I have to safeguard this side of myself I only recently discovered. When I have the chance, which isn't often anymore as there are only so many hours in a day, I have sex with other men and I tell #6 when I do. He is apprehensive, but I tell him I love him, and I do. I struggled with sharing my feelings for him, terrified to reveal myself so nakedly. Too timid to say the words out loud, I drew him a cartoon of a teddy bear holding a heart, in the style of the notes I make every morning for Georgia's lunchbox that he admires, and tucked it into an envelope that I told him not to open until I had walked away, further instructing him not to feel obligated to return the stated feelings. He, as it turned out, felt no such compunction, and in the weeks until he revealed that he loved me too, I spent hours perseverating over whether or not I should have said anything at all. Now, he understands that he either accepts me as a complicated, against-the-norm package, or we part. He has embraced the full package, which might change someday, but we don't worry about it – we are here now, and it works.

Time is truly an amazing wonder, how the passing of it allows healing and recovery. I am at peace with Michael now, able to acknowledge that I love him deeply; he is half of the recipe we used to cook up our kids and a goofy, loving dad. Is he the great love of my life, who I tragically lost? My true soulmate? I don't know that I can answer that yet, with so much of my life still ahead of me as I round the bend to my fiftieth birthday. We no longer have a physical connection to each other, but we do have a kinship that binds us unlike anyone else in our lives. There is no one in the world like Michael and I love him for it, but I don't want to be married to him ever again and I assume he would say the same about me. The wounds that I have from the fallout of his affair have hardened into scars; I suspect the feelings of hurt will stay with me for the rest of my life, having made an impression with their depth and profundity.

Just to clarify: when I say there are only two sets of people I hope won't read this book, that doesn't mean I don't feel stabbing twinges of discomfort imagining some of the other people I know who may read it and thus be privy to my most private thoughts and moments. The embarrassment factor is formidable. I'm not impervious to feeling self-conscious or worrying that I've revealed parts of myself I should have kept private. I blush when I tell people about the book, and my description of it emerges haltingly, ineloquently. But like all the other things in the past few years that terrified me but that I faced down, here I go yet again. I'm learning to skate anew, jumping into icy-cold water, stripping off all my clothes to present myself to my first new lover in decades. As Pema Chödron writes in *When Things Fall Apart*, bravery stems not from fearlessness but from being afraid of things and doing them anyway.

I'm proud of the life I've rebuilt for myself, but also often melancholy that I didn't get to "have it all" in the way I thought I would when I was younger. I fervently hope that anyone who reads this book – whether middle-aged and newly single like me or just starting to dip their toes into the murky, alluring waters of relationships at any age, young or old – takes from it that it's possible to have it all, if only you're flexible about what that actually means. For most of my life, I believed that meant having a loving husband staunchly by my side, children, good health, financial stability, a cadre of loyal friends. That belief, embedded in me for decades, has not simply dissipated because my circumstances have changed. It's a work in progress, but that's all I can ask of myself: put one foot in front of the other and keep moving forward. Divorce is an ending and a terribly painful one at that, but it's also a beginning. My advice to anyone looking at that door and trying to decide whether it's opening or closing is, don't overthink it. Shave your legs, spritz on some perfume, don that lace thong you bought in an optimistic moment, slip into a pair of heels that make you feel sexy and bold, and let the momentum carry you ahead.

I can't answer easily the question that started this all: is this too much? It is, and it isn't. It may be too much for other people, but I am enough for myself, neither too much, nor too little. I am on both sides of the seesaw, and only I can maintain the aerial trick of equilibrium for myself. I feel, I appreciate, I experience, I observe on a level many layers beneath the surface I used to placidly coast along, and I'm grateful for every second of it.

Acknowledgements

This is as close to an Oscar acceptance speech as I will ever get; like those actors that continue to talk over the closing music, I'm determined that no one will cut me off. I am thankful to a boat-load of people and I intend to thank them all.

My children expressed that they were proud of me as I wrote this book even as they shared their misgivings. I am sorry if I have embarrassed you in these pages, but each of you is a force to be reckoned with and you'll be fine. I appreciate that you try to see me as my own person even though first and foremost what I am to you is your mother. I love you so much, and the love you return to me is the lifeboat in which I have bounced over some daunting waves.

My mother, Carol Friedman, has been my ultimate role model and has always unconditionally loved, supported, and encouraged me to such an extent that I came to believe I could do just about anything (as long as it was safe and close to home). Thank you Mom for always having unabated faith in me.

My soon-to-be ex-husband gave me love and security when I craved it above all else. You and I made a family together that will always bring us joy, and I am grateful to have you as a co-parent in the cockpit with me. Thank you for giving me your blessing to write this book.

My father, Robert Friedman; my siblings, Jennifer Donohue and Matthew Friedman; and my sister-in-law Breeda Wool, have been an endless source of love and support for me and my kids. Thank you for always being there to catch us when we falter and for your tireless enthusiasm for my book.

Caryn Karmatz Rudy of DeFiore & Company was my friend decades before she became my agent and it was not until then that I fully understood her talent and the fierceness of her allegiance. You spurred me along countless times, but calmly and wisely. Your concern that our working together might put a wedge in our friendship was the opposite of what turned out to happen. I respect and trust you even more now than I did before, if that's possible. Thank you also to Caryn's fellow agent Meredith Kaffel Simonoff for securing this book with Borough Press.

My editor, Ore Agbaje-Williams, has been the gift that keeps on giving. Brilliant, funny, dedicated, and astute, you work so hard but seemingly without another care in the world. You asked me to rewrite the entire book twice, but so gently that not until I sat down to do it did I realize exactly how much work you wanted done. Sometimes I silently cursed you, but then I saw that what you asked me to do was spot on. Thank you for your keen eye, attention to both the big picture and every little detail, and for your willingness to compromise with me.

The whole team at Borough Press has been caring and enthusiastic;

I did not imagine it would ever be possible to be on the receiving end of this level of commitment. Cover designer Claire Ward created two beautiful covers and redefined how I will look at certain fruits and vegetables forevermore. Publicist Jen Harlow is so lovely that she makes me feel like I'm doing her a favor even though she's doing the heavy lifting. The marketing savvy of Abbie Salter helped to create a fresh look and campaign for the book. Proofreader Sarah Bance and copy-editor Jane Donovan are grammar goddesses, and I bow down to them. Editorial Assistant Margot Gray has managed the behind-the-scenes with great efficiency.

Literary scouts Molly Maguire and Aram Fox championed this book when it was a slender proposal and got it into Ore's magical hands – without that bit of handselling, this book would not have come to be. Thank you eternally.

My friends, oh my friends.

Lauren Moss, head cheerleader – there has not been a time that I have needed you that you haven't been ready, willing and able. You never once gave me critical feedback beyond "I love every word you write," but that was helpful in its own way. Thank you for your devotion to me.

Erika Brown-Campbell is amongst my oldest friends and a therapist, and if you put those things together you have what she has been to me: a confidante, voice of reason and advisor for going on almost forty years now. I would be broke if I had to pay someone else for all the brilliant guidance you have given me.

Jessica Pell is also amongst my oldest friends and has long been a sister to me. We've been through some serious trials and travails together, but always manage to laugh even in our darkest moments.

My other oldest friends, Heidi Valenzuela, Leslie Blauner and Julie Weill have been stalwart supporters going back to the '80s, and have been steadfastly kind, consistent and generous with their love.

I often asked Mara Hatzimemos to remind me of some of the memories that had faded for me, and she did so enthusiastically and with amazing recall. You were there for me when I needed you most, and have always lavished love on all my kids.

Jacqueline Brachman, Tina Zelinski Pollack, and Karen Berlind have not only held my hand and cheered me along, but have been like sister wives, giving me copious help with childcare – the kind that only the best friends can give in which you mothered my child as if that child was your own.

Jennifer Economou was kindhearted and patient with me, reading pages, giving me feedback, listening to me with a finely attuned ear, and always making herself available when I needed her.

Stephen and Johanna Lindsay gave both me and my ex the gift of unflagging friendship. You have gracefully and genuinely stayed firm for both of us.

Alex Chandler, Beth Dobrish, Simona Levin, Katherine Locker Scharlatt, Rebecca Oyer, Alexandra Conley, Sarah Wayland-Smith, Christina Ohly Evans, and Carolyn Clark Creekmore have been devoted friends and sources of comfort and laughter, the kind of strong, smart, funny women we all hope to have in the foxhole with us.

Christy Ottaviano was adamant that I write this book – thank you for being so pushy, I'm not sure I would have done it if you hadn't hounded me about it.

Daniel Pollack is a dear friend and brilliant photographer who gave me the gift of his time and talent.

My newest and most unexpected friend Desiree Murnane has been one of my most enthusiastic champions and has fallen down more rabbit holes with me regarding cover designs than could fairly be asked of anyone.

And last, but certainly not least, #6 took it upon himself to feed me, stock both my fridge and my lingerie drawer, and provide outlets for quiet time so that I could get this book done. You have carefully listened to every detail, addressed every concern, and been tenacious on my behalf during every moment in which I've wavered and wanted to hide. Your happiness for and pride in me fill me up as much as your bountiful meals.